DATE DUE		
AUG 1 7 1987			
JAN 1 1 1988			
MAR - 2 1990			
MAR 26 1990			

AUG - 3 1984

Religion and Politics
in the Modern World

RELIGION AND POLITICS IN THE MODERN WORLD

EDITED BY

Peter H. Merkl and Ninian Smart

NEW YORK UNIVERSITY PRESS
New York and London
1983

Library of Congress Cataloging in Publication Data
Main entry under title:

Religion and politics in the modern world.

"This book arose from a symposium on religion,
myth, and politics held at Santa Barbara in the
spring of 1979"—Foreword.
Includes bibliographical references and index.
1. Religion and politics—Congresses. I. Merkl,
Peter H. II. Smart, Ninian, 1927–
BL65.P7R4324   1983   322'.1   82-22572
ISBN 0-8147-5389-2

Clothbound editions of New York University Press books are Smyth-
sewn and printed on permanent and durable acid-free paper.

Contents

Contributors

DAVID J. BIALE is Associate Professor of History and Judaic Studies at the State University of New York at Binghamton. He is the author of *Gershom Scholem: Kabbalah and Counter-History* (Harvard University Press) and is currently working on a book on Jewish attitudes toward love, marriage, and the family.

KEES W. BOLLE is Professor of History, University of California, Los Angeles. A specialist in the history of religion, he is the author of *The Freedom of Man in Myth, the Bhagavadgita, A New Translation* the article on "Myth and Mythology" in the latest edition of the Encyclopedia Britannica, and of various studies and essays on mysticism, secularization, and on religion in India.

MICHAEL J. CAREY is Assistant Professor of Political Science at Loyola Marymount University, teaching Western European Politics and International Relations. He has published several works on European politics.

WILBUR M. FRIDELL lived in Japan from 1948 to 1959. Returning to the United States, he took the M.A. and Ph.D. in Japanese history at the University of California, Berkeley. After receiving the Ph.D. he spent one year at the Center for the Study of World Religions, Harvard University. In 1967 he began to teach East Asian religions in the Religious Studies Department, University of California, Santa Barbara, where he is presently an Associate Professor.

LEONARD GREENSPOON teaches in the Department of History at Clemson University in South Carolina. Greenspoon received his Ph.D.

in Near Eastern Languages from Harvard University, and has done research primarily on the Greek translations of the Hebrew Bible. His work on the Book of Joshua has led to consideration of issues such as Biblical attitudes towards war and concepts such as the Divine Warrior and Holy War.

MICHAEL D. KENNEDY, a doctoral candidate in sociology at the University of North Carolina, Chapel Hill, is presently working on his dissertation, which is a comparative study of political instability in industrial socialist societies.

JAROSLAV KREJCI is Professor in the School of European Studies at the University of Lancaster. Born in Czechoslovakia in 1916, he worked in the State Planning Office and taught macroeconomics at the Economic Faculty in Prague. During an enforced break in his professional career (1954–67) he turned to the broader field of social science. When the Soviet armies occupied Czechoslovakia in August 1968 he moved to Vienna. Since 1969 he has lived in Lancaster.

GARY LEASE received the Dr. theol. from the University of Munich in 1968. Since then he has worked at the John XXIII Center for Ecumenical Theology, Loyola University, and for the past nine years at the University of California, Santa Cruz. In addition to a book on Newman's theory of a church's teaching function, he has published an edition and study of Harnack's and Sohm's letters; a study of Hitler's National Socialism as a religious movement; and contributions to the ANRW on so-called Jewish mysteries and Mithraism's relationship to early Christianity. He is currently working on studies of the interactions between church and state in the nineteenth and twentieth centuries.

EDWARD TABOR LINENTHAL is an Assistant Professor in the Department of Religion at the University of Wisconsin-Oshkosh. He has recently finished a book concerning the enduring attractions of war and the warrior in American history.

PETER H. MERKL is a Professor of Political Science at the University of California, Santa Barbara. Recent publications are *The Making of a Stormtrooper, Western European Party Systems: Trends and Prospects,* and *American Democracy in World Perspective.* Current research interests are comparative political violence, comparative local government, and comparative political parties.

BARBARA METCALF has taught history and South Asian studies at the Universities of Pennsylvania and California, Berkeley. She is the author of *Islamic Revival in British India: Deoband, 1860–1900* (Princeton, 1982) and the editor of *Moral Conduct and Authority: The Place of Adab in South Asian Islam* (Berkeley and Los Angeles, 1983).

RAIMUNDO PANIKKAR, born 1918 in Barcelona, is Professor of Religious Studies at the University of California, Santa Barbara. He studied philosophy, chemistry, and theology in Spain, Italy, and Germany and holds doctorates in these three fields from the Universities of Madrid and Rome respectively. Among his more recent works are *The Intrareligious Dialogue* (1978), *Myth, Faith, and Hermeneutics* (1979), and *Il Silenzio di Dio* (1979).

MAURICE D. SIMON is an Associate Professor of Political Science at the University of North Carolina at Greensboro. He is co-editor of *Background to Crisis: Policy and Politics in Gierek's Poland* (Westview Press, 1981) and *Developed Socialism in the Soviet Bloc: Political Theory vs. Political Reality* (Westview Press, 1982). He is also the author of numerous articles on Polish politics and is currently doing research on political alienation in socialist societies.

NINIAN SMART is Professor of Religious Studies at the University of California, Santa Barbara. He founded England's first department in the field, at Lancaster in 1967, and has written widely on the philosophy of religion, Indian religions, and the phenomenology of religion. His recent *Beyond Ideology* (1981) related traditional beliefs to modern ideologies.

Foreword

This book arose from a symposium on religion, myth, and politics held at Santa Barbara in the spring of 1979. We are grateful to participants, some of whom contributed papers to this volume, and to others who wrote for us. It will be obvious that we have only covered some of the areas where the interplay between religions and politics is a powerful ingredient in events. But the general principles of how such an interplay is to be understood have been sufficiently discussed for the volume to have, we hope, very wide relevance. Too often in academe we treat separately what in life is intertwined, and the book is intended as being a major crossing of such artificial boundaries. We are grateful to Colin Jones of New York University Press for his considerable help in bringing the book to publication.

Peter H. Merkl
Ninian Smart

Introduction

Peter H. Merkl

Nationalism and religion. What dramatic images may be conjured up in our minds by these words in our troubled age? The raging of the Ayatollah Ruhollah Khomeini against "the great Satan, America," which is accused of having corrupted Iranian Islamic civilization and subjugated the Iranian nation to alien interests? The burning of the American embassy in Islamabad by Pakistani mobs led by the students of an Islamic academy and triggered by false rumors of American complicity in the seizure of the holy shrine in Mecca by Moslem extremists? The images need not be this exotic; they could be much closer to the everyday world of Western experience. We might think instead of the enthusiastic reception given the newly elected Pope, John Paul II, in his native Poland, where deeply ingrained national sentiment is united with Catholic resistance to Russian communist domination. Or, closer yet, of the strident, patriotic appeals of "Americanism" in the religious preachings of certain Protestant fundamentalist evangelists in the United States. United or opposed to each other, virulent nationalism and religious myths have been major political factors throughout most of the nineteenth and twentieth century and are likely to remain so in the foreseeable future.

The contributors to this book attempt to shed light on their subject from a variety of angles, beginning with a mapping out of the relationships among differing concepts of nationhood and church-state relations. Ninian Smart's article on religious myth and human identity heads the contributions to Part I with a catalog of ideas and situations associated with the rise of the tribal religions of modern nationalism. His essay links the French national tradition of the *citoyen* and mass education to the "performative construct" of the nation and its rituals, its tongue and "sacred space," and its sense of identity grown from common triumphs and sufferings. Like all great popular faiths, nationalisms require the invention of symbols, heroes, even martyrs, and perhaps a cosmogony of land and people, or at least a history of national origins that bends the facts to the purpose. The nationalist religion thrives best on real or fancied oppression by alien demons, from which the nation must free itself with a superhuman effort. The act of national liberation, or renaissance, if it is to be the foundation of a lasting political community, requires total human dedication and something akin to individual conversion experiences: "Yesterday still merely New Yorkers and Virginians, today we have become Americans!" This dedication to the new identity must be repeated daily, as in Ernest Renan's *plébiscite de tous les jours*.

Ninian Smart's phenomenology of nationalism as a tribal religion is counterpointed by Jaroslav Krejci's sociology of ethnicity in the existing nation-states of the world. Even though nationalism as a state-building force has been a universal phenomenon in these last two centuries, history and circumstances have created several distinct types of nation-states. Hardly any contemporary state is ethnically homogeneous, nor has national consciousness developed simultaneously in all social strata. The interplay of social and political mobilization of the population, the accident of the original ethnic distributions, and frequently, religious and dynastic conflict produced many different patterns, including nation-states in which one ethnicity dominates another and others where they live side by side in harmonious "consociation." An ethnic melting pot is rarer to observe in the history of nation-building, except perhaps among Europeans in overseas settlements or in situations of rapid urbanization.

Given the political loyalties of citizens of the nation-state, we still have to determine the role of the institutionalized religious community, the church, amidst the national political community. Raimundo Panikkar describes the variety of options that range from theocracy, or totalitarian identification of the religious and political obligations of the individual over monism (wherein the state controls the church or vice versa) to dualism, or the interdependence of relatively autonomous communities. Humans thirst for meaning and tend to be deeply dissatisfied with a "desacralized politics," or with "political technocracy," or with a "depoliticized religion." The two great community-building forces of our age must each be given their due, and this in harmonious symbiosis.

With the elementary relationships thus sorted out, we can turn, in Part II, to the variety of nationalist experiences and their religious or quasi-religious forms in particular countries. As Ninian Smart has pointed out at the beginning, there is nothing truly transcendent or universal about the tribal religions of nationalism except for their ubiquity. This points to the deep longing of all uprooted modern humanity for meaning and community, or better yet communal meaning and identity. A brief glance at the contemporary Middle East shows the extraordinary range of likely relationships between nascent nationalisms and particular religious patterns. There are the relatively secular nationalist movements, frequently spearheaded by military men rather than popular upheavals, that made anticolonial revolutions and never-ending coups from Algeria to Syria and Iraq. Frequently socialist and, in a fashion, even democratic, they permitted the Islamic clergy and its traditionalist spokesmen very little influence. Some were outspokenly anticlerical, such as Turkey's Kemal Ataturk or the late Shah of Iran; others only showed their disdain by concentrating solely on pragmatic social and economic goals of development in their countries. Today, many of them have reason to worry about a rising tide of popular, religious fundamentalism that threatens to wash away the secular leadership of such diverse countries as progressive Egypt, conservative Saudi Arabia, or socialist Syria and Iraq. There are striking differences, moreover, between the radical egalitarian and often revolutionary and Messianic strain of Islam—which insists on guiding the everyday life of the faithful, including of course their political behavior, in such countries as Shiite Iran—and the conservative communal and cultural emphasis still dominant among Pakistani Moslems, other Sunnis, and even among Afghani insurgents against communist usurpation.

Nationalism, especially anticolonialist nationalism, again varies in the extent to which it becomes identified with these varieties of politicized Islamic religion. In revolutionary Iran, xenophobia and religious radicalism are wondrously identical, though other factions from former President Bani-Sadr's liberal following to the Marxist left differ in their nationalism only by degree. In Pakistan, on the other hand, stirrings of religious radicalism run athwart the conservative Islamic nationalism of the dominant political forces. Shiite radicalism throughout the region outside Iran is rather internationalist, directing its eyes and ears to the Imam, Khomeini, while the latter is adamant in his religious and political defense of Iranian national unity against the rival nationalisms of the Kurdish, Arab, and Beluchi minorities of his country. The complexities of national and religious loyalties of Southwest Asia are not all that different from those of Central and Eastern Europe in the nineteenth century, when conflicting nationalisms often found themselves at war with each other and with the ultramontane claims of the Roman Catholic church. The unhappy Kurds of Iraq, Iran, and Turkey, and the rebellious Arabs of Khuzistan had their predecessors in similar situations in yesterday's Europe, not to mention their contemporaries in parts of Africa such as Ethiopa, Kenya, and Somalia.

There are other dimensions as well that may impinge on the interaction between religion and nationalist movements. Some religions, such as Islam or Catholicism have been more inclined towards institutionalization and centralization. Others, such as Hinduism, have penetrated life almost without the formation of churches or canonic codes of law. Institutionalized religious authority usually has come under pressure to accommodate itself to the existing political regime as in a state church or union of throne and altar. Thus it may become part and parcel of the official patriotism or, more likely, an object of hatred of minority or rival nationalisms. In nineteenth century Catholic areas in Central or Eastern Europe, this identification of Catholicism with the legitimate *ancien regime* often led its nationalist opponents and would-be revolutionaries to consider conversion to Lutheranism. The presence of more than one religious community, in any case, complicates the identification of nationalism with the prevailing religion of a country.

Part II begins with an essay by Gary Lease that probes the depths of German nineteenth-century romantic nationalism and racism, from Richard Wagner's pseudoreligious epics to the *voelkisch* movement of the early twentieth century. Some contemporary German Catholic theologians and Adolf Hitler himself are cited as eloquent witnesses to the tortured striving for the creation of a new German religion, *voelkisch* and patriotic at the expense of conventional religious piety. The author has already presented persuasive evidence elsewhere that Hitler's "national socialism" was a religious movement,[1] as are other ideological crusades that insist on establishing a representative and all-inclusive interpretation of social reality. What Lease says about certain German intellectual elites at the time is supplemented by Peter Merkl with a description of popular German nationalist attitudes and organizations during World War I and the Weimar Republic: popular nationalism as a militant, passionate faith complete with conversion experiences, a mystic sense of community, proselytizing, and the cruel persecution of heretics (i.e., pacifists, Marxists), infidels, and devils. The description culminates in the self-image of Nazi storm troopers as battling archangels—not unlike the storm troopers of other interwar fascist movements, Hindu storm troopers or Turkish

Gray Wolves, China's cultural revolutionaries of the 1960s, or the Iranian revolutionary guards of today—and descriptions of the lituragy and revivalist style of Nazi rallies before 1933.

From Germany, the book turns to two European Catholic nations, Ireland and Poland, where centuries of national and religious oppression seem to have welded together "faith and fatherland" (see Michael Carey on Ireland). The external enemies and oppressors undoubtedly helped to preserve this unity and solidarity. In both countries, the Catholic religion is still a "folk church" for a largely integral peasant and worker society, in which secularism is restricted to metropolitan and, in Poland, Communist minorities. In both countries, the union of nationalism and religion rests in considerable part also on the historic role of the lower clergy in the nationalist movements and as pillars of patriotic piety. Every local priest, it seems, still is a veritable Don Camillo, ever ready to do the patriotic battle against alien forces and rival faiths. In this connection, again, there is a striking parallel among the Shiite clergy of Iran, the mullahs and their role in the nationalist revolution and in the anti-Western regime that has succeeded the secularist Shah. The political violence of Irish and Iranian revolutionaries and their exalted expressions of hatred for their alien adversaries also have more the earmark of tribal religious fanaticisms than of any universal religious values.[2] This is not to deny that universal churches, too, have on occasion justified or defended massacres and even genocide. Both Irish and Polish nationalism, according to Carey, Simon, and Kennedy also have had their romantic phases in which religion, culture, history, language, and poetry, not to mention Polish music, merged into heroic or messianic nationalist myths and symbols reminiscent of Wagnerian German mythology.

During the seven years of crisis since 1975, the Polish church reached a pinnacle of influence as the official Polish United Workers Party went into a steep decline and the rising independent trade union movement Solidarity struggled for legitimacy. Maurice Simon and Michael Kennedy describe the popular perceptions of Polish patriotism and the popular trust in church and Solidarity as compared to the PUWP. The frantic efforts of government and communist party to rein in the forces moving toward national independence and economic self-management—in the face of decades of mismanagement—cast the church in the role of an impartial arbiter and, more and more, of a guardian of the human rights of food rioters, strikers, and a political opposition. In spite of its moderation and cautious emphasis on the non-violent resolution of conflicts, such a stance could not but be interpreted as the championing of the national traditions against the communist and, finally, a military dictatorship.

Hardly less effective than these Catholic nationalisms is the subject of Wilbur Fridell's contribution, the "societal" or "culture religion" of Japanese Shinto. Complete with a cosmogonic myth of the creation of the sacred land, emperor, and people by spirits in the High Plain of Heaven, Shinto was most effective as a patriotic cult, not unlike American "civil religion" (Robert Bellah), the religious dimension of American nationalism. That such a civil religion can create heroes and fanatics, and lead to the persecution of infidels and devils, is borne out by such phenomena of American history as the Alien and Sedition Laws of the end of the eighteenth century, Know-Nothingism and the Klan, the persecution of anarchists, Wobblies, and alleged communists, the bible-thumping patriotic crusades of yesterday and today.

Religion and nationalism in Pakistan as described by Barbara Metcalf form something of a missing link between several of the countries already mentioned. There is the element of past national and religious oppression, although with far less homogeneous national substance. Urdu, the "national language," is spoken by only four percent of the population and the uncertainty of borders and divided loyalties of much of the population, even after the secession of Bangladesh, leaves little of a national core. On the other hand, there is the competition between the conservative, communal Islamic emphasis of an Ayub Khan or the current government of Zia ul-Haq and the egalitarian Islamic radicalism of the late Ali Bhutto. Under the former, economic development and law and order have been far more of an object of national pride than were the religious traditions of the Prophet and the Koran. Implicit skepticism of these traditions, in fact, was matched by a government usurpation of religious endowments and tithes comparable to the Shah's policies against Iran's mullahs. On the other hand, Pakistan's religious and national self-image, at least until the 1970s, was dominated by its role as a refuge and national home for the Moslems of the subcontinent, fifty million of whom were left behind in hostile India. With this sense of religious and national persecution through the ordeals of partition, secession, and defeats at the hands of India—where Moslems still suffer discrimination and, at times, local persecutions—Pakistan most resembles Israel.

This brings us to the last of the contemporary societies covered in this book, Israel, and Zionism, by David Biale. The author gives particular attention to the militant and yet messianic secularism of the Zionist movement on the one hand and the emphatically religious messianism of Gush Emunim, the movement responsible for the expansion of Israeli settlements on the West Bank, on the other. The settlement idea itself originated with Zionism but the leader of Gush Emunim, Rabbi Zvi Yehuda Kook, gave it an overwhelmingly religious meaning as a first step into the dawn of a messianic age of the people of Israel in their ancient homelands.

This survey of religion and nationalism in seven countries has pinpointed an extraordinary variety of relationships and phenomena. It would have been tempting to add further examples, both from history and from other areas. In particular, an examination of other countries in which communist regimes have added one more official religion to those of nationalism and existing religion might have added further depth. The Soviet Union, with its toleration of an "accommodated" orthodox religion and revived nationalism, but also with its suppression of other faiths, not to mention the religious fundamentalist and old patriot, Aleksandr Solzhenitsyn, comes to mind. China with its new religious tolerance would have been interesting, too.

But any list of desiderata must end somewhere and leave further explorations to future endeavors.

The third and final part of the book is devoted to the humanistic and moral dimension of the subject, especially the religious and political obligation of the individual in a world governed by powerful collective myths that demand human loyalty and, at times, even human sacrifice. In the first of the essays, Leonard Greenspon describes the warrior god of the ancient Hebrews who was thought to "reveal himself through the processes of human history," as a leader of his people in "holy wars" or "just wars" against their enemies, riding a chariot or giving divine signals through startling upheavals in the order of nature. Having God on your side, however, had to be demonstrated by victory against overwhelming odds, by nothing less than a miracle. In one form or another, the warrior god is still alive today wherever armies and their leaders pray for divine favors or in crude displays of popular faith in divine partiality.

For Americans, in particular, Edward Linenthal describes the image of the American warrior through the "holy wars" of 1776, the "Homeric period" of the Civil War, and the two world wars of this century. But in Korea and Vietnam, the divine spell no longer seemed to work against the meaninglessness of the war experience in the technological age. Instead, there was a deep-seated emotional need to make communism into a devil, and to restore honor and pride in American arms by grand gestures. These in turn were counterpointed by the quasi-religious urge of "winter soldiers" and war resisters to express deep guilt feelings over the rationale and nature of the American involvement. It was a simpler world when citizens of a political and religious community could follow their warrior god into "redemptive sacrifice" without the moral ambiguities of today's wars. But all forms of dedication to a collective myth, religious or political, also imply the possibility of human alienation and of a refusal, for whatever reason, to follow the call.

It is a sense of alienation and yet another powerful collective myth of our time, materialism, that Kees Bolle explores in the last chapter of Part III. Karl Marx was both a philosopher of alienation in his earlier days and then the philosopher of materialism par excellence who "stood Hegel ['s idealism] on [its] head." The spell of materialism as the fulcrum through which all other collective myths of states, ruling classes, and churches could be overthrown clearly won out over the philosophy of alienation of Marx, the humanist. The alienation that is sometimes expressed in the visions, and even poetry, of Marxists is only an alienation from the ruling rival myths of nationalism, bourgeois hypocrisy, or religious piety, and never an alienation from the materialist millenarianism of Marx, the materialist, and his camp followers of a century. This has been the undoubted strength of Marxism as the ideology of mass movements in industrialized and post-colonial, underdeveloped societies alike. But it is also its weakness and irrelevance in the eyes of a new, rebellious generation of intellectuals and especially of middle-class youth in post-industrial societies. This new generation also feels deeply alienated, and has already felt so for half a century and more, wherever youth movements and youth cultures have erupted spontaneously. But its alienation was usually aimed at materialism as well, at the idolization of possessions and of the baubles of a technological society, durable consumer goods, and the consumer attitudes that go with them. Instead of such shallow preoccupations, they strove for authenticity in human relations, for a sense of community, and frequently for a pristine utopia of nature unsullied by human affluence and the desecrations of the machine age. These new preoccupations, however, would not with necessity exclude a rededication to nationalism and, perhaps also, to religious myths. The cycle of human dedication to collective myths, and from there on to alienation and back again to new commitment, thus may well continue.

NOTES

1. See Gary Lease, "Hitler's National Socialism as a Religious Movement," *Journal of the American Academy of Religion,* XLV (Sept. 1977),

793–838. See also Werner Timm, *Die heilige Revolution: Das religiöse Totalitätskonzept der Frühromantik,* Frankfurt: SAV, 1978, and Friedrich Wilhelm Graf, *Die Politisierung des religiösen Bewusstseins.* Stuttgart: Frommann-Holzboog, 1978.

2. In particular, neither Catholic catechism nor Islamic teaching ever gave justification for any form of terrorism against innocent bystanders, or for hostage-taking.

I

OF GOD AND NATIONHOOD

Religion, Myth, and Nationalism *

Ninian Smart

Professor Zeman remarks, in his account *The Twilight of the Habsburgs,*[1] "Like the Hungarians, the Czechs had had a long history behind them before they came under the rule of the Habsburg. . . ." This shows us something about the concept of a people's history. For from one point of view everyone has as many ancestors, roughly speaking, as anyone else. What is implied in this passage is that Czechs as a collectivity had had quite a long time together; presumably they were in some general way aware of that time. A number of notions are entwined here: the sense of belonging to a group, the awareness of the past of the group, identification with that past. Of course, in regard to the rise of Czech and other nationalisms—a large part of Zeman's theme—the group not merely acknowledges its collectivity, but desires to establish a nation-state, to achieve (in other words) self-determination. Crudely: a nation wishes to possess its own territory and to administer itself, undominated by others.

I wish to explore these notions, for they are relevant to ques-

*Version of this essay appeared in *Scottish Journal of Religious Studies*, vol. I, no. I. Reprinted by permission.

tions of identity and myth that are encountered in the field of religion. But first, let me say something briefly about modern nationalism. It is, of course, a very powerful force—the most powerful perhaps in politics. It is at heart the theory that each nation should have its state, but more existentially it becomes the sentiment that our people should have our state. Renan said that a nation is a daily plebiscite, but we could go beyond this to say that the creation of a national consciousness is a necessary feature of true nationalism, and such consciousness is a blend of awareness, sentiment, and sacrament.

Various theories[2] of modern nationalism have been propounded. Its origins clearly owe much to the following factors: the French Revolution and the conception of "the citizen;" the Enlightenment; the spread of education, implying centralization and national language formation; the oppression of ethnic groups in Europe; the oppression of groups outside Europe, and the exporting of European ideas through imperialism; and so on. Modern socialism, incidentally, often reinforces national identity, because "the people" has to be defined nationally, and because centralization and the welfare state increase internal cohesion and dependence. But perhaps we should note above all that industrialization and modernization themselves tend to dissolve intermediate bonds—intermediate that is between family and nation—and thus play a central role in the emergence of nationalism.

One other preliminary: clearly, many nations are not more or less homogeneous groups. But for the sake of simplicity I shall take as the classic model of a nation and a nation-state one where the territory is unitary and occupied largely by people speaking one language. With few exceptions, incidentally, there are troubles where this model is not operative. But I shall take linguistic nationalism as the primary form.

First, then, let us look to the notion of a group, for a nation is a sort of group. Belonging to a group has an external definition, in the sense that we can nominate some mark or property in virtue of which members of a group are indeed members of that group. For instance: the people sitting on the right-hand side of the room are a group; or all black people; or one-armed piano players. But of course the mark that demarcates the class may not be considered specially important by the members of the class. I am of medium height, but I have no very great feelings of solidarity with others of my height (though I feel *some* solidarity and I am resentful of games like basketball best played by giants and so discriminatory against me). So belonging to a group in a meaningful way implies an acknowledgment by the individuals of the importance of the mark that defines the group.

What does "acknowledging the mark" mean? Briefly, it means celebrating it. Thus in acknowledging my belonging to the Scots group, I celebrate Scottishness. I can do this by recommending Burns, boasting of whisky, giving wondrous accounts of the '45, telling people how beautiful the Highlands are, wearing a kilt, and so on.

To celebrate is a performative act—a kind of ritual when formalized. Unfortunately there is no very good vocabulary to cover those acts, gestures, and symbolic moves which at the formal end are ritual but at the informal end are to be found in winks, smiles, turning your back, and so forth—bodily and more-than-bodily acts having an emotional significance. "Symbolic act" is not a good phrase, because the symbolic is often identified with what is merely symbolic. So I shall on occasion employ the rather redundant expression "performative act."

Celebrating is a performative act that enhances what is celebrated: it as it were conveys a positive charge to the focus of celebration. Still, though it is right to look at acknowledging the mark as being a performative act, it is not just using words, but using words and other means performatively. It also involves acknowledging the focus as somehow mine or ours. So for the member of a group to acknowledge the mark that defines the group, he celebrates it as his mark. "I am proud to be a Scot" is a way of declaring my participation in the mark. (I can of course try to do the opposite, by repudiating my nationality.) My substance thus in an important way is enhanced or diminished by reference to the substance of Scotland.

Briefly then, belonging to a group involves performatively acknowledging the mark. What of feelings? I assume about human life the following: that feelings are expressed performatively, and that many performative acts are intended to have feeling effects. If I feel contempt for someone I sneer, and the sneer is an attempt to induce a bad feeling, of inferiority. Sincerity is where feelings match their performative expressions.

If one were to write an alternative to *I and Thou* called *Us and Them,* us-ness—the bond that makes us use "we"—would best be seen as a mutual acknowledgment, a mutual celebration of substance, a joint performative. True us-ness implies sincerity of feeling behind such performative belonging to one another.

Consciousness then of belonging to a group involves the feelings that go with acknowledging the mark that defines the group.

But what is the mark when it comes to a national group? The simplified model we are considering involves that the folk occupy a territory and speak predominantly a given tongue. But they also have a history (typically). To understand something of this history is to understand something important about myth. For a nation of the sort we are considering is well summed up—or rather its spirit is—by the opening phrase of the great Welsh national song: land of our fathers. Why do we glorify the past?

Part of the reason appears to be as follows. The individual arrives in the group by birth and his belonging is performatively reinforced by education and the various and multitudinous celebrations of the mark of the group (its Scottishness, Italianness or whatever). Being born into the group though is not just a simple biological event. It involves performative aspects: the child is acknowledged as legitimate by the parents and the community, and derives therefore his identity from his father and mother. The chain of legitimation thus points backward in time. Thus our ancestors are part of the group, and have the property of imparting the mark downward to us.

Celebration of ancestors is then natural enough. If we celebrate our forefathers we enhance the substance of the nation, and so indirectly we enhance ourselves.

This is of some interest if we consider the great flowering of cultural and historical creativity in the nineteenth century in Europe. It was a period when national histories were being written, philology explored, folk music rediscovered, national-flavored symphonies composed, and so on. Ethnic consciousness was reinforced by the arts, and often the creative artist, poet, or musician was seen as hero, for in giving dignity and glory to the nation he performatively diffused glory to all who belonged to the group. The most spectacular of such heroes, of course, was Wagner, and the most loved.

The logic of the national hero is worth considering. He has to perform some act or acts that are positively charged. Pele, to take a modern hero, played wonderful football, helping Brazil to glittering victories. In supporting their team with lively and frenetic enthusiasm, the Brazilians conferred upon their men a glorious substance, but one linked indissolubly to those supporters, and to the nation. The cheers of Brazilians helped to enhance the team; the team by its victories shed glory backward upon Brazilians. It was a good exchange. Fickle supporters turn on their heroes. The team is abused if it loses—meaning that its substance is diminished, and by rituals of hostility the bad substance is kept away from the wider group.

To return to our emerging nations of Europe: the histories that were written became in a sense myths relating to national identity. Historiography became a kind of modern myth-making. This suggests a way in which, from one perspective, we can treat the concept of myth.

The history of a people is the real counterpart of a story, or perhaps we should say that what is told in the story of a people reflects at least a putative series of events. I shall call that an event-pattern. The storytelling is the way the event-pattern is conveyed to us. But that "conveying" is not just a question of the transfer of information: it is a performative act of celebrating the event-pattern; for indeed the event-pattern is not just flat events, but ones charged with meaning. They include victories over oppression, heroic deeds, and so on. A myth thus may be considered simply as a *charged story;* in this sense, history is myth, for it is (albeit objectively and scientifically undertaken up to a point) a story that has a charge for the people for whom it is the history. Alas, however, scientific history seems often to defuse the charge.

Of course, nationalism often arises most strongly in the situation of oppression. The Greek struggle for independence against the Turks, Garibaldi's campaigns, the various phases of the Polish struggle for liberty and independence—many such examples can be cited. Thus often the history of a people is charged not just with glory but with suffering. From a performative point of view, how is such suffering to be treated? It is after all celebrated in a sort of way. For one thing, the dead can be mourned. What is mourning? It is enhancing the value of the dead by weeping and other performative expressions of sadness. Death is losing the loved one: the loss is a blow that finds the response of grief, and the depth of grief is a sign of the worth of the loved one. In other words mourning enhances the dead. And the dead, solid with us in nationality, thus have a glory they can vouchsafe to us. That is the meaning of the cenotaph.

Thus the national story is not so much one that explains how we came to be, though it does that, as one that provides a past cement of identity and an enhancement of present substance.

History as myth is something conveyed performatively, for modern nationalism, in the schools. The spread of education, first among the better off, and then throughout the community, is a means of solidifying the past story. Of course, education does much else besides. Cheating about a group's history, though indeed frequent, also has limits, since a nation needs to be "modern" and modernity implies some deference toward objectivity and science.

The whole notion of modernity is an element in the mythic aspect of nationhood. Certain institutions and entities have a positive charge, from this point of view, as being concretizations of modernity: the airline, the university, the steelworks, the rocket launcher, the palace of the people. Such entities have a ritual or performative function. One might regard such symbols (perhaps all symbols) as frozen acts, congealed performatives. The airline dumbly and yet eloquently tells us something: it tells us how good we are, technologically proficient, glamorously modern, organizationally impressive. In expressing modern machismo it helps to enhance the nation's substance.

All this helps us to understand Goethe's dictum about history: the best thing about it is the enthusiasm it arouses. We also need to change Renan's remark that a nation is a daily plebiscite: one could say better perhaps that it is a daily sacrament—the communication of substance throughout the group through the very language itself and through the innumerable assumptions and celebrations of identity.

Let us now turn to consider the territorial aspect. It is easy for us now to believe that man is a territorial animal, since the nation-state has given us a special way of looking at the ancestral land. This becomes a kind of sacred space, from various points of view. It is the nation's home, i.e. the place where the people are secure (they hope). It is also the land of the ancestors, the fatherland (or mother, as in Mother Russia). To tell the story of how the ancestors settled the land and defended it, developed it and beautified it, is to express the charge the land has for the group. Its magic is enhanced because it is *ours:* "By yon bonnie banks and by yon bonny braes. . . ." Although in modern times the numina have vanished from the streams and the forests, and the gods from the mountains, there is still something of their spirit left. The aesthetic properties of one's country (America the beautiful) are a source of substance that we celebrate. The land too is made holy, especially if it is also defended with great suffering: the blood of the dead adds solemn charge to the soil. And at the edge of the land is the frontier, to be a demarcation: woe betide the one who infringes on that line.

I have used the term "sacred" once or twice in connection with the nation's land. Sacredness in such a context appears to be a relational property: my country is sacred to me in a primary way, and only secondarily to others who are not co-nationals. Among other things it implies that I have a duty to defend the land, and others commit an outrage in invading it. I do not, incidentally, think that sacredness is anything very special, as if one can use the conception to demarcate the religious. The point is that some spaces and people and things are sacred in the sense that they are charged in a solemn manner in such a way that a certain sort of conduct in relation to them is demanded. It is to do with depth of feeling and defined behavior, and that behavior has to do with enhancing or preserving the substance of what is sacred and with not diminishing it. It is thus to do with appropriate performatives.

Sometimes sacredness is in the literature more reified, as though the sacred "irrupts" into the world, or pulsates in rocks and ikons. From a phenomenological point of view there is something to be said for saying that we have external counterparts, so to speak, to our feelings. A person with authority seems to emanate power, for instance, and a film star radiates beauty. The power exists in things to affect us, and since the sacred is solemn, it emanates a solemn, serious, deep power. This is where it is useful to use such an expression as "charged." When something is performatively highly charged, then it has the properties of the sacred (or its opposite). Nationhood tends to reinforce a feeling for the territory of such depth that the land becomes highly charged, and so sacred space. If the Shah takes away from Iran a casket of Iranian soil then this is to be used by him as a performative whereby he celebrates his land, and mourns its passing from his power.

A nation also draws substance from its future as well as its past. The death of hope is where the future has no charge for me: likewise when a group has no spirit left and sees no future, it disintegrates in despair—like some smaller ethnic groups in the face of white conquest and powerful new values, good and bad. Such national accidie is, however, rare; especially in the course of the struggle for freedom peoples have a strong interest in the future. This is partly the attraction of revolutionary ideology. The very notion of a revolution is a new start, a rite of passage, in which the humiliations of outside dominance will be replaced by the glory of a new order. A successful war of liberation, a revolution—these are purifying processes in which the old nation is put off and the new nation put on. They are collective cases of being twice-born. Indeed, one might point to great wars as of sacred significance in that the fellowship of suffering and the promise of a new deal help to give the people new solidarity and new hope.

So far in this analysis of the nation I have made use of various ideas. I think they might be useful ones in simplifying our understanding of the emotional and practical life of humankind, and of religion in particular. As a more general category than that of ritual, I have spoken of the performative act; as a more general category than that of myth I have used the idea of a charged story; as a more general category than sacred I have used the idea of a certain sort of charge. Let me explore this last point a little further.

Things and people can have special powers. These powers cause or suggest certain reactions of feeling and action in us. They are either beneficent, neutral, or malevolent; good, indifferent, or bad; or as I shall say, positive, neutral, or negative. Thus a threatening dog has a negative charge; a wheedling one a positive charge; one trotting past a neutral charge. Typically, that is: circumstances can change this. It is a natural response to enhance or maintain positive values and to diminish or restrain negative ones—maximizing the positive, minimizing the negative. The sacred may be regarded simply as that which has fairly intense positive value: it has a high positive charge.

A main type of performative act (and a typical piece of ritual) can be said to be a conveying or communication of value. Thus when I enter a church, a sacred space, I speak in whispers, and do not act arrogantly or with disrespect. By a kind of self-deprecation or self-restraint I reduce my value somewhat and communicate sacrificed value to what is sacred. But such proper behavior opens up the interface between me and the sacred, and in exchange for my self-deprecation I gain the charged blessing of what is sacred. There are thus transactions across the interface between what is highly charged, sacred, and me.

This perhaps helps to illuminate the idea of mystical participation. It can either be *gaining a share of* or *being a part of*. Roughly speaking: the believer can gain a share of God (if God so permits—he can gain the grace of God, which is God's good substance in action); while the patriot is part of his nation. Thus a vital part of the mark of such belonging is the territory of the nation, and in a certain sense the land and the patriots mutually inhere. Thus from the point of view of *our* substance the invasion of our territory by hostile outsiders is a desecration and a direct attack: a desecration because the value of the land is diminished *for us,* and sacredness is *for us;* it is a direct attack because our substance is directly diminished. The nation is, so to speak, a performative transubstantiation whereby many individuals become a superindividual.

I use the word "transubstantiation" a little advisedly. I have also on occasion used the idea of substance. I do not mean it in any technical sense, as used in philsosphy. Rather, by "substance" I mean the sum or balance of performatively communicated value, as it inheres in an individual or entity. Identification with a group involves pooling part of my substance with that of others. Such a pooling is a performative matter: pledging my loyalty, etc.

Let me now illustrate some of my analysis by considering the logic of certain phenomena in religion and nationalism. I'll begin this part with an analysis of a passage from Marshal Mannerheim's memoirs. He writes of the famous Winter War against the Soviet Union:

May coming generations not forget the dearly bought lessons of our defensive way. They can with pride look back on the Winter War and find courage and confidence in its glorious history. That an army so inferior in numbers and equipment should have inflicted such serious defeats on an overwhelmingly powerful enemy, and, while retreating, have over and over again repelled his attacks is something for which it is hard to find a parallel in the history of war. But it is equally admirable that the Finnish people, face to face with an apparently hopeless situation, were able to resist a feeling of despair and, instead, to grow in devotion and greatness. Such a nation has earned the right to live.[3]

His words here are a celebration of heroic deeds. They are manifest in that the Finns showed disproportionate power. Perhaps the Russians may have admired the Finnish resistance, but they could not be proud of it: for pride is feeling good about what I/we have done. "Looking back on" a past good deed is a kind of celebration in the mind. We say "looking back" by analogy with gazing at in admiration: to gaze in a certain way is to expose oneself to the impact of an object. It opens an interface, through which the power of the object flows. So, then, the Winter War has generated the positive value that flows via celebration in the mind to future generations. This enhances their Finnish substance, for they look back not on random individuals but individuals bonded performatively by consciousness of being Finnish and fighting for Finland. But why is displaying courage so good? (And incidentally, how ought Finnish courage to impress the Russians?)

Courage in war is fighting without avoiding the risks: it at least mimics fearlessness. It is preparing to meet death, the ultimate self-sacrifice. Dying for one's country is using up one's substance (or much of it, as we shall see) on behalf of the national group: performatively it enhances the substance of the nation.

Courage, effectively expressed in the business of fighting, often elicits admiration in the enemy by the following logic: combat is itself a performative struggle issuing ultimately in one side or the other acknowledging defeat. The courage of the enemy is in principle daunting, for preparedness to die makes for the effective exercise of fighting power. So, an enemy's courage is impressive. That it in addition can attract praise arises because the military men, or fighting men in general, become somewhat performatively bonded by fighting each other. Speaking from that transnational constituency it is natural to praise its primary virtue. Praising an enemy is also a way of enhancing one's own victory.

I have suggested too that death in battle is, if undertaken in the right spirit, a noble sacrifice, and thus communicates the individual's sacrificed value to the store of substance accruing to the nation. In fact, the more people that die for their nation without weakening the nation's capacity to sustain itself in relevant ways against other nations, the better. Provided that they can also be commemorated. The absolutely anonymous dead are not much use, for their death-value cannot be celebrated and thereby communicated to the nation. The commemoration in fact serves a double purpose, for it does something, through our mourning, to convey substance to the dead (so they live on in a kind of way, and so are not utterly devoid of substance, great though their sacrifice of substance has been); it conveys their sacrificed substance to the nation.

My analysis suggests also that a nation—such as the Finnish people, who according to Mannerheim have earned the right to live—is a complex performative construct, sacramentally bonded: it is perhaps like a person, for it has a body, namely the land; it has a mind, namely its population; it has a biography, namely its mythic history, its charged story; it has clothes, namely the flag, the monuments, the poetry of its tradition. It has a future.

From a philosophical point of view such an organic, even idealist, account of a nation may be open to criticism. But phenomenologically it is vital to note that the nation is in its own strange way present to the minds of its members, and to members of other nations. Thus a nation is a phenomenological focus of loyalty, hostility, etc.

Here, as an aside, an important point emerges. A vital aspect of psychology is how such constructs as a nation actually enter into a people's experience. The flow of human events in history and society, in individual living, is such that there is impinging upon consciousness and feeling entities that have phenomenological reality and a special shape, independent of whether they have actual existence. Nations belong to this class of construct.

The nation as performative construct transcends the individuals who belong to it. This sometimes makes the sense of duty to the nation seem as if it is a duty to something Other. It mimics divine duty.

Here it is appropriate to see how nationalism is, and how far it is not, like a religion. Or rather, perhaps I should say "patriotism." Nationalism from one point of view can be defined as the theory that each nation should have its nation-state. Patriotism is devotion to my own nation-state, and incorporates the view that my nation should have its rightful (whatever that is) place in the world. If one were to try out the six-dimensional analysis on it that I have used above, one could see patriotism as involving a rather weak doctrinal dimension (already summed up as the view of my nation's rightful place); strong in myth—the charged story of my people; strong in ethics, for I have a duty to die for my country; intermittent in ritual (I stand for the national anthem, give suitable praise to the royal family or whoever, etc.); moderately strong in experience, for I feel glory as a patriot at my nation's achievements; and strong in social form, for so many institutional pressures and expressions guide me to do what I should do—pay taxes and so forth. But it is not a universal religion: it is more akin to a tribal religion. Moreover, it has nothing truly transcendent.

This is why the Christian, Marxist, or Buddhist—not to mention others belonging to universal viewpoints—will have a certain ultimate scepticism about patriotism. But it happens that often such ideological forms are used as reinforcements of nationalism. This is above all true of Marxism, since "the people" inevitably gets defined in national terms where states are sovereign, and socialist centralization strengthens immeasurably the organs of the state and so the power of the nation against its members.

But people need the security of a group. In modern society groups intermediate between the family and the nation tend to dissolve—through industrialization, mobility of folk, the voracious demands of the state, new communications and mores. So ethnic identity is important and should not be attacked. But (if I may permit a valuation of these matters) it ought to be transcended. To transcend is to go through something to something beyond. There used to be the patriotic bumper sticker "America: love it or leave it." Maybe it should have read "Love it and leave it." But my aim in this paper has been essentially to analyze, not to judge.

This analysis has a number of components—performative

acts, positive and negative charges, charged story as myth, substance, and the idea of a phenomenological construct. A nation is a superindividual that is a phenomenological construct resulting from performative acts in which individuals communicate and pool positively charged substance, including the charged space of territory and the charged story of their past.

NOTES

1. Z.A.B. Zeman, *Twilight of the Hapsburgs* (New York: Heritage Press, 1961), p. 31.

2. See especially A.D. Smith, *Theories of Nationalism* (London: Duckworth, 1971).

3. Marshal Mannerheim, *The Memoirs of Marshal Mannerheim* tr. Count Eric Lewenhaupt (London: Cassell, 1953), p. 373.

What Is a Nation?

Jaroslav Krejci

As is well known, "nation" is an elastic concept. Its elasticity has three dimensions: cultural, political, and psychological. The cultural and political dimensions can be assessed by objective, i.e., externally observable, criteria. The psychological dimension is a subjective one; it consists of the awareness of belonging to a certain collectivity sustained by successive generations and bound together by what may be called a collective historical memory.

Some observers have noted that this type of awareness possesses myth-like qualities.[1] This is especially the case when the national consciousness acquires such an intensity that one's own nation becomes an idol, the greatness and prestige of which are worth any sacrifice. Through such a sacrifice the myth becomes a reality of everyday life, a reality that is likely to produce innumerable moral challenges to those who are called upon to bear witness to it with their own lives.

Yet the national idol is not always so demanding; it does not always form the focal point for societal loyalty. Throughout the world, history has seen periods when national consciousness was so weak that nations could be considered as mere ethnic categories, often without clear-cut boundaries. In such cases, the supreme societal idol was erected elsewhere. Loyalties were focused primarily on a religious community or on a monarchical institution which often had only loose links with what might have been called a nation.

So whether based on the nation or not, societal myths and idols have always been with us. The same can be said of society's demands for utter loyalty and readiness for self-sacrifice on the part of its members. It is well known that there have been historical periods that saw in different parts of the world an alternation of different focuses for people's primary loyalties. The sequence of religious, dynastic, and national wars exemplifies the shifts in values which provided the subsequent basis for the ideational integration of societal units.

For our observations it is significant that both these alternatives to national loyalty—i.e., religion and dynasty—operated within the same three dimensions as "nation," yet in different proportions. Religious loyalties may be classified as predominantly cultural, dynastic loyalties as predominantly political. In the case of a nation both these types of loyalty tend to be blended so that the result increases the intensity of the third, the psychological dimension of the collectivity.

Within a nation, the cultural dimension finds its main expression in ethnicity, which is as a rule manifested in a particular language. The political dimension is determined by the existence of a sovereign state or a similar territorial power unit. This of course presupposes a more or less compactly settled territory. If an ethnic group lives scattered throughout a wider area, the political aspirations of that group are forced (as will be shown later) to find other forms of self-assertion.

The relative frequencies of the main forms of expression of the cultural and political dimensions of a nation may be illustrated using the case of Europe. In a study of ethnic problems in Europe,[2] 69 ethnic groups were identified in that part of the world toward the end of 1977. Identification marks in the two objectively assessable dimensions were as follows:

On the cultural plane:
  56 were identified primarily by their own literary language
  5 by a specific religious allegiance
  7 by a particular politico-historical development
  1 by a special way of life

On the political plane:
  24 were identified by their own formally sovereign state
  20 by a federated status (membership in a federation)
  16 by an autonomous status (within another nation-state)
  9 currently lacked any political identity.

With respect to the geographical conditions:
  56 were settled in compact territories
  11 were settled in ethnically mixed territories
  2 lived scattered in diaspora

In all 69 cases a fairly highly developed national consciousness was noted, though its intensity or levels varied according to the individual social groups or geographical areas (vertically and horizontally stratified consciousness). Cases of a two-tier national consciousness such as, for instance, Scottish and British, or Bavarian and German, were also noted. In several cases linguistic ethnicity has been combined with a particular religious affiliation; as a result of such a combination the psychological dimension of a nation tends to become particularly accentuated (national consciousness attains a high degree of intensity).

In defining the concept of nation, contemporary official terminology favors the political dimension. Each sovereign state, however minute, is considered a "nation," irrespective of whether it is based on an ethnic group or not. Such a "nation," however, may lack a full cultural and psychological identity. The cultural and psychological dimensions may be more developed within another aggregation of people; national consciousness may be based on a different bond from that which forms the basis of a given state; ethnic nationality need not be identical with political nationality, i.e., citizenship.

If we consider the world as a whole we discover innumerable nuances of ethno-political relationship: multinational states that in turn may be federations of whole ethnic nations, as in the case of the U.S.S.R. and India, or federations of parts of ethnic nations, as in the case of Switzerland and Belgium, or federations of states each of which is inhabited by a (broadly speaking) differently structured mixture of a dominant nationality and several ethnic and/or racial segments, as in the case of the U.S.A. and Brazil; on the other hand there are multistate ethnic nations such as the Arabs and the Germans. Further, there are ethnic nations that do possess their own one-nation states, but also have fragments living in other states; these fragments may be either in the position of equal confederates, such as the French speakers in Belgium and Switzerland, or in the position of an ethnic minority, such as the Hungarians in Rumania and other neighboring states, and the Chinese in Malaysia.

Then of course there are one-nation states which at the same time are one-state nations, such as for instance Japan, Norway, and Poland, and one-nation states with ethnic minorities, like Italy or Finland in Europe, and Iran and Burma in Asia. Further, there are ethnic groups that are identified primarily by their specific religious allegiance, such as the Jews, or by a specific juxtaposition of religion and language, as are the Yugoslav Muslims. Finally, there are ethnic groups whose identity is given merely by their specific historical experience, such as the Scots and the Eritreans.

Needless to say, all these different ethno-political combinations are reflected in differences in the psychological dimension. Particular juxtapositions of ethnic and political claims on loyalty are likely to bear dysfunctional consequences. Stateless ethnic groups strive for their own independent states or at least for a federated or autonomous status. People in states whose population is part of a wider ethnic nation are inclined to envisage either unification of their lands in one state or federation as a desirable end. The Italians and to some extent the Germans achieved this aim in the nineteenth century, but the Germans again became divided as a result of World War II, in which Hitler transformed the drive for still more unification into an imperialist expansion. The Indonesians achieved their unification in the teeth of the opposition of their constitutive ethnic groups, which under different political conditions might have well developed into separate ethnic nations with several distinct literary languages. For the Arabs, political unification is still in the cards, but so far several partial attempts in that direction have met with failure.

On the whole the states whose populations consider themselves as part of other or wider ethnic nations can best base their identity and their claims on their citizens' loyalty on the longeval existence of a separate state, which may eventually lead to a specific collective consciousness. This need not necessarily be a straightforward process—witness, for instance, the case of the Austrians. Even if such states draw support from ideological sources for their claim to national identity, as do, for instance, East Germany, North Korea, and South Yemen, the crystallization of a specific collective (national) consciousness may take a long time. Any ingenious crosssection analysis which is based on a mere thirty-year period, such as Schweigler's, can hardly be taken as a reliable forecast.[3]

In the prevailing opinion, historical experience is the decisive factor for the combination of the three existential dimensions of a nation, i.e., the cultural, the political, and the psychological. I would like to demonstrate this point by looking at the different development of the ethno-political relationship in Europe and in America. Referring to the currently prevalent sense of the term nation, we can describe the respective experiences as two different patterns of "nation-building."

The most usual pattern of nation-building in Europe proceeded from a tribe (patriarchal organization based on kinship) through a dynastic state (monarchic organization based on feudal bonds or hierarchy of estates) to a nation-state (organization by means of representative or bureaucratic institutions based on an enlarged, more or less linguistic kinship). Exceptions to the rule were provided in the earlier stage by the city-state, later by the multinational empire.

This simplified picture requires some qualification. As one of the supposed virtues of monarchs was the enlargement of their realm both in terms of territory and wealth, the conquest of other tribes was actively pursued. So, dynasties either united kindred tribes or imposed the rule of their own tribe on alien tribes. In providing their kingdoms with an increasingly more coherent administration, judiciary, and police, the kings gradually built up state apparatuses that, as Francis[4] correctly perceives, could eventually do without a monarch. Moreover, these apparatuses, being in need of written documents, eventually became instrumental in providing a common literary language.

As long as the Catholic Church was the main sociocultural force in the greater part of Europe, Latin could be used for this purpose. As a result of the Reformation, however, vernaculars started to take over this function; consequently state apparatuses also started to use national languages, the standardization of which was based either on Bible translations or on outstanding works of literature. So gradually, long before the French Revolution, a national consciousness reaching far beyond the original tribal framework started to crystallize, especially among the literate strata. (Outside the Catholic orbit there was in Europe only Orthodox Christian Russia and the Orthodox Christian Balkans, the latter with a superimposed Islamic layer; here the development was similar to that in other parts of Europe but with different timing.) Yet this was a period where only the literate elite could keep the national consciousness alive; consequently there was some scope for the assimilation of even less closely related ethnic groups.

Through the involvement of broader masses in the political struggle the French Revolution and the subsequent trends of liberalism and democratization brought about a growth in national consciousness. The emerging "mass society," stratified de facto rather than de jure, was increasingly receptive to nationalistic attitudes and symbols. In fact, the shift to nationalistic values was often stronger than the call for that kind of democracy which mainly stressed individual liberties and representative government. This facilitated the raise of popular movements subject to a more or less authoritarian leadership. Nationalism thus became an additional force of "social mobilization." The interplay of mobilization and socialization processes became a crucial factor in so-called nation-building.[5]

Where the dynastic state was, geographically speaking, approximately identified with a linguistic community (a society using one and the same literary language), the transition from a legally stratified society in a dynastic state to a nation-state and a mass society was only a matter of political restratification: an extension of citizenship and a representative government, or some other type of government capable of promoting "social mobilization." When the dynastic state either encompassed only a fragment of a linguistic community, or stretched over two or several such communities, the political restratification was complicated by ethnic issues.[6] In the first case (the dynastic state smaller than the linguistic group) there was the struggle for unification into one nation-state; in the second case (the multi-ethnic state) there was the struggle for self-assertion by each individual linguistic community, and possibly the emancipation of the weaker ones from the domination of the stronger.

After the French Revolution there was an attempt to revitalize religious and dynastic loyalties; yet the liberal and democratic movements gathered momentum and those dynastic regimes that wanted to preserve their power had to make concessions in one or other or even both directions. With the weakening of religious and dynastic loyalties, it was the sociocultural bond of ethnicity that became the main integrative force, a force based on what for human beings is the most important means of communication—language. In that epoch no other societal force could provide a more efficient basis for spontaneous integration within the boundaries of a state. Although the multistate nations did not fully disappear from the map of Europe, the multinational state had either to become federalized or to go.

A pattern of ethno-political relationships quite different from that in Europe can be observed in lands overseas settled by Europeans. At the outset the new settlers considered themselves as offshoots of their respective mother nations. Only after a century or even longer did they realize that they had grown different and that they no longer needed the tutelage of the mother country, which on occasion became too burdensome. They emancipated themselves, becoming independent states, and because their leaders were in many respects inspired by the European example, they envisaged a possible development on nation-state lines. This, however, was hampered by several serious obstacles. First, in most cases, these states were far from ethnically homogeneous, and second, they did not include all the settlers of a single immigrant ethnic group. Moreover, individual states became, to different degrees, subject to extensive additional immigration by widely varying ethnic and even racial groups. These groups became scattered all over the respective countries without creating, as a rule, areas of compact settlements. Nevertheless, in spite of considerable pressure for the acculturation of immigrants, full assimilation and absorption was achieved only if immigrants were similar to the host nation either ethnically or with respect to their own social stratification.[7]

Furthermore, in most Latin American countries there has remained a considerable body of indigenous Indians who have still not been assimilated, in spite of a continuing process of mixing through intermarriage. As most Indians belong to the lowest social strata of the population, ethnic and racial differences acquire strong class connotations. In these conditions, the culturally unassimilated Indians are "vertical" ethnic groups. So the population of a state has to come to nationhood along a path that is quite different from the European one. This happens through the absorption of the numerically weaker or culturally less self-assertive groups in the melting pot. In the light of this the stress on nation-building is more easily understandable.

This situation is also reflected in the term "ethnic" used as a noun, introduced by Warner[8] to indicate a member of a minority ethnic group. The idea that members of majority ethnic groups should not be labelled ethnics may seem bizarre to any ethnologist, but for sociologists, it may well be acceptable. This term then stands only for an additional element in the stratification pattern.

In this context a further difference vis-à-vis Europe has to be stressed: in Europe most ethnic groups are demarcated by distinct geographical boundaries. In the Americas such a situation is an exception. A geographical demarcation is a natural obstacle to ethnic mingling. An ethnic melting pot is possible only where people of different ethnic and racial origin live close together and have unhampered opportunities for mutual contact. In such a case only social barriers based on different types of ideological motivation for preserving the group identity may slow down or even halt the process of mingling.

Whether an ethnic minority lives in a compactly settled territory or not is most relevant for its aspirations. With a compactly settled territory there is a case for national independence or, at least, territorial autonomy. Where the minority is scattered, it strives primarily for equal opportunities with the dominant ethnic majority (equal access to better jobs and higher rewards). The need for autonomy, if any, is reduced to the cultural-personal sphere. In the whole of America there is virtually only one ethnically conscious minority with its own compactly settled territory in which it constitutes a majority: the French Canadians. Otherwise, there are what American scholars call ethnic segments, who are so scattered that they are a minority everywhere; consequently they are interested primarily in equal rights with the dominant ethnic group or compound.

The peculiarity of the American situation can also be seen from a brief glance at the political map of North America. Boundaries between the states or provinces are often drawn according to the parallels and meridians; this is often also the case where other, more sensible borderlines (following rivers or mountain ranges) could easily be drawn. Such straight boundaries bear witness to the fact that when they were drawn, either the respective areas were sparsely populated by the European settlers, or it did not matter on which side of the border their inhabitants turned out to be. It shows that the demarcation of provinces and states preceded their ethnic content, which was eventually structured according to other circumstances as a result of later immigration.

Moreover, in the U.S.A. multi-ethnicity is complicated by the wide range of different religious denominations, sometimes identified with particular ethnic groups like the Mennonites, or even gradually assuming similar features like the Mormons.[9] More often than not, however, religious affiliation cuts across racial and ethnic distinctions.[10]

As long as the absorption of ethnic minorities, whether primary (indigenous) or secondary (immigrant) is not completed and as long as there is, as far as Latin America is concerned, a plurality of sovereign states with identical or similar ethnic structures, it may be apposite to label these American countries territorial rather than nation-states. If Americans themselves call them nations too, they have to realize that here nation means something quite different from what it means in Europe.[11]

The main differences between the European and American ethno-political (nation-state) relationship can be visualised in a form illustrated in the following table.

The development in other parts of the world seems, with the sole exception of Australia and New Zealand, to follow the European pattern. Most Asian states are one-nation states, some with considerable ethnic minorities; in Indonesia the attempt is being made to weld kindred ethnic groups into one nation; India is a multinational federation. In Africa, the one-nation state is an exception; although there is only one larger dynastic state, most of the African republics are ruled by presidents as if they were absolute monarchs. The modern African states emerged more often than not from the administrative divisions of European colonies, carved out from the African continent irrespective of its ethnic or religious structure. Consequently some

Patterns of Ethno-Political Relationship

	European Pattern		American Pattern
Stages*	Standard lines of development	Exceptional lines of development	Alternative lines of development

1.

tribes

tribes

Foreign occupation and primary immigration

2.

dynastic states		city-states
over kindred tribes	over non-kindred tribes	

c o l o n i e s	
with natives evicted or exterminated	with natives subjected

Liberation and new demarcation

3.

one-nation states with sizable non-autonomous ethnic minorities	multi-national states (empires)

territorial states	
of new-comers only	ethnically stratified

Secondary immigration

4.

one-nation states, possibly with ethnic minorities**	multinational federations

territorial states with additional ethnic segmentation and struggle for nationhood

Transitions
from stage 1 to 2   Polities (states) are superimposed on ethnies (tribal nations)   colonization upsets ethnic ties

2 to 3   Polities (states) deviate from ethnies (cultural nations)   colonies become states

Transitions
from stage (*continued*)

3 to 4	Polities adapt to enlarged ethnies with national consciousness (full-scale nations)	states aim at creating nations (political nations)
	States are built on nations (ethnicity precedes polity)	nations are built on states (polity precedes ethnicity)

---

*The different timing of these stages in individual parts of Europe or America does not upset the general lines of development.

**These, as a rule, either enjoy or strive for some kind of cultural or regional autonomy.

of the states unite kindred tribes and others different tribes; the former are likely to be transformed into one-nation states, the integration of the latter depends on whether they succeed in developing a federal structure or not.

In Africa, as was earlier the case in Europe, changes that have occurred or might occur in the future result either in the emancipation of ethnic nations, which thereby acquire their own states, or the amalgamation of kindred tribes into bigger nations. This is a process that in Europe was experienced in the hundred years between 1820 and 1920.

The African repetition of the European experience may give rise to the question whether the variety of nation-building patterns is not exhaustible. However much the concept of nation may vary in time due to changes in emphasis from one to another of its different dimensions, there is nevertheless a clearly observable tendency towards what may be described as the harmonization of the ethno-political relationship.

This harmonization, however, assumes different forms according to the respective historical patterns of nation-building. In Europe and in much of Asia, where most ethnic groups are geographically demarcated, this harmonization may be described as a tendency toward a situation where each ethnic nation has its own state or at least some reasonable degree of autonomy, and where each state is based on one nation only or on a genuine federation of nations. If for geographical reasons a particular state encompasses fragments of other ethnic groups living in a compactly settled territory (ethnic minorities), it grants them an adequate amount of cultural and political autonomy. In countries where most ethnic groups live in mixed territories, the harmonization presupposes generally equal opportunities for different ethnic or racial groups.

Within the European historical pattern the tendency towards ethno-political harmonization has, during the last 150 years, been pretty successful, but often at a disastrous cost in human lives and suffering. In 1820 more than half the population of Europe belonged to ethnic nations who either lacked a territorial political status of their own (state or autonomy) or were scattered among several dynastic states uninterested in their national aspirations. By 1920, the proportion of the total population represented by such ethnic groups (whole nations or their fragments) had declined to about seven percent. As a result of World War II, this figure dropped to only three percent. Yet, on the other hand, a new source of ethno-political disharmony was created through the division of Germany. The most recent harmonization arrangements include the federalization of Czechoslovakia (1968), Catalonian and Basque autonomy (1977 and 1979 respectively), the creation of the Jura canton in Switzerland (1978) and the continuing ethnic federalization of Belgium.[12]

Looking to other parts of the world we may draw the following conclusions. Since 1945 almost all European overseas colonies have become independent states. Yet this has not always happened in accordance with the ethnic structures of the countries concerned. Consequently, new tensions emerge, which are likely to persist as long as the necessary harmonization of the ethno-political relationship is not achieved.

So far there has been only one decolonized new state (it happens to be the most populous one—the Indian federation) that has thoroughly remodeled its member states' structure along ethnic lines. The provinces and dynastic units of the colonial era gave way to new territorial units based on individual nationalities. Pakistan, whose unity was based on a common religion, broke in two for ethnic and geographical reasons.

In Africa, where most of the former colonial provinces became independent states, such an adaptation is much more difficult. The ruling power elites want to perpetuate their rule, which more often than not relies on particular tribes or ethnic groups within the respective states. The Organization of African Unity tries to preserve the existing boundaries rather as the Holy Alliance tried to do in post-Napoleonic Europe. So far, peaceful actions have not met with success; neither have wars aimed at national liberation or at a redrawing of boundaries according to ethnic criteria. Yet the Sudan has granted a sort of autonomy to its southern ethnic minority and Nigeria has drawn up a federal constitution. It remains to be seen how far these arrangements will satisfy the minority groups.

Opposition to the ethnic readjustments of the new African states is lent weight by the fact that for the majority of official and educational purposes most of them use one of the languages of their former European masters. This helps them to avoid controversies between speakers of different domestic languages, controversies which in Europe were, and marginally still are, at the root of ethnic struggles. This gives the nation-building process in black Africa a chance to follow the Latin American rather than the European historical pattern.

Yet whatever pattern of nation-building the Africans eventually develop, it cannot evade the three-dimensional nature of that phenomenon. Political, cultural, and psychological factors have to be adequately harmonized with each other if fully fledged nations are eventually to emerge from these processes.

NOTES

1. B.C. Shafer, *Nationalism, Myth & Reality,* (New York: Harcourt, 1955).

2. J. Krejci, "Ethnic Problems in Europe," in *Contemporary Europe, Social Structures and Cultural Patterns,* S. Giner and M.S. Archer, eds. (London: Routledge and Kegan Paul, 1978) p. 135.

3. G.L. Schweigler, *National Consciousness in Divided Germany* (London: Sage, 1975).

4. E.K. Francis, *Inter-ethnic Relations, an Essay in Sociological Theory* (Amsterdam: Elsevier, 1976) p. 61.

5. K. Deutsch, *Nationalism and its Alternatives* (New York: Random House, 1969), pp. 21–27.

6. The interplay of mobilization and assimilation processes and the relevance of their respective timing for the nation-building has been reinterpreted by Stein Rokkan, "Dimension of State Formation" in Ch. Tilly, ed., *The Formation of National States in Western Europe* (Princeton: Princeton University Press, 1975) p. 562 ff.

7. Francis, op. cit., pp. 223–225.

8. W.L. Warner and P.S. Lunt, *The Social Life of a Modern Community* (New Haven: Yale University Press, 1941).

9. For arguments to this effect see Francis, op. cit., pp. 172–189.

10. For a conceptualization of this see M.M. Gordon, *Human Nature, Class and Ethnicity* (New York: Oxford University Press 1978) p. 110.

11. In view of European historical experience it sounds odd when American scholars treat ethnic groups in Europe as "segments" where problems have to be analyzed at "subnational level." For instance: Milton J. Esman, ed., *Ethnic Conflict in the Western World* (Ithaca: Cornell University Press, 1977).

12. For more detail on the European experience, see J. Krejci and V. Velimsky, *Ethnic and Political Nations in Europe* (London: Croom Helm, 1980).

THREE

Religion or Politics:
The Western Dilemma[1]

Raimundo Panikkar

In Western history the relationship between politics and religion has been beset by the following dilemma: either religion
and politics are considered to be identical (Caesaro-papism,
theocracy, *sacrum imperium* and all types of totalitarianisms),
or else one is pitted against the other as if religion and politics
were mutually incompatible and antagonistic forces (Church and
State, sacred and secular, God and Caesar, and all types of lib-
eralisms). In the first case, the union between the two not only
embroils religion in compromises that reduce it to a sectarian
status, but also loads politics with responsibilities that drive it
toward totalitarian attitudes. In the second case, the separation
of the two weakens religion by relegating it to a more and more
insignificant role, and gives rise to degeneracy in politics by
reducing it to a mere application of techniques or by converting
it into a religious ideology.

I would like to put forward the following hypothesis: the
problem of the relationship between politics and religion as it
presents itself in our contemporary world is one particular and
sometimes historically tragic instance of the monism/dualism
dilemma that has tormented Western civilisation since the Pre-

Socratics. I shall indicate the broad lines of my hypothesis both in sociological, as well as philosophical parameters. Furthermore, I approach the dilemma from an angle which, though situated within Western history, also sees the problem reflected in an Eastern mirror and therefore refracts it in such a way as to present a perspective which is simultaneously internal and external to the Western problematic. I would call this a cross-cultural approach.

In order to be brief, let me be precise: I understand "politics" to be the sum total of principles, symbols, means, and actions whereby Man endeavors to attain the *common good* of the *polis*. This "common good" is defined as the realization of human plentitude in the life of the city—the city being here the symbol of life lived in society. I understand by "religion" the sum total of principles, symbols, means, and actions whereby Man expects to reach the *summum bonum* of life. This *summum bonum* is defined as the realization of the plenitude of human life.

To preserve the parallelism with the *polis,* I should have added "in the Kingdom," the Kingdom being here the symbol of a universe that has been divinized. But I hesitate to use these words because the New Testament image of the Kingdom and the expression "divinized" of the Christian religion is foreign to many other cultural and religious traditions. One noteworthy characteristic of our epoch is that secular (and political) language seems to be far more universal than the language of the traditional religions.

To reformulate the hypothesis: Politics is the art of the means and ways for the realization of a human order. Order is the integration of each part into the whole. Religion is the art of the means and ways for the realization of the ultimate order. The tensions between the "a" and the "the," the "human" and the "ultimate," express the polarity between politics and religion. The different conceptions of the whole make for the different human traditions.

Our interpretation will say that we are approaching the close of the modern Western dichotomy between religion and politics, and we are coming nearer to a nondualistic relation between the two. All the burning religious issues are at the same time political, as the examples of Ireland, Lebanon, Israel, Iran, Latin America, etc. sufficiently show. Likewise, all the important political questions are at the same time religious, as the examples of Marxism, liberalism, capitalism, socialism, etc. make sufficiently clear. Religion without politics becomes uninteresting, just as politics without religion turns irrelevant. It is when both come together that they gain the power to affect human lives, and accordingly, it is when the two are mixed together that they can become explosive and dangerous.

SOCIOLOGICAL REFLECTIONS

Up to the present day, sociological formulations of the relations between religion and politics have been attempted almost exclusively in terms of institutions: Holy See and Empire, Church and State, church school and state school, religious marriage and civil marriage, Vatican and State of Italy (or anywhere else), etc. Also connected with this tendency is the concrete language in which the historical circumstances are couched, such as the questions of the "secularization" of ecclesiastical properties, the "state" of Israel, the problem of "Christian political parties," etc. All of these have become chronic areas of tension in Western civilization. One knows all too well how these problems have affected the conscience of our own day, particularly of the last two centuries. In this article I would like to go beyond this perspective, which is too limited in its expression and too inadequate, to articulate other possible avenues of approach to these problems.

Current language usage already betrays a dialectical bent: professional clergy is put in opposition to laity, religious to civil, secular to sacred, etc., just as if the *laos* were incapable of both professing and adhering to convictions, as if religion had no part to play in the city, as if temporal life must must always be profane, and so on. These are dichotomies that I would like to challenge in order to re-establish a certain orderliness which, while admitting valid distinctions, refrains from making artifical separations—separations that end by being of fatal consequence for both parties. I suspect that not a few of our contemporary totalitarianisms were brought into being mainly by violent reactions against the dichotomy between politics and religion; the human impulse seems to fly against such schizophrenic attempts to re-unite the poles by short-circuiting and lapsing all too easily into monism (heteronomy).

Let us try to outline a certain typology. Either the relationship between politics and religion is an extrinsic one, and in that case dependent upon a third factor that puts them in relationship; or it is an intrinsic one, that is to say, one rooted in the very nature of religion and politics. In the first instance, when it is a question of a purely extrinsic relation between religion and politics, one presupposes an autonomy within each of these two spheres of human activity. However, since religious and political activities are often intertwined, a superior and independent factor is required to regulate their relationship. Reason has often been advanced as the classical example of this third factor. Its role consists, it is said, in telling us what the function of politics is, or what the mission of religion is. Yet difficulties both theoretical as well as practical have hindered the establishment of a simple pragmatic *modus vivendi*.

In the second instance, when it is a question of an intrinsic relation, one is presupposing a *heteronomous* relationship in which either religion lays down what is the common good or the goal of life, and leaves it to, or even dictates to the politicians the means of attaining it. Sometimes just the reverse is the case: it is politics that decides what this common good and this goal is, and leaves to religion its particular sphere, dictating its function to it.

The relationship can also be *ontonomous;* that is to say, it can be one of constitutive interdependence regulated by the very nature of both religion and politics as being two elements of one and the same human reality. Elsewhere I have gone more fully into this concept of ontonomy, distinguishing it both from heteronomy (which is monolithic) and autonomy (which is atomistic).[2]

Let us offer the following scheme:

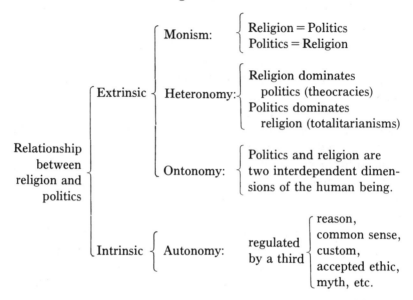

Relationship between religion and politics

- Extrinsic
  - Monism: Religion = Politics / Politics = Religion
  - Heteronomy: Religion dominates politics (theocracies) / Politics dominates religion (totalitarianisms)
  - Ontonomy: Politics and religion are two interdependent dimensions of the human being.
- Intrinsic
  - Autonomy: regulated by a third — reason, common sense, custom, accepted ethic, myth, etc.

By studying the development of the modern Christian West from the socio-historic point of view one can discern a certain dynamism which clearly shows how the political has progressively usurped the place of the religious. For the sake of brevity, I will confine myself to a slight sketch limited to the West.

We can observe in the West a revealing parallelism: religion controls the relationship of men with the divine. It is the bond, link (*religio*) between the human and the superhuman (God). It belongs to the sphere of the supernatural, the sacred, the eternal, and also to the church: *religatio divina*. Politics, for its part, controls the relationship of men with society. It is the link (*religio*) of the human being with the inter-human (man and men). It belongs to the sphere of the natural, the profane, the temporal, as well as to the state: *religatio humana*. In this way of thought, vertical *religatio* consists in religion, whereas horizontal *religatio* consists in politics. But can one admit such a cleavage either in man or in reality?

The supreme value for both attitudes is expressed by an ambivalent word: salvation, *moksha, soteria.* Well-being is *beatitudo, ānanda* and can be interpreted either as a religious "well-being" or as social "welfare;" as a religious liberation or a political liberty. In this sense, religion would be termed the relationship with the Other or the Transcendent, while politics would be the relationship with Others or Exteriority.[3]

I stop at this point because my concern is not so much with an analysis of the relationships between "religion" and "politics" as with a consideration of the real nature of these two concepts. Indeed, I fear that these two words, when understood in dialectical opposition, have lost their meaning. It appears to me that it is necessary to find a new meaning in them, so as to express the polarity of an ontonomous (intrinsic) relationship.

PHILOSOPHICAL REFLECTIONS

Philosophical reflection on the problem of the relationship between religion and politics should question at the outset whether it is only when the relationship is considered to be of a dialectical nature that such a problem appears.

All too often it seems to be taken for granted that religion is only concerned with the divine, the supernatural, the eternal, the sacred and, in the Christian view, with the ecclesiastical sphere and the Christian individual; while, similarly, politics is only concerned with the earthly, the natural, the temporal, the profane and, in Christian belief, the lay and human.

Now these are dualisms I would like to challenge. We could put it somewhat brutally by citing the overabundance of concrete historical exceptions: Buddhism does not accept the divine, Hinduism shuns the supernatural as such, mysticism goes beyond the cleavage eternity–temporality, humanism is ill at ease in the sacred, and we may further add that a certain brand of Christianity tends to protest against a professed ecclesiastical monopoly on salvation or some kind of privileged status for Christians. In other words, *separation* between politics and religion is only understandable in the climate of dualist thought, while their *identification* is only understandable in a world of monism.

However it may be with these examples and with the complexity of the problems raised, I would suggest a different approach to the problem of the relationship between religion and politics, and that neither dualism nor monism will be of any help to us in finding a solution to our problem.

My hypothesis intends to go beyond the dualist presuppositions of earlier arguments without, however, falling into monism. Obviously, time is not eternity, nor God, man; the sacred is not the same as the profane, we must not confound Church with State, or God with Caesar. But epistemological distinctions do not imply ultimate ontological separations. The *fundamentum in re* of distinctions is not the *res*. Reality is neither purely temporal nor exclusively eternal; it is not "for the moment" temporal and "afterward" eternal; God and the world are not two realities, nor are they one and the same. Moreover, to return to our subject, politics and religion are not two independent activities, nor are they one indiscriminate thing. There is no politics separate from religion. There is no religious factor that is not at the same time a political factor. There is no question of substituting one for the other, nor of sterilizing them by turning them into mere techniques (political and religious) at the service of some higher ideology. The divine tabernacle is to be found among men; the earthly city is a divine happening. A politics that is soulless (areligious) is as cramped as a religion without a body (apolitical)—though I am not thereby defending the theory of religion as the soul of politics or the thesis of the soul and the body.

Religion has not to do with an eternal deprived of temporal roots, nor has politics to do with a temporal stripped of transtemporal repercussions; for reality is not cut in two, nor is man temporal on the one hand and eternal on the other. Though it would help illumine our problem, I will not explain the concept of *tempiternity* here in this paper, since I have done so elsewhere.[4] It is sufficient to observe that every real human question involves the total nature of man: and, we may add, that to attribute insecurity, gropings, and the provisional to politics while reserving security, stability, and the definitive for religion wrongs the first as much as the second. This type of hypocrisy where, for example, religious authorities claim to keep themselves unspotted from all worldly contact by leaving the administration of justice to the "secular arm," or where a civilian government absolves itself from its responsibilities by leaving the task of maintaining public order or national peace to a police-military system is no longer acceptable in this day and age. Nor does it carry conviction nowadays that a Buddhist monk should put on gloves out of fidelity to the rule not to handle money. One cannot totally separate politics from religion any more than one can separate the civil from the military.

To sum up: the distinctions natural–supernatural, temporal–eternal, secular–sacred, human–Christian, individual–personal must be reconsidered in depth and, in any case, cannot be turned into ultimate ontological divisions. Here, however, I must stop lest I develop a whole metaphysical thesis.

A NON-DUALIST VIEWPOINT

The history of the relationship between religion and politics in the West resembles the history of a marriage: at the outset the partners promised an eternal fidelity; then came a mutual disenchantment, accusations were levied on both sides with recriminations; there followed a legal divorce, after which each side began to respect the other; and now attempts are being made to declare the marriage null and void. Politics and religion should never have been married; there must have been a misunderstanding on the side of one or the other party that now must be cleaned up *a radice*.

Without abusing the metaphor, I would like to submit that the situation we face is rather a question of legitimizing or of recognizing the son born of this union: a son in which the two natures of the parents unite in a hypostatic union in such a way as to offer us today a new intuition about both politics and religion. This son is not yet baptised, and thus has no name; but I shall try to describe his physiognomy.

First, let us take a look at some of the signs of our times. People speak of a politics of engagement and of a religion of incarnation. We are discovering the sacred character of secular engagement and the political aspect of religious life. Secular work reveals its own mystical dimension, and the monk understands his vocation as a *monachos* not as an isolated being but rather as one that is integrated, that is to say, become-one-with everything.

It is not only the political activity of man that contains a sacred thrust and a religious energy; the modern religious ideal contains within it a secular interest and a political involvement. I am thinking here not only of the religious zeal of communist cells or the political zeal of the "secular institutes," but also of the numerous Eastern movements transplanted to the West which no longer preach a *fuga mundi* or a *contemptus saeculi*. I am thinking of the growth of a Christianity that is less and less ecclesiastical, and of civil and political activities that are less and less subject to party disciplines.

This is not new in what concerns the absorption of the political by the religious, or of the religious by the political, i.e., in a heteronomic relationship. What is new is the ontonomy between the two, that is, the intuition that there is no authentic religion without a political dimension, and no true politics without a religious dimension. *"Dios toma la forma de pan"* was the slogan of one Eucharistic congress; "Work is worship" is a slogan of contemporary India.

Now let us try to outline certain fundamental characteristics.

From the side of religion, there is the question, for example, of an awareness being born that heaven and hell are not in a "beyond" of either space or time, but that they constitute a dimension inherent in the human being and in reality; that God is not a totally separate or separable being, above and outside human life in all its complexity, but that the divine is incarnate and involved in that very life in which man plays his part; that the celestial city is not a second city for the elect, but that it represents, so to speak, the channels of communication and the joy of earthly paradise constantly lost and refound; that love of God is love of the neighbor and vice versa. We could continue.

From the side of politics, there is the question, for example, of an awareness taking hold that political activity cannot be reduced to a simple choice of means towards the common good, but that it emerges from both a search for as well as the creation of this same common good, for which, furthermore, it assumes responsibility; that secular activity can be just as sacred as so-called religious activity; that one cannot separate bread for the body from nourishment for the mind or from the elixir of life for the heart; that cities have not only the need for green zones, but also a need for free zones, etc.

Concretely, this means that the problem of religion and politics cannot be identified with the question of Church and State. One may need to distinguish the institutions, but one cannot separate religion from life, just as one cannot separate politics from life.

To quote the phrase of Galileo: "The Church tells us how to go to heaven; Science, how the heavens go." This separation is no longer tenable (in an ontonomic sense, not in the heteronomic sense of the arguments of that day). Now the circle is coming to a close. The path *to* heaven can no longer be divorced from the path *of* heaven: one does not arrive *at* heaven, at human–divine plenitude, except by walking *with* heaven as well as with men and the earth, in order that the whole of reality should get closer to truth, justice, and love. One does not enter heaven alone; it is necessary that somehow the earth enters with us. Those who are deaf to the cries of men are blind to the presence of God. There is no true religion without an incarnation in politics, nor is there true politics without its assumption by the religious.

The religious fulfillment of the human being is not achieved by escaping from the community, by abandoning the world, or by negating one's links with what I would call the "tribe" (a word expressing family, church, race, people, region, nation, group, etc.). The human being is not an individual who is *also*

"social." It is in the person where we find the very locus of
I/Thou/It/We/You/They. There is no personhood in isolation.
To think that I can go to God or establish friendship with him,
to think that I can reach *nirvāṇa, moksha* or heaven by cutting
all my ties with the rest of reality has certainly been a constant
temptation for the religious soul, but this kind of world-negat-
ing attitude leads to the degradation of religion. In other words,
the truly religious persons are involved with their fellow beings
and with the human problems of the community. Even if it
entails going up to the mountain or down into the cave, this is
a genuine religious act only if the recluse is somewhat sent or
sustained by the community that believes it needs him in that
particular place. The moment that the people cease to believe
in the "acosmic" monk, the monk ceases to be a true monk and
becomes a mere egoist, escaping from his duties. There is no
moksha without *dharma*. The religious attitude encompasses a
political stance, like any true political situation always has a
religious dimension.

Analogously, the political fulfillment of man is not achieved
by eschewing the ultimate issues of life or with some kind of
provisional success in excogitating the best theoretical means
for running a township or governing a state. The true *homo
politicus* is involved with the deepest concerns of his fellow
beings, and ultimately with the religious concerns of his constituency. Even if he advocates some very concrete technical
solutions for immediate problems he does not forget that those
problems are such only against the background of a much
larger, ultimately religious problematic. It is the moment when
the political man loses his almost "religious" aura and people
do not trust him, that the politician appears to be a mere egoist
who is looking after his exclusive interests or those of his particular clan.

Now for some reflections on the subject of the subtitle.
The paradox of the religion of the Incarnation par excellence
is that it has set in motion a reaction in the opposite direction,
and sometimes it has given the impression of being a spiritu-

ality purporting to keep itself on the sidelines of political problems. Historians outline the reasons for this, and sociologists try to persuade us that it is not so much a question of religion and politics as of the institutions of Church and State. Meanwhile the man in the street assures us that the distinction is purely theoretical, because in concrete life religion is mixed up with politics and politics meddles in religion.

Nonetheless, it is our task to ponder in depth the very nature of what is named politics as well as of that which is named religion. If the dichotomies I have mentioned can no longer be maintained as such, it is clear that the notion of "politics" meaning temporal and secular affairs, affairs that may be called natural, and the notion of "religion" meaning eternal and sacred affairs, that which may be called supernatural, are no longer valid. Man does not have two natures, two countries to which he belongs, two vocations. Religion is eminently political, and politics essentially a religious matter. Religion has to do with a concrete man, a political animal, while politics cannot ignore the nature of man, who is a religious animal. A religion for our times must be political, and thus cannot keep itself on the edge of problems of injustice, hunger, war, exploitation, the power of money, the function of the economy, armaments, ecological questions, demographic problems, etc. A politics that is really concerned with the human *polis* and desires to be something more than a technocracy at the service of an ideology (of whatever sort) can not only not ignore the religious roots of problems presented, but must take into its reckoning that human happiness is not exclusively a matter of intake of calories, that peace does not automatically result from a balance of power, that distribution of wealth is not a purely economic problem, nor questions of demography simply of a technical, medical or even moral sort, and so on.

I am not saying that institutions should be abolished, nor am I making any direct pronouncements on Church or State. I am, however, affirming that one must not identify religion with the church or politics with the state. I am affirming that modern life must be disentangled from its over-institutionalization and, consequently, that the same goes for both religious and political life. The elements of mystery and prophecy cannot be institutionalized, and they have their place in both religion and politics.

The urge to institutionalize stems from the dimension of *logos* in human life. *Logos* requires institutionalized structures in order to come to full flowering. I am not desirous of impugning either *logos* or institutions, but just want to point out that man is also spirit, *pneuma,* and that human life also has need of a free space (which is something more than a space of freedom). The spirit blows not only where it wills, but *how* it wills.

Nowadays, there has been much mention of demythization. Now myth has no need of institutions. Even in the concrete, there is a distinction between religion and church. Christianity tends to maintain the proposition that religion cannot subsist without a church. In the sacramental, and indeed in the mystical sense, this is certainly true for all religions: *mythos* and *logos* are de facto co-extensive. But this is not the case in the ecclesiastical sense of the word: *mythos* and *logos* are not identical, and de jure not comparable. Hinduism is a striking example of a living religion that is capable of penetrating the very marrow of the life of a people without any rigid form of ecclesiastical organization.[5]

To conclude, let us consider how to formulate this non-dualistic relation between religion and politics.

On the one hand, it must be stressed that it is not a question of there being two independent and separate activities: every political activity has its religious repercussions and vice versa. This is the case not only because the human being is a unity, but also because human destiny is unique. I am not here discussing what this final goal of human life may be, but am simply affirming that it is unique for each person, and involves the total being of each in his or her own way. As human beings we do not have a twofold end.

Politics deals with relationships between human beings, but

if religion means something more than mere superstition, these relationships are also religious. Religion opens us up toward the transcendent, but if politics means something more than mere technocracy, this openness is a conditioning factor in each and every human relationship, and thus religion is also political.

On the other hand, religion and politics are certainly not identical either. The city is not only built on plans devised by individuals, but in the final analysis, human life cannot be regulated simply by human wills, for even this "will" is something given. For those who believe in the transcendent, there remains a factor that is not to be reduced to any human whim. For those who do not so believe, there also remains an imponderable factor, or even a mystery that is equally irreducible to any political forecast. This mystery does not spring from a separate source of its own, but nonetheless pervades everything. There is always "something more."

The term "non-dualistic" that I use to describe this relationship causes us to take another step forward. It suggests, in fact, that the relationship between religion and politics can not be reduced to one of pure *theoria*. Thus fully to understand this relationship would be to destroy it and turn it into a dialectical relationship. It would then be open to manipulation from either the political or the religious side. Yet this relationship is not reducible to *praxis* either. Thus to control this relationship with pure *praxis* would destroy it and turn it into a mere ideology. Here we are dealing not with a vicious circle, but with a vital one. The real exists prior to a man's thought of it, even though it is formulated by this same thought. The relation between politics and religion can be defined neither a priori, nor once for all. It is not objectifiable, for it is innate in human nature, in people striving after their fulfillment.

No contradiction is involved in taking note of and expressing this non-duality. There would be so, however, if human speech were only a *logos* without spirit; i.e., if the word had only an autonomous intellectual content. Non-dualistic awareness of reality is not the awareness of an object (i.e., of reality—objective genitive), but rather the actual awareness of reality (subjective genitive) in us that is conscious of its own limitations.

Politics is always more—or other—than just "politics," and we are cognizant of this: it involves that which men have always called religion. Religion is always less—or other—than "religion;" it contains within itself that which men have called politics. The tension between the two is part of the very polarity of human existence and, indeed, of the real.

Summing up we could present this internal link between religion and politics from an anthropological angle. The human being has a thirst for fulfillment, no matter how we may interpret it. People want to be useful and to have a meaningful existence. Fulfillment, usefulness, and meaningfulness are not isolated values. They imply, or rather, demand an environment, a world. A "depoliticized" religion would strive for this fullness via the *communio sanctorum,* prayer, sacrifice, vicarious action, suffering, and the like. Hidden in their caves, buried in their monasteries, performing sacred rites—people still believe that they have some kind of power over the world, that they are working for the welfare and improvement of all humanity. A "desacralized" politics would tend toward bettering the human condition (as part and parcel of human fulfillment) via political action, mass media utilization, social involvement, revolution, financial power, and the like. Whether from their party headquarters or their financial desks, whether picketing or engaging in guerrilla warfare, people still believe that they have power over the world and are capable of eliminating the negative factors in human life.

The separation of these two realms has been deleterious for both. On the religious side, the acosmic monk tends to bury his talents and becomes ineffective; ritualistic action severed from life becomes irrelevant, masochistic mortification and world-denial become barren acts, etc. Likewise on the political side, the sheer politician faces despair and becomes cynical seeing that he has not reached the goal; the power of money turns out to be countereffective; industry, self-destructive; revolution, the seed of a more radical counter-revolution, and so on. The fight is to the bitter end because there is no transcendence.

But the manipulation by the one or the other is equally self-destructive of both religion and politics. On the one hand, to use prayer for social means, mortification for political power, or ritual for profane goals, etc., are typical examples of the degeneration of religion into magic, superstition, abuse, and so on. On the other, to manipulate political factors to foster or combat religion, to use the banking system for the kingdom of God, the Church for the State, or the State for the Church, etc., are equally degenerations of the very nature of politics. In the long run, moreover, such tactics simply do not work.

In other words, the relation is an "advaitic" relation, a non-dualistic relationship of the nature I have tried to describe. It is an intrinsic and thus nonmanipulable relationship that distinguishes but does not separate, allows for diversity but not for rupture, does not confuse roles, but equally does not raise roles to ontological status. "Political Theology" and "Theology of Liberation" are two examples of modern trends in the West, but the problem lies deeper in the very foundations of modern civilization. A cross-cultural approach may be welcome here, at least to diagnose the situation, if not to indicate a direction for a remedy.

NOTES

1. This paper is a revised version of an article published in *Religion and Society,* XXV/3 (September 1978) and will also appear in its original French in the proceedings of the Centro Internazionale di Studi Umanistici and the Istituto di Studi Filosofici di Roma. I have dealt with the same problematic "in actu exercitu" and from a Christian theological viewpoint in my book *Patriotismo y Cristianidad. Una investigacion teológico-histórica sobre el patriotismo cristiano* (Madrid: Rialp, 1961). The topic was, in fact, a central issue in post-World War II Europe. Cf. the *VI Conversaciones Católicas Internacionales,* San Sebastian, 1951, which inspired the above-mentioned book.

2. Cf. "Le concept d'ontonomie," *Actes du XIème Congrès International de Philosophie,* Bruxelles, 1953, vol. III, p. 182 ff.

3. Not without reason does a certain philosophy of liberation denounce

interiority and affirm exteriority as the fundamental category. Cf. e.g., E.D. Dussel, *Filosofia de la Liberación* (México: Edicol, 1977), p. 47 ff.

4. Cf. "La Tempiternidad. La Misa como 'consecratio temporis,' " *Sanctum Sacrificium,* Actas del V Congreso Eucarístico Nacional, Zaragoza, 1961, pp. 75–93. Also "El presente tempiterno. Una apostilla a la historia de la salvación y a la teología de la liberación," A. Vargas-Machuca, ed., *Teología y mundo contemporaneo* (Homenaje a K. Rahner) (Madrid: Ed. Cristiandad, 1975), pp. 133–175.

5. Cf. my essay "The Hindu Ecclesial Consciousness. Some Ecclesiological Reflections," *Jeevadhara,* Vol. XXI, 1974, pp. 199–205.

II

OF PARTICULAR TRIBES
AND MORTAL GODS

FOUR

The Origins of National Socialism: Some Fruits of Religion and Nationalism

Gary Lease

I

Recent geopolitical events in Iran, and the continuing struggle for the control of Palestine, have focused attention once again in this troubled century on the relationship of religion to national and political order. Commentaries in the press remark on the specter of Iran, presumably due to a nationalistic movement openly identifying with a particular Islamic religious belief, representing a retreat from current levels of civilization to those of an earlier age and a greater inhumanity.[1] On another front political pundits note with ghoulish humor an Israeli prime minister defining the boundaries of his country by the use of Jewish religious scriptures. But the problem of the delicate relationship between religious beliefs and their institutions on the one hand, and political identity and order on the other, is not a phenomenon restricted to our own time. At the very dawn of recorded history in the Near East and the Mediterranean basin these two facets of human life were found inextricably linked to one another.

As early as the Nile valley and Mesopotamian valley monarchies, cultures and civilizations in the Western world have striven to unite the forces and powers inherent in large-scale religious movements with the necessity of maintaining an ethnic and national identity in order to survive as a political entity. These early monarchs, often seen as representing the place and power of the universe's divine origins here on earth, left a model that has been emulated throughout Western history.[2] In Persia by the fourth century B.C.E. the early Iranian light god Mithra had already become the house god of the ruling dynastic family.[3] Carsten Colpe has recently theorized that the origins of the Hellenistic Mithraic religion lie in the far-flung Roman province of Pontus where a local king devised this unique religion as a tool to gain independence from Roman hegemony.[4] In Palestine in the second century B.C.E., the Maccabean revolts were fueled by the fusion of the desire for political freedom with the drive for religious separateness. In the fourth century of our common era, Christianity appropriated the governmental structures of the declining Roman empire and called for holy war against those who did not share the ruling beliefs.[5] In the seventh and eighth centuries the newly forged religion of Mohammed swept north through the Near East and west through northern Africa identifying its conquered foes and lands under a unique religio-political rule. Medieval Europe reached a crescendo in the thirteenth century under Innocent III's and Innocent IV's extended battle with the Hohenstaufen for both political and religious control of western Europe. The goal: a final and lasting churchification of society.[6]

Since the sixteenth century, however, Europe has been wracked by a series of devastating wars, often termed "religious," but which in reality represent the struggle to divest religion and its institutions of any identification with the political order. The most poignant example is Richelieu, a prince of the Roman church, hiring Protestant troops to destroy Catholic troops in the Thirty Years' War.[7] The attempted messianic revolt of Sabbatai Zvi in the late seventeenth century was brought to a rude halt in Turkey when the sultan realized the danger to his political control of a religious movement that united people in a common identity and struggle.[8] Finally, the American revolution and the consequent experiment in a new form of republic brought forth the demand that religion and the political order be formally, carefully, and lastingly separated one from the other so that each might thrive unencumbered by such an added burden.[9]

Yet, as I have tried to show elsewhere, the attraction of religion to national identity continues apace and the usefulness of each to the other has been exploited time and again in our modern era, most notably in the National Socialist movement in Germany of the 1920s and '30s.[10] "Authority," said Hobbes, "forges the law, not truth,"[11] and one of the key insights that has fueled German political developments since the late nineteenth century is that authority is best achieved and continued under the guidance of religious belief. As an early National Socialist ideologue, Carl Schmitt observed in our modern age the political has been totally subsumed by the theological and vice versa.[12] It is my contention that religion and the propensity of people living together and united in the same struggle for survival to identify on a level larger than that of the family (nationalism) forms a lasting and powerful union; and that this century's National Socialist movement in Germany is a prime example of how religion and nationalism reinforce and aid each other in a common striving for power and control. After some preliminary remarks concerning the nature of religion I will direct my attention to several figures from Germany's social, political, and intellectual life during the past century to illustrate how this commingling of religion and nationalism in National Socialism was prepared, furthered, and accepted.

II

In another place I proposed a description and definition of religion that culminated in the statement that religion represents "the ultimate act of an imperialistic totalitarianism which must claim for itself validity for all reality."[13] My work since

I wrote that has confirmed rather than weakened my persuasion that this is an accurate description of religion's function.

In brief summary, I maintained that the key task of any religion is to provide a satisfactory resolution to the essential problems of human existence, namely those of self-identity and place, or in other words, provide answers to the questions "Who am I?" and "Where am I?" I further maintained that religion attempts to do this by establishing coherent relationships between the self and other reality, i.e., other selves, the world, the cosmos, and indeed the self itself. The ability of a religion to maintain itself seems always to hinge upon its power to provide as broad a system of such relationships as possible to as many members as possible in a given community. In other words, religion has, as far as we are able to tell, no major role or function for the isolated human being, but rather is part and parcel of humanity's community nature.[14]

Like community identity itself, religion strives to maintain a continuity between the past and present and between the various members of the religious belief system. This is achieved in three major steps: (1) All religious systems attempt to provide an explanation of reality. In common with the general communal existence within which the religion takes shape, it attempts to supply an intelligible explanation for both observed and nonobserved reality, and tries, in other words, to make sense out of the entirety of human experience. (2) As noted above, religion also attempts to establish relationships, or to construct a coherent pattern that interrelates the various parts of the human experience, and in a concrete situation the various parts of the human community within which that experience takes place. (3) Finally, religion attempts to construct a framework or organized context within which these relationships are worked out. At times this constitutive context is separate, or apparently separate, from the community at large within which it operates, but at other times it is coextensive with the entire human context of the people who adhere to this religion.[15]

The logical and indeed historically observable consequence

is that any religion that tries to meet these needs of explanation, relationship, and context becomes thereby an absolute world view that cannot allow any other to intrude upon it. In other words, it is the *only* explanation of reality; it has the *only* relationships possible for human beings; and it provides the *only* context within which these relationships can be pursued. By its very nature religion defines reality; insofar as that definition of reality becomes coextensive with the community in which it has taken shape, that religion becomes identical to that community. Or, to put it another way, the nationalism that results from a large (or in some cases not so large) group of human beings identified one with another socially, culturally, and above all in the form and extent of their political order, becomes equal to the religious structure shared by that community. This is, I am convinced, what Schmitt meant when he said that our age has finally achieved the insight that in the last analysis the political is identical with the theological and vice versa. It is the final claim of any developed religion that it and it alone can supply the guidelines for the totality of human reality, that human reality shared by its believers.[16] Such a religion thus becomes coextensive with the political persuasion that the social, cultural, and at times ethnic identity of that community is the final arbiter over its reality and its fate (nationalism). I conclude that for a people to establish themselves as absolute in their world leads inevitably to an identification with the religious persuasions of that same community; that is, religion and nationalism in their final apex and development are the same.[17]

III

Hitler, long known to be an enthusiastic fan of Wagner's operas and writings (he deemed *Lohengrin,* Wagner's first opera, one of his greatest inspirations and also one of the clearest statements of German superiority), made the claim that "whoever wants to understand national socialist Germany must know Wagner."[18] Sadly, this is one of the truer remarks made by him. In his early sketches for the famous Ring cycle Wagner had contended that the Germans represented the noblest of humanity's races; but he also felt compelled to point out the pollution of this noble race by its intermingling with those of less noble blood, and particularly with the Jews. He saw his art as a redemptive act for the Germans celebrated in the great temples of the opera houses. Only sacrifice and a return to the wellsprings of pure and true race would allow the German *Volk* to gain salvation. This cleansing would occur in the sacramental ritual of Germanic myth, which would allow the German nation to achieve once again its divine wisdom and strength.[19]

In one of his last essays (1881) Wagner prepared the way for his opera *Parsifal* through a discussion of "Heroism and Christianity."[20] It is one of the most bizarre of his many bizarre writings in its attempt to establish a quasi-religious element as a foundation for German romantic nationalism and racism. Drawing on the racial speculations of Count Gobineau,[21] Wagner established the superiority of some races, and in particular the white Aryan race, to all other races. This "divine" human race is the only one capable of conquering the desires and demands of the will through the intellect. This heroic characteristic, marked by a capacity for "conscious suffering," is to be found most clearly in the Aryan race of the Germans.[22] The present-day task of the German nation is "to rediscover itself as a race of divine heroes living in a sanctified world."[23] The Christian church, so claimed Wagner, has preached such a noble and heroic martyrdom of self-sacrifice but its proclamation of this redemptive message has been weakened almost to the point of death by racial intermixture.[24] And yet how can this be? For the very blood of Christianity that is now ruined is dependent upon the blood of its savior. In a mind-boggling jump, Wagner proclaims that Christ himself did not possess Semitic blood but rather a kind of super-Aryan blood which, if allowed the flow, will cleanse humanity of its pollutions and infirmities.[25] It is impossible to assume that history will end with all humanity becoming equal or the same; rather the heroic German Aryan race is given the task of mastering and exploiting the lower races.[26] It can only do this, however, through the full use of the redeeming Christian religion, which will finally cleanse the German nation of its debilitating elements.[27] In that guise religion and the German nation have become one.

In the intricate story of *Parsifal* (1881), the redeeming knight who saves the tight-knit little band of humanity's noble rulers gathered together on the mount of salvation (Monsalvat), who can forget the power of the final scene, when Parsifal touches the ailing and long-suffering Amfortas with the holy spear, cleansing him of his sins and restoring his health after many years of pain and sorrow?[28] As Parsifal then approaches the altar and raises the Holy Grail for the intrepid knights to worship they cry out "O wonder of greatest holiness, redemption to the redeemer!"[29] A white dove descends to sit over Parsifal's head and the sinful Kundry, purged of her impurities and now redeemed, dies as Parsifal swings the Holy Grail over the assembled knights. In this climax *Parsifal* attempts to be both a "Christian" myth and a "Christian" liturgy while at the same time pointing the way beyond that religious tradition to a new non-Christian one.[30] Wagner himself, shortly before his death, praised this, his final work, as "the image of a prophetic dream . . . prophesying redemption."[31] A select nationalistically pure people, cleansed by the redemptive effect of religion, is led to the heights of its divinely promised perfection, thereby also becoming the way of salvation for the rest of the world.

IV

As illustrated by Wagner, the late nineteenth century and early twentieth century in Germany was characterized, as was the rest of Europe, by an enthusiastic and at times exaggerated commitment to the ideal of the *Volk,* that community of interest and shared nature (blood) that transcends the mere external bonds of a common government, but instead forms the foundation or substance of that political order and in addition of religious persuasion.[32] This *völkische* movement reached a peak just prior to and after World War I in Germany. The youth organizations and physical exercise groups took on a quasi-mystical tone that was enhanced by such marginal figures as Rudolph Steiner, who had his temple to Goethe in Switzerland, where *Faust* was annually performed as a liturgy to celebrate the German people and the German race.[33] This supportive atmosphere of a common origin and common interconnectedness created by the bonds of social, cultural, and ethnic identity found strange bedfellows indeed. Some of the oddest and most surprising supporters of such a nationalistic viewpoint, particularly under the influence of the Wagnerian movement, are to be found among the leading members of the German Jewish community of the war years and the 1920s.

Walther Rathenau (1867–1922) is one of the most remarkable of these figures. Born into wealth and capitalistic power as the son of the founder of the German Edison Company, he became the director of that firm's successor in 1889 at the age of 22, and its president in 1915. This firm pioneered the use of electricity both in Germany and in the rest of Europe, and indeed exported its electric plants and technology to such far-flung places as South America. Rathenau was a millionaire many times over and his genius and organization prompted the government to appoint him director of war material early in World War I. His efficiency at this task saved Germany from industrial collapse and indeed prolonged the war to its bitter end in 1918. It is not therefore surprising that among other things, Rathenau denounced General Ludendorff's call for an armistice in early 1918 as rash.

Soon after the founding of the Weimar Republic, Rathenau was persuaded to assume the post of Minister of Reconstruction and Foreign Affairs (1921); he was convinced that duty to his country and his people transcended his desire for a private retirement and concern with his intellectual pursuits. He immediately dedicated himself to the task at hand and set about achieving a reconciliation with France and Russia, which culminated in the Treaty of Rapallo (1922). His achievements, however, earned him the enmity of a variety of different classes within Germany. As a critic of capitalism the hatred of his own capitalistic class and colleagues fell upon him; as a Jew and Republican patriot he became the object of the hate of rising racists; finally, to many he appeared to represent the Bolshevist forces that had brought Germany to woe in the recent war and that would lead it to further destruction. In 1922 he was assassinated on his way to work by right-wing reactionaries.

The recent appearance of Rathenau's complete works[34] brings to light once again the apparent contradiction between Rathenau's public life as one of the more ruthless architects of German, and by extension European, capitalism during the pre-World War I period through his monopoly of electric works, and the almost world-denying mysticism and religio-nationalism apparent in his wartime essays. His work from 1913, on "The Kingdom of the Soul" and his essay of 1917, "Concerning the Future Age," especially highlight that he seems to have abhorred the very world of industrial society that his own financial wizardry helped bring about. At the same time his writings accentuate his persuasion that the highest human calling is one which will leave behind the world of matter and live entirely in the world of the spirit.[35] In "The Kingdom of the Soul" he talks of a purity of spirit that is possessed "only by the conquerors or masters" and that therefore a demand is made on any society to protect "the nobler blood against interbreeding." He finds it a sad thing to have seen how the earth has "squandered its noblest racial stocks" and he discovers that we are faced with the terrifying question: "Is it really the goal of tens of thousands of years of effort to brew a gray, decaying mixture out of all the colorfulness and individuality of the races of mankind?"[36] His appreciation and love for the "blond, blue-eyed men of courage" led him to postulate a new age of the spirit based on the German stock, a new age that would return to the older spiritual and artistic values and lead to a complete reorganization of the economic and social levels of society.[37] The result would give the ruling elite the power to enforce its puritanical and esthetic values on the masses. In his final essay this theme becomes a major topic for a blueprint of a capitalist utopia; the pamphlets sold briskly and received favorable reviews by such minds as Hermann Hesse and Ernst Troeltsch.[38]

Rathenau's idealistic philosophy, mixed with religious overtones and having as its goal a nationalistic democracy that
would provide social and moral judgments for society's life,
seems to derive a good deal of influence from that *völkisch*
stream of German romantic thought stemming from Wagner
and others at the end of the nineteenth and early twentieth
centuries.[39] Indeed, as we have seen, his praising of nationalistic racial purity smacks heavily of Wagner and even Houston
Stewart Chamberlain. In a real sense, Rathenau represents the
unwitting supportive atmosphere for the rise of National Socialism. What is even more ironic is that his assassination occurred as much for his well-known Jewishness and homosex-
uality as it did for his political acts as Minister of Foreign
Affairs. His combination of religious achievement and nationalistic identity clearly points the way to the final synthesis
achieved in National Socialism of the 1930s.

An even more enigmatic person than Rathenau is the strange
appearance of Hans Joachim Schoeps (1909–present), a Berlin
Jewish intellectual who claimed that his confession of the Jewish faith and his Jewish racial identity could be fully combined
with membership in the German and Prussian national states.
Elsewhere I have sketched the peculiarly Jewish sources of
Schoeps's thought and above all some of the tragic consequences of his call for Jews under the National Socialist regime
to remain at their places, not as loyal Jews but as loyal Germans in the belief that this nationalistic fervor and identity
could be combined with the Jewish religion.[40] In a 1933 debate
with a major National Socialist commentator, Hans Blüher,
Schoeps clearly stated his persuasion that such an identification
between the Jewish religion and the German nationalistic
membership could be achieved.[41] Blüher's response was that
"Christianity inextricably and originally belongs to Germanness and that therefore Jews and Muslims and Buddhists may
be members of the German state but can never belong to the
state *Volk* nor ever be *Reichsvolk.*" In other words, "Only as a
Christian or as a secularized citizen who has gone through

Christianity can one be German."[42] We see here in all clarity how the lines were drawn along the front of religious identification as the final criterion for a nationalistic community. Schoeps claimed that his Jewish faith was as supportive of the German nationalistic state as the Christian; but his opponents denied him this and claimed that only the Christian religion could be identified with that nationalistic state and in fact only as a member of that Christian belief system could one also be a member of the German national people. Religion had become the hallmark of nationalistic identity. In our final section we will see how this persuasion assumed tragic consequences.

V

In 1933, shortly after the assumption of governmental control by Hitler's National Socialist German Worker Party, a periodical series was founded named *Reich und Kirche,* published in Münster. According to its initial advertisement this series was to serve "the building of the Third Reich from the united forces of the National Socialist State and Catholic Christianity."[43] It was borne by the persuasion that "there is no fundamental contradiction between the natural *völkisch* rebirth of our time and the supernatural life of the church." In fact, the founders of this series were convinced that the "reestablishment of political order precisely calls for its completion in the fundamental support of religion."[44] Contributors to this series included Josef Lortz, the famous Reformation historian; Michael Schmaus, the young student of Grabmann and newly appointed professor at Münster; Franz von Papen, the leading Catholic layman and vice chancellor under Hitler; and Josef Pieper, the noted philosopher and ethicist. These leading German Catholic theoreticians and historians saw their task as serving through their religion the nationalistic movement then sweeping Germany.

One of the first to appear was Schmaus's monograph on "Contacts Between Catholic Christianity and the National Socialist World View," which already had experienced a second

edition in less than a year.[45] I have analyzed this material in
an earlier publication[46] but note here that Schmaus's fundamental point of departure, like that of his colleagues, was the
conviction that God has given every national people a particular task in history: "one of the most noble duties of a people
is to recognize and to fulfill the mission given it by God."[47]
Since God's will stands behind all historical happenings one
must recognize without fear that "God has given the German
people one of the greatest tasks in human history." Christianity
can do no better than to serve this people in the fulfillment of
its task: "If world history is not to remain meaningless, if it is
not to fulfill itself outside of God's will, then one must acknowledge that the German nation has a different and higher
rank in history than, for example, that of the African Republic
of Liberia."[48] Schmaus concludes that the similarities between
Catholic Christianity and the National Socialist state are so
striking that Catholicism can be one of the strongest and most
useful supports for the realization of the National Socialist goals
and ideals for all of German society.[49]

Even more striking, however, is the monograph from Lortz
entitled "Catholic Entree to National Socialism."[50] This pam-
phlet achieved an astounding third edition less than a year from
its publication! Lortz himself, though born in Luxembourg
(1887), took his training at Würzburg and had become a professor at Braunberg in 1929 with the publication of his famous
History of the Church, Considered as a History of Ideas.[51]
Shortly after the publication of his tract on National Socialism,
he was appointed (1935) to the church history chair at Münster, where he joined Schmaus for the next twelve years. His
most noted achievement was a reevaluation of the Lutheran
reformation from the Catholic viewpoint in his famous *The
History of the Reformation in Germany.*[52] Like Schmaus, he
took his stand on the Catholic doctrine of the natural and
supernatural orders and pointed out, in contrast to the Lutheran position, that the natural order is not overwhelmed and
isolated by God's supernatural grace and action, but rather is
led by it to greater heights of achievement within history. In

supporting the nationalistic movement of National Socialism Lortz was persuaded that only in Hitler and Hitler's movement would Europe have a victorious opponent to the glowering specter of barbaric Bolshevism.[53] In his mind, Hitler's act "is the salvation of Germany and therefore the salvation of Europe from the chaos of Bolshevism and the destruction of Christian Europe."[54] As far as Lortz was concerned this was an historical and therefore eminently "churchly act" that demands Christian acknowledgement of it as such.

This is all the more easy since National Socialism has made out of a political positivism a world view that encompasses the entire human experience; only the recognition of this totalitarian demand on the one hand, and a positive coping with it through the cooperation of the church on the other, will lead to a resolution satisfactory to both sides, namely fulfillment of common goals.[55] Lortz is at pains to point out that Hitler himself was a Catholic and that Catholicism's rejection of Hitler in the beginning was a false one; it does not hold within itself the danger of a heretical nationalism or a separatist state church.[56] In fact, since 1933, and above all since the completion of the Concordat between the German government and the Vatican, it is clear that the "totality of German Catholics are able to become one with the National Socialist state."[57] Since this movement of National Socialism has, however, become for all practical purposes the state itself, Catholicism has one task and one task only: namely, to acknowledge this saving act on the part of the National Socialist movement and to place itself at the service of that movement for the future of Germany.

Among the reasons for the church to acknowledge the role to be played by the National Socialist Party are to be found the many similarities between Catholicism and that movement. Among these Lortz mentions the emphasis on national identity; from the earliest times of the church's presence in Europe, Germany and Christianity have enjoyed an especially deep and unique relationship.[58] In addition, to be Catholic means fundamentally to be confessional, i.e., to express one's commitment through a complete and unrestricted faith in the church's

principles and leaders. Thus, though the church will not totally
identify itself with a particular state since it is in fact universal,
it can on the other hand do nothing else but greet the German
nation as a comrade in arms in a common struggle.[59] In fact,
in many essential things only Catholicism is able to fulfill the
beginning steps of the National Socialist movement. And one
of the deepest duties of Catholicism in this contemporary period is to work for the realization of the authentic essence of
National Socialism.[60]

The results of such cooperation were obvious to Lortz. For
one thing the church ideal of a new human being will emerge
from this struggle precisely because of the cooperation between
Christianity and National Socialism. In addition, the absolute
political unity demanded by National Socialism will be followed by church unity.[61] This is so because National Socialism
has been able to awaken the nerve of a national consciousness
that will allow the Germans to transcend the deep wound of
the Reformation.[62] On the other hand, Lortz is convinced that
"National Socialism has prepared the way in the deepest possible fashion for faith to be spread, and for that matter even
for the idea of the church to gain new life."[63] In fact, he looks
with great sorrow on those attempts to separate the nationalist
commitment of Catholics from their Christian church membership. If this were to happen, he claims, then "in one form or
another our absolute, unrestricted and fanatical fidelity to the
Reich would be doubted."[64] One must remember, he continues, that the growth and process of the church is inextricably
bound up with the national consciousness of those races and
nations in which the church has performed its work most effectively.[65] One sees this particularly in the example of the Middle
Ages, where the powers of the German nation ruled the field
of church history in a manner that only our contemporary age
is likely to see once again.[66] Thus, the final goal should be the
absolute centralization of all forces for the service of the church
as well as the nation; as other peoples in Europe have experienced, the result will be a "living and enthusiastically emphasized national church unity: to be a German Catholic or, a
Catholic German."[67]

All this is possible, concluded Lortz, because National Socialism is not a system of thought but rather an elementary life force, an unfailing growth and development; it thus represents the fulfillment of the deepest and most profound forces of our time.[68] If the greatest commitment to the human task is demanded, namely that of sacrifice, then every Christian should be prepared to make that commitment. National Socialism is not just the legal government of Germany, it is Germany itself and therefore all Germans, particularly German Christians, must say yes to this movement. Of even greater import, however, is that either "this movement will be able to struggle and achieve the salvation of Germany and Europe, or we will all land in chaos." Lortz is convinced that no one will deny any longer that these are the alternatives facing Germany. "Chaos, however, would mean the destruction of the nation and the ruin of the German church. That closes the discussion."[69] German Catholicism, the church, and National Socialism are one in their service to the unified national consciousness.

Even more clear, and in many ways more startling, is the position taken by the famous German theologian Karl Adam (1876–1966). Already famous because of his publication in 1924 of *The Spirit of Catholicism* and his study of 1928, *Christ and the Spirit of the Western World,*[70] he also was an ecumenical pioneer and after the war became a leader of the *Una Sancta* movement. At the same time, however, that Adam was pursuing his theological work at the University of Tübingen (1919–1949) he also published a study in a well-known periodical entitled "German Volkstum and Catholic Christianity."[71] He felt compelled to do this because the current "national revolution"[72] concerns all Germans and indeed the best of German society. In contrast to contemporary scholarly work, the National Socialist revolution is leading the Germans back to those "primeval powers, which created and formed our nationalistic consciousness: blood and spirit, blood and religion, German blood and Christianity."[73]

Ever since the terrible disaster and poison of the Treaty of Versailles, Germany has been a suffering national body; some have tried to heal it but only externally and not internally.

Adam is convinced that only from within, only with a renewal and rebirth can health be once again brought to Germany.[74] Only a living person who has contact with those hidden forces, those secret sources of life for a people and is able to awaken those powers will be able to lead Germany to its salvation. "Such a man who totally and completely was of the *Volk* and nothing but the *Volk,* a people's chancellor, had to come if the German people were to be touched in their most inner recesses and awakened to a new will to life. And he came, Adolph Hitler. From the south he came. From the Catholic south he came, but we knew him not.[75] For he had gone through suffering and terror and had fought for Germany's salvation against those who had called themselves our leaders up to then. . . . But the hour came and we saw him and recognized him. . . . He now stands before us as the one who has been prophesied by our poets and our wise men, who is the liberator of the German genius, who has taken the blindfold from our eyes, and has led us through all political, economic, societal, and confessional traumas to see the one essential moment: our unity in blood, our German self, the homo Germanus."[76] Finally, and in primeval fashion, religion and fatherland are once again joined in the ideal unity desired by all Germans, for it is clear "that whoever wishes to speak to German *Volkstum* must also speak of German Christianity."[77] The German nation entered into history as a Christian people and it must be recognized as such. Thus the call to a new existence as a national *Volk* is at the same time a call to a new and living Christianity.

But Adam does not want Catholic Christianity identified simply as an instrument of nationalism; rather he sees it as the vehicle of God's supernatural power entering into the natural world and using a particular historical people and national construction to achieve supernatural goals. As both Schmaus and Lortz, so also Adam sees Christianity and German National Socialism mutually fulfilling each other, thus aiding each one to reach the final realization of their common goals. In contrast to Lutheran Christianity, Catholic Christianity understands the necessity of renewal from within through the union of blood and spirit, of nature and the supernatural. "Thus redemption in its full meaning is an act of God and a work of humanity at the same time, a God–human act—blood and spirit in one."[78] This is so because "the [spirit] only becomes effective through blood, in blood, and by blood."[79] Particularly in the area of education, Christianity receives through the National Socialist movement a new task, an essentially national, yes, even *völkisch* influence, to which a response must be made.[80] In a crescendo of emotionally laden language, Adam claims that not only is there a German Catholic theology, but there is a German Catholicism and a German Catholic spirituality just as there are German saints: "And there is all of this because there is German blood and because Catholicism does not want to dry up this German blood but rather wishes to purify it and sanctify it in the blood of Christ. The Catholic church fulfills its God-given mission to the German people by calling forth the best of that people through its proclamation of the gospel and permeating it with the forces of that gospel."[81] Thus, the Catholic religion is dependent upon the national identity of blood relationship in order to achieve its own goals and to fulfill its God-given mission. It needs a nationalistic people in order to be a living Catholicism, "and therefore there is no inner contradiction between nationalism and Catholicism."[82]

As could be expected, Adam closes his study by defending the National Socialist race laws in the same manner that Cardinal Faulhaber and Schmaus had before him.[83] Any nation is bound to maintain the purity and freshness of its blood and to protect that through its laws. In fact, like his predecessors, Adam seized on the Jews as a classic example of a people that fought to maintain its purity of blood; the German attempt to do the same is nothing more than respecting the fourth commandment, "honor your father and your mother."[84] When one considers, Adam continues, how the Jewish immigrants from the east have flooded Germany since the end of the war and the November Revolution, and how that Jewish spirit has become all-powerful in the German economy, its press, its literature, its art, and its scholarship, "then one must understand the action of the German government against this Jewish flood, no matter how painfully it is viewed by nationally minded German Jews, as an obligatory act of Christian German survival."[85] Of course, insofar as the reduction of the Jewish influence in Germany is also a victory over the Communist-Bolshevistic world view, then of course this "political anti-Semitism" is doubtless in the very deepest interest of the Christian religion and church.[86]

This theologian, Karl Adam, became famous after the war for the "opposition" he led against the National Socialist government. In an obituary of the *London Times*[87] his "uncompromising attitude to the Nazi movement" was praised, and though "he was frequently threatened with arrest" and "finally removed from office at his university by government order," he nevertheless remained strong in his denial of the National Socialists. And yet the Munich professor for church history, Hermann Tüchle, who had been Adam's colleague at Tübingen and was present at his death, reported to a hushed seminar in 1966 that the last words of Karl Adam, the great Catholic systematic theologian, were: "Heil Hitler!" given with a trembling but raised right arm.

VI

To paraphrase Lortz, the materials I have assembled speak most forcefully by themselves. Stretching from Wagner to leading Catholic theologians of the 1930s, we have the record of a cultural-spiritual development leading to a conceptualization of a new nationalistic racist ideology by expanding it to a universal level in conjunction with religion. As such these figures are both the immediate and antecedent participants in Hitler's National Socialist movement, which itself strove to be the ultimate completion and at the same time transformation of the Judeo-Christian tradition in the Western world.[88] These thinkers illustrate with stunning effectiveness the ease with which nationalistic strivings may be absolutized by combination with religion and the fearsome consequences of such an identity.[89]

Certainly Hitler himself did not share the Christian idealism of his theological helpmates. Though convinced that religion lay at the roots of Germany's nationalism, he felt that only French and Italians could be both pagan and Christian at the same time; a German, however, must be one or the other. For Germans therefore it is decisive whether they have "the Jewish-Christian faith" or a "strong, heroic faith in god in nature, in god in their own people, in god in their own fate, in their own blood."[90] He never announced his own abandonment of the Catholic church publicly, but did intend to do so when the war ended. Hitler viewed that public revelation as a symbolic act: Germany would thereby close an historical epoch and with the Third Reich begin a new one. After the war, therefore, the "last great task will be the solution of the church problem."[91] This final identification of National Socialism as a religion, rather than as a political movement conjoined with the Christian religion, was already signalled in regulations issued in 1936 forbidding the singing of patriotic or National Socialist melodies with religious texts in churches; just as the churches themselves do not allow their devotional melodies to be used with worldly texts, neither will the NSDAP allow that usage by the churches.[92] In other words, the very motif that led Adam, Lortz, Rathenau, and Wagner to envision such a union of the Judeo-Christian religion and nationalism—the unity of blood—was the very factor Hitler saw as unique to National Socialism, and not to be shared with others. The sacrificial nature of Christ's blood, and its key redemptive role in Christian thought, made such an identification easy for nationalistic theologians; Hitler, however, saw this redemption to lie in the movement itself. Yet the way to transcending those Christian bounds had been prepared mainly by Christians themselves.

The National Socialist movement in Germany of the 1920s and '30s most certainly had a large number of sources upon which it drew; the causes for its rise and preliminary successes are also legion. Clearly among those sources and causes one of the most potent and obvious was the tendency among a wide variety of influential German thinkers to see in the union of religion and nationalistic consciousness a possibility for mutual fulfillment. In the process of religion and nationalism serving each other, each would achieve a completeness and fulfillment that might otherwise remain closed to them. This fatal and final combination leading to an inhuman totalitarian claim must provoke us, as I have written elsewhere, "to reevaluate seriously the place such an event, namely religion, may be allowed to occupy in a world striving to become more, not less, human."[93]

NOTES

1. Cf., for example, the revealing interview of the Ayatollah Khomeini, religious leader of the current revolution in Iran, by the Italian journalist, Oriana Fallaci, in *San Francisco Examiner,* 7 October 1979.

2. Cf. Francis Dvornik, *Early Christian and Byzantine Political Philosophy: Origins and Background,* 2 vols. (Washington: Dumbarton Oaks, 1966), especially Volume I. Also, Eric Vögelin, *Order and History* (Baton Rouge: Louisiana State University Press, 1956), Volume I.

3. Hugo Gressman, *Die orientalischen Religionen im hellenistisch-römischen Zeitalter* (Berlin: de Gruyter, 1930), p. 141.

4. Carsten Colpe, "Mithra-Verehrung, Mithras-Kult und die Existenziranischen Mysterien," in *Mithraic Studies,* ed. J. R. Hinnells, Vol. II (Manchester: Manchester University Press, 1975), pp. 378–405.

5. Adolf von Harnack, *Militia Christi* (Tübingen: Mohr, 1905), pp. 44–45.

6. Innocent III: "Petro non solum universam ecclesiam sed totum reliquit saeculum gubernandum" (*PL* 214, 759). Cf. Ernesto Buonaiuti, *Le Modernisme Catholique* (Paris: Rieder, 1927), p. 82.

7. Both his internal and his foreign policies were aimed at the establishment of French control of Europe and the destruction of the Habsburg-Spanish power, not at the elimination of non-Catholics per se.

8. Gershom Scholem, *Sabbtai Sevi: The Mystical Messiah* (Princeton: Princeton University Press, 1973).

9. Yet this experiment has not been successful: ". . . the separation of church and state has not denied the political realm a religious dimension." On the contrary, there is a "religious dimension for the whole fabric of American life, including the political sphere." Cf. Robert Bellah, "Civil Religion in America," *Daedalus* 96 (1967), pp. 3–4.

10. Gary Lease, "Hitler's National Socialism as a Religious Movement," *Journal of the American Academy of Religion* 45 (1977), Supplement, pp. 793–838.

11. Thomas Hobbes, *Leviathan* (Oxford: Blackwell, 1946), p. 143.

12. Carl Schmitt, *Politische Theologie* (Munich: Duncker and Humbolt, 1934), p. 7.

13. Gary Lease, "The Origin and Nature of Religion," *Metanoia* 10 (1978), p. 11.

14. Ibid., pp. 9–10.

15. Ibid., pp. 10–11.

16. Ibid., pp. 11. Cf. Peter Berger, *The Sacred Canopy* (Garden City: Doubleday Anchor, 1969), p. 28.

17. Aurobindo Ghose (1872–1950) exemplifies this point of view in a non-Western context (but remember that his major schooling took place in England!). His famous speech in Bombay (1907) could not be clearer: "There is a creed in India today which calls itself Nationalism, a creed which has come to you from Bengal. This is a creed which many of you have accepted when you called yourselves Nationalists. Have you realized, have you yet realized what that means? . . . What is Nationalism? Nationalism is not a mere political program; Nationalism is a religion that has come from God; Nationalism is a creed which you shall have to live." Cf. W. T. de Bary, *Sources of Indian Tradition* (New York: Columbia University Press, 1958), Vol. II, p. 176.

18. Robert Gutman, *Richard Wagner: The Man, His Mind, and His Music* (New York: Harcourt Brace Jovanovich, 1968), p. 426.

19. Ibid., pp. 121–122, 421.

20. Richard Wagner, "Heldentum und Christentum." Originally published in Wagner's house organ, the *Bayreuther Blätter* in 1881, it is now to be found in *Richard Wagner's Schriften und Dichtungen* (Leipzig: Siegel, 1903), pp. 275–285.

21. Joseph Arthur, Count de Gobineau (1816–1882), who had written his *Essay on the Inequality of Races* some 25 years earlier (1854), became famous through Wagner's espousal. Houston Stewart Chamberlain (1855–1927), Wagner's son-in-law, redid Gobineau's theories in his *Foundations of the 19th Century* (1899) and promptly became Wilhelm II's court intellectual.

22. Richard Wagner, "Heldentum und Christentum," op. cit., pp. 275, 277–278.

23. Ibid., p. 279.

24. Ibid., p. 280.

25. Ibid., pp. 281, 283.

26. Ibid., p. 283.

27. Ibid., pp. 284–285.

28. *Parsifal,* Act 3. After touching him, Parsifal cries out: "Sei heil, entsündigt und gesühnt! . . . Gesegnet sei dein Leiden, des Mitleids höchste Kraft."

29. Ibid.: "Höchsten Heiles Wunder: Erlösung dem Erlöser!"

30. Termed "the gospel of National Socialism," *Parsifal* is equally "a reli-

gion of racism under the cover of Christian legend." Cf. Robert Gutman, op. cit., pp. 431–432.

31. Ibid., p. 426.

32. The *narod* movement in Russia is part of this same phenomenon. For further development in Germany, cf. Fritz Stern, *The Politics of Cultural Despair* (Berkeley: University of California Press, 1974), p. 87 (Paul de Lagarde); pp. 138–139 (Julius Langbehn).

33. For example, a contemporary flyer of the *Bund für Leibeszucht* (Gemeinschaft für naturnahe und artgemässe Lebensgestaltung), claims that "eine solche Erziehung des gesamten Menschen vom Leibe her und eine solche Entwicklung aller seiner Kräfte von der körperlichen Haltung aus, zu einem hervorragenden Mittel der rassischen Auslese wird, weil sie körperlich und willensmassig bestimmte Anforderungen stellt, die nur ein leistungsfühiger und somit erbgesunder Mensch, in dem sie wahrhafte Schönheit zur Entfaltung und Offenbarung bringt, erfüllen kann." (Private possession.) The *völkische* movement brought with it a revival of youth organizations; highly flavored with a romantic nationalism, it also smacked of natural religion: Cf. Fritz Stern, *The Politics of Cultural Despair: A Study in the Rise of the German Ideology* (Berkeley: University of California Press, 1974), pp. 176–180. Hans Blüher, mentioned below was a leading figure in this German youth movement, while Hans Joachim Schoeps, also treated below, has a melancholy and nostalgic description of his own personal experiences in the tow of this national "return to nature:" Hans Joachim Schoeps, *Ja—Nein—und Trotzdem* (Mainz: v. Hase u. Koehler, 1974,) pp. 176–180. Steiner's (1861–1925) "Goetheanum" in Dornach (Basel) was begun in 1913 as a university for the "Geisteswissenschaften," and was built according to his own architectural principles. As a coeditor of the Goethe Weimar edition (1883–1897), Steiner had developed a lifelong fascination with Goethe's thought; it was partly this influence which led him to found the anthroposophical society in 1913 and transfer his activities to the new building in Dornach. Among other innovations, he pioneered his concept of "Eurhythmie," or visible language through body movement, particularly as a therapeutic measure. In the same vein, Stefan George (1868–1933), the influential poet, gathered around him a close and intimate circle that included such figures as Friedrich Gundolf, the classicist and a doctoral advisor to Goebbels; von Hofmannsthal, who eventually broke with George; and von Stauffenberg, who played such a prominent role in the July 20 attempt to assassinate Hitler. George saw himself as the prophet of a new age that would purge both mind and body of accumulated evils; this was to be carried out by a "heilige Jugend." Interestingly, the logo for his and the circle's publications was the *Hakenkreuz* (Blätter für die Kunst) in a form that is remarkably similar to the later National Socialist use of the same symbol. The contribution is undeniable and particularly ironic in view of the fact that many of George's closest associates were Jewish writ-

ers and intellectuals—such as Gundolf! Cf. Karl Dietrich Bracher, *The German Dictatorship* (New York: Praeger, 1974), pp. 87, 144.

34. Walther Rathenau, *Gesamtausgabe,* Vol. II: *Hauptwerke und Gespräche,* H. D. Hellige and E. Schulin, eds. (Munich: G. Müller, 1978).

35. "Zur Mechanik des Geistes oder vom Reich der Seele" (1913) and "Von kommenden Dingen" (1917).

36. James Joll, "The Contradictory Capitalist," *The Times Literary Supplement,* 25 August 1978, pp. 942–943.

37. Eduard Heimann, *Encyclopedia Americana* (New York: Americana Corp., 1966), Vol. 23, p. 230b.

38. James Joll, op. cit.

39. Ibid.

40. Gary Lease, "S. L. Steinheim's Influence: H. J. Schoeps, A Case Study," in press; also, *Papers of the 19th-Century Theology Working Group* 4 (1978), pp. 134–154. Cf. H. J. Schoeps, *Rückblicke: Die ersten dreissig Jahre (1925–55) und danach* (Berlin: Haude und Spener, 1963), pp. 32–57: "Die Jugendbewegung," where he notes that the German nationalistic Youth Movement (cf. above) was "ein spiritualistischer Aufbruch gewesen, wie er sonst nur aus religiösen Erweckungsbewegungen bekannt ist;" it reached "tief hinunter in die irrationalen Untergründe und auch Abgründe des deutschen Lebens." After the fact Schoeps realized the ambivalent character of his admonition to German Jews and expressed strong doubt that he had done the right thing by enjoining them to remain in Germany until the end (ibid., p. 101).

41. Hans Blüher and Hans Joachim Schoeps, *Streit um Israel* (Hamburg: Hanseatische Verlagsanstalt, 1933), 6.

42. Ibid.

43. Joseph Lortz, "Katholischer Zugang zum Nationalsozialismus," *Reich und Kirche: Eine Schriftenreihe* (Münster: Aschendorff, 1934²), 28.

44. Ibid.

45. Michael Schmaus, "Begegnungen zwischen katholischem Christentum und National-Sozialistischer Weltanschauung," *Reich und Kirche: Eine Schriftenreihe* (Münster: Aschendorff, 1934).

46. Gary Lease, "Hitler's National Socialism as a Religious Movement," *Journal of the American Academy of Religion* 45 (1977), pp. 818–823.

47. Michael Schmaus, op. cit., p. 30.

48. Ibid.

49. Ibid., pp. 30–31; parenthetically Schmaus notes that for these reasons the idea of the League of Nations is very likely opposed to sound Catholic doctrine!

50. Cf. note 42 above.

51. *Geschichte der Kirche in ideengeschichtlicher Betrachtung: Eine geschichtliche Sinndeutung der christlichen Vergangenheit* (Münster: Aschendorff, 1934, 1953). In an introductory note to his monograph for "Reich und

Kirche," Lortz remarks that the justification for his remarks therein are to be found in his earlier, larger work.

52. *Die Reformation in Deutschland* (Freiburg: Hurder, 1939–1940), 2 vols.

53. Joseph Lortz, "Katholischer Zugang zum Nationalsozialismus," op. cit., p. 3.

54. Ibid., p. 4.

55. Ibid., p. 5.

56. Ibid., p. 6.

57. Ibid., p. 7.

58. Ibid., p. 13.

59. Ibid., p. 14.

60. Ibid., pp. 14–15.

61. Ibid., p. 16.

62. Ibid., p. 17.

63. Ibid., p. 18.

64. Ibid., p. 19: ". . . unsere absolute, restlose, fanatische Reich-streue. . . ."

65. Ibid., p. 20.

66. Ibid., pp. 20–21.

67. Ibid., p. 23: ". . . in der lebenden und begeistert betonten national-kirchlichen Einheit: Deutscher Katholik oder: katholischer Deutscher."

68. Ibid., p. 24: ". . . elementare Welle des Lebens, ist unbeirrbares Wachsen. . . ."

69. Ibid., p. 26.

70. *Das Wesen des Katholizismus* (Düsseldorf: L. Schwann, 1924; 1949), titled in emulation of Harnack's *Das Wesen des Christentums,* as Schmaus was later to write *Vom Wesen des Christentums* (Ettal: Buch-Kunst Verlag, 1954). Adam's second success was *Jesus Christus und der Geist unserer Zeit* (Augsburg: Haas u. Grabherr, 1935).

71. "Deutsches Volkstum und katholisches Christentum," *Theologische Quartalschrift* 114 (1933), pp. 40–63. Adam had long been a nationalist: during World War I he published several books of poetry aimed at maintaining pride in Germany in the face of suffering and defeat; cf. for example, *Im Friedenssonnenglanze empor! Ein Jugendgeleitbuch. Wege und Worte zur höherführenden Ertüchtigung und zum Neubau des Lebens* (Graz: Verlag der Schutzvereine "Südmark" und "Nordmark," 1918).

72. Ibid., p. 40.

73. Ibid., pp. 40–41: "Blut und Geist, Blut und Religion, deutsches Blut und Christentum."

74. Ibid., p. 41.

75. The similarity with John 1:10–11 is unmistakable.

76. Karl Adam, "Deutsches Volkstum und katholisches Christentum," op. cit., pp. 41–42: ". . . unsere bluthafte Einheit, unser deutsches Selbst, den homo germanus."

77. Ibid., p. 43.

78. Ibid., p. 53: "Blut und Geist in einem."

79. Ibid., p. 53: ". . . dass der 'Geist' an dem Blut, im Blut, durch das Blut wirksam wird." Compare Hitler's phrasing during a speech to the Hitler Youth at the Party Congress of 1934: "Ihr seid Fleisch unseres Fleisches, Blut unseres Blutes . . . Um uns liegt Deutschland, in uns marschiert Deutschland, hinter uns kommt Deutschland." Df. Lease, "Hitler's National Socialism," op. cit., p. 811.

80. Ibid., p. 56.

81. Ibid., p. 58.

82. Ibid., p. 58: ". . . das Blutmässige . . ." allows this mission to succeed; p. 59.

83. Cf. Lease, "Hitler's National Socialism," op. cit., pp. 813–823.

84. Adam, op. cit., p. 60.

85. Ibid., p. 62: ". . . einen pflichtgemässen Akt christlich germanischer Selbstbehauptung. . . ."

86. Ibid.

87. London Times, April 20, 1966.

88. Lease, "Hitler's National Socialism," op. cit., pp. 823–829. Cf. John Toland, *Adolf Hitler* (New York: Ballantine, 1977), pp. 491–492, where he reports Ambassador Dodd's diary entry for 23 August 1934, that during the 1934 Oberammergau Passion Play members of the audience exclaimed, as Jesus was raised on the cross, "Es ist unser Hitler!"

89. It should be remarked that the pieces considered here from the pens of Catholic theologians were formulated early on in the National Socialist effort to consolidate power in the German state. Later, many of those who had been enthusiastic in their support of a church/National Socialist Party unity for the betterment of the German nation expressed grave disappointment in subsequent developments, or even outright opposition—particularly after the summer of 1934 and the elimination of the SA. Especially Schmaus has remained adamant that it was only after 1934 that one was able to see the actual direction the National Socialist movement was taking; up to that point, so he emphasizes, he and his colleagues truly believed that they would be able to turn the genuinely healthy forces in the National Socialist movement away from the danger of evil goals (letter, Schmaus to Lease, 17 March 1977). Lortz, on the other hand, remained notorious in his support of the NSDAP, while we saw above how Adam retained his inner commitment to the very end of his life. And who would forget Cardinal Faulhaber's Christmas card to Hitler in December of 1937, "after four years of National Socialist government and church harassment," in which the good bishop called the Führer Germany's "apocalyptic peacemaker"? (Cf. G. Lease, "Hitler's National Socialism," op. cit., p. 815). While it would be both unfair and untrue to characterize Catholics in general, and Catholic theologians specifically as automatic Nazis, it remains true that the unreflective support of such a nationalistic

movement, which came so easily to Catholic thinkers of the moment, and which went far in aiding the success of the National Socialist movement, did in fact stem from the propensity of that form of Christianity to combine with nationalistic fervor and goals.

90. In conversation Hitler let it be known that eventually Christianity would have to be eliminated in Germany ("ausrotten"); the faith spoken of was to be "ein starker, heldenhafter Glaube an Gott in der Natur, an Gott im eigenen Volk, an Gott im eigenen Schicksal, im eigenen Blut." Cf. Hermann Rauschning, *Gespräche mit Hitler* (Zürich: Europa Verlag, 1939; 1950), p. 50.

91. Hitler: "Der Krieg wird ein Ende nehmen. Die letzte grosse Aufgabe unserer Zeit ist dann darin zu sehen, das Kirchenproblem noch zu klären." Cf. Hans Buchheim, "War die katholische Kirche eine vom nationalsozialistischen Regime verfolgte Organisation?" *Gutachten des Instituts für Zeitgeschichte* (Munich: Selbstverlag, 1958), pp. 13–45. Rosenberg reported that Hitler intended an "Endlösung" to the church's problem at war's end: he would not forget what they had done during the war (ibid., p. 45).

92. In particular, the SS oath song and the Hitler Youth song; cf. the Munich Rundschreiben from 21 October 1936, #134/36 and the Berlin-Anordnung from 28 August 1936 to the Reich and Prussian Minister for Ecclesiastical Matters, *Anordnungen des Stellvertreters des Führers* (Munich: Zentralverlag der NSDAP, 1937), pp. 337–339.

93. Lease, "The Origin and Nature of Religion," op. cit., p. 12.

FIVE

German Nationalism
in the Weimar Era

Peter H. Merkl

The word nationalism is used with many different meanings by historians, social scientists, and the general public. Obviously, many of these meanings have nothing to do with religious attitudes and experiences.[1] Our reference instead is to nationalism as a militant, passionate faith complete with conversion experiences, a mystic sense of community, proselytizing, and the persecution of heretics and infidels. Nationalism in this virulent form was rampant among many nationalities during World War I and in the Weimar era, often rivaling and even replacing established religious beliefs and the sense of identity and solidarity the masses had derived from them.[2] It took on perhaps its most virulent form in the German Nazi party and its propaganda, but was by no means limited to the Nazis. Some Nazis, including Adolf Hitler himself, in fact soon shifted from German nationalism toward identification with a supranational Aryan race.[3] But the official Nazi propaganda and the enthusiasms of rank-and-file NSDAP members, voters, and the wider German public continued to focus on German nationalism pure and simple.

This kind of fanaticism may be the only explanation we can

find for contemporary statements such as the following made
by the famous sociologist Max Weber in 1918–1919. Weber was
an aspiring politician of the liberal and pacifist Democratic Party
(DDP) at the time:

[If any territory other than the Alsace is taken from Germany, say in the
East or on the Belgian border], the epoch of pacifism caused by defeat will
come to an end and be followed by one in which everyone, down to the last
worker . . . will turn into a national chauvinist. Hatred among nations will
become permanent and a German irredentist movement . . . will use all the
customary revolutionary means.

I

German nationalism in the Weimar era, to be sure, had been
formed by unique circumstances that may explain much of its
virulence. Germany's sense of national identity had first been
awakened by the Napoleonic conquest and its influence in the
German states. The nationalistic passion had reached its first
popular peak in the wars of liberation against the conqueror,
after which it was suppressed by the restored princes. It was
revived timidly in the years of revolutionary stirrings, in 1830
and especially in 1848/1849, only to suffer once more the same
fate at the hands of the particularistic interests of Prussia, Austria, and other crowned heads.

Bismarck's wars of unification once again kindled popular
nationalism and this time legitimized it with the creation of a
powerful nation-state that could stand up for the national interests at home and abroad. In the fifty years of social and
economic development that followed, the separate identities of
Prussians, Bavarians, and Saxonians indeed grew into a national community with a distinctive sense of national identity
and solidarity. This was the exuberant nation that marched
into World War I in August, 1914, demanding recognition of
its military, economic, and most significantly, its cultural
prowess as a nation. There are endless testimonials by German
soldiers about the final hardening effect that the war experience had on their identification with that nation and its fate in
the struggle for national survival and predominance.[4]

The intensity with which national feelings became a consuming passion during the war also brought out a series of fatal flaws in German nationalism and national identity. To begin with, there was the problem of delimiting the nation and its territory, a problem that had already bedeviled the Frankfurt Assembly of 1848 until it decided to shut out the German Austrians from its intended, new, German nation-state.[5] Similar problems of ethnic delimitation complicated the national borders in the north (Schleswig-Holstein), west (Alsace, Lorraine), south, and especially in the east in the Polish areas of Prussia and along the ethnic frontier in Austria. The awakening nationalisms of the Poles, Czechs, Magyars, Italians, and other ethnicities under German domination forcefully dramatized this uncertainty of German national identity in the east once the defeat in World War I had ended German (and German-Austrian) control and replaced it with a congeries of successor states.

The intense national animosities aroused by the war everywhere else where Germans and non-Germans encountered each other similarly heightened the sense of embattled identity at the same time that it made it attractive for some people to switch their national loyalties from German to non-German.[6] Such a "betrayal" of Germanness was seen in pro-French separatist movements, as in the Rhineland, during the occupation, or in Polish secessionism in Silesia. The very uncertainty of the ethnic identities of others often provoked extremes of violent passion in German ethnic patriots. Like embattled religious communities, nationalism demanded the persecution of heretics and infidels and was not above venting its frustration with ethnic ambiguity by inquisitions and even terrorism against advocates of interethnic understanding, such as Social Democrats, or Catholic priests (heretics), or the Poles (infidels).[7]

All along the ethnic frontier in East Prussia, Danzig, along the Polish Corridor, and around the rim of new Czechoslovakia, ethnic passions, power politics, and partisan politics to the right of the Social Democrats (and frequently including them) were embroiled in the new militant faith of German nationalism which would suffer no other gods beside it, much less above it. In the occupied parts of the Rhineland, and especially during the Franco-Belgian occupation, the same passions were kindled by the presence of the alien occupation and by incidents of friction with it.[8] Just like the war, these conflicts were supported on the German side, by broadly shared and deeply felt sentiments, and fought by the entire patriotic right wing, not just Nazi extremists. The Nazis, however, became the eventual heirs of all this passion long after the actual conflicts had quieted down, for a simple reason: As Pan-Germans, they had a cogent solution for the problems of competing ethnic loyalties and the heresies of interethnic understanding, namely domination by the German master race. This solution also was bound to appeal to German and Austrian conservatives and to an older generation that remembered the years of German ethnic domination in the east[9] and the victory of 1871 in the west.

II

Pan-Germanism in various forms occupies a key position in the complex world of German and Austrian nationalist foreign policy ideas. It was a kind of missing link between old-fashioned conservatives and Nazis, and between elements that otherwise seem antithetical, such as the modern Prussian military-dominated state and the older, greater German idea of the universal European federal empire. The Pan-German League of 1891, along with the Naval and the Colonial Leagues,[10] was a typical product of post-Bismarckian, expansive German nationalism and expressed in aggressively political form the sense of ethnic superiority felt by increasing numbers of the educated and semi-educated.

The *voelkisch* literati spelled out at considerable length and with an odd mixture of populism, medieval romanticism, and anti-Semitism what it meant to many of these people to be German. The Germans, in their eyes, had suddenly become *the chosen people* though there was considerable doubt about who was doing the choosing—a god, social Darwinian selection, or they themselves.[11] *Voelkisch* writers became immensely popular in the two decades before World War I when a large part of the educated youth and of the so-called national bourgeoisie fell under their influence. To be sure, there were gradations in the *Hurrahpatriotismus* of the national bourgeoisie and not all its strident nationalists deserved to be called *voelkisch* or to be likened to religious devotees. Up until the beginning of the war, in fact, the *voelkisch* faith was more typical of academic youth, anti-establishment intellectuals, and backward pockets of the petty bourgeoisie, such as in small towns and certain professions. The great trial by fire of the war and the disillusionment of the German defeat suddenly raised the doctrine of a German mission in the world to the heights of popularity. Large numbers of *voelkisch* clubs, associations, and even parties were founded in 1918 and thereafter and literally inundated all political and cultural opinion to the right of the center.[12]

The Pan-German League had not been idle in the last years of the war and during the defeat. It was intimately involved with Admiral von Tirpitz's Fatherland party[13] of 1917/1918, which united the Conservative and National Liberal holdouts against the parties of the Peace Resolution of July, 1917, Social Democrats, the Catholic Center party and the Democrats, the same parties that later founded and defended the Weimar Republic. The Fatherland party became a great popular movement of one and a quarter million members, a telltale sign of the depth of the political mobilization of the right that up until then had been of very limited popular participation in its parties and politics. The Pan-German League also experienced a tremendous postwar expansion of membership and was instrumental in the foundation of several of the postwar *voelkisch* groups, such as the German *Voelkisch* Defense and Protection League, another militant mass organization.[14] Pan-German and Fatherland Party influence was also prominent in the early years of the Nazi party, which maintained close ties to the German racialist movements of the ethnic frontier in Poland, Silesia, Czechoslovakia, and Austria.[15] Hitler himself came from the Austrian ethnic frontier and had grown up under the influence of Pan-German figures such as Georg von Schoenerer and abstruse German racialist propaganda.[16] Even though Nazi doctrines and policies were from the beginning more mindful of workers and the lower middle class than those of the original Pan-Germans, Nazi foreign policy was guided almost exclusively by Pan-Germanism.[17]

III

To come back to our original analogy between German nationalism and religion, there remains the task of showing that this equation is based on more than a simile. To begin with, we need to emphasize that this was an extremely ideological period in European politics, an era full of passionately felt and conflicting *Weltanschauungen,* ranging from the utopian millenarianism of the communists and socialists to fanatic nationalists and racialists on the right. There were, furthermore, many new religious cults moving into the vacuum left by the decline of religious faith and observances among Protestants and among urbanized Catholics in Germany.

New messiahs, religious or secular, appeared throughout the Weimar Republic, emphatically appealing to the new mood of irrationality and the longing for dependence and salvation that was sweeping the country. Astrology and occult arts were greatly admired. Gone were the days of tribute to German scientific and industrial development. Among German youth in particular, an intense youth culture of spontaneous group life and group leadership had grown up, with overtones of *voelkisch* romanticism and a profound distaste for rationalism and pragmatism in politics and economic life. These were the legions of organized youth groups[18] and veterans who wanted no part of Weimar party politics and democracy, but who later fell for the new politico-religious Messiah, Adolf Hitler.

Hitler's younger years clearly show a sharp separation between the relationships of his personal life and the emerging ideological stereotypes that later came to rule his politics with such deadly effect. The devil image of his ideology, the Jews, did not keep him from maintaining friendly relations with his Jewish family doctor[19] and several Jewish art dealers in Vienna. The dogmatic hatred for his heretics, Marxist socialists and especially the Communists, veils a close acquaintance with Austrian socialism and its press, born of years of proletarian existence in Vienna. Political Catholicism, the other heresy in his ideology, he likewise encountered first in his Vienna years when he felt considerable admiration for the Christian Socialist mayor of the city, Karl Lueger, who may also have been his model as a skillful anti-Semitic demagogue. He undoubtedly knew a number of Marxists and Christian Socialists and may well have carried on the interminable political discussions of the Men's Home with men of these persuasions.

In his later political life, the Jewish devil becomes the chief object of hatred. He is exposed as the secret force behind all evil, the "wire pullers" behind the German defeat in World War I, the fall of the Empire, the Treaty of Versailles, the republican parties, and the economic troubles of the republic. This devil finally has to be killed off systematically in extermination camps. The Marxist and Catholic Center party heretics become the object of the street violence of his storm trooper army. The latter are the "sacred freedom fighters" of the cause, in the words of their storm trooper chief Pfeffer von Salomon, while the Nazi party members were the missionaries who recruited new members and spread the gospel.[20] If we consider the sudden mushrooming of the storm troopers and party members by a factor of at least seven in the two years and four months before the appointment of Hitler as Chancellor,[21] we can appreciate the character of the brown host as a proselytizing missionary movement. Add to this the increase in votes, say from the 810,000 of 1928 to the 17.3 million of March, 1933,[22] and the effectiveness of the Nazis' missionary propaganda becomes plain indeed.

There can be little doubt, from all accounts, that nearly all of these party and storm trooper members and many of the voters looked upon Hitler as a quasi-religious savior of the nation from degradation and humiliation.[23] It is not easy to specify how and from what he was expected to save them, but there is a good deal of consensus that his monster rallies resembled enormous religious revival meetings of evangelical crusades at which people felt deeply stirred and had conversion experiences. This "politics of ecstasy" was most carefully stage-managed and clearly outclassed even such ecstatic, utopian rallies as those of the Communists. There were already well-established nationalistic rituals of other right-wing, veterans', and youth organizations that harked back to the mass enthusiasm for the patriotic cause at the outbreak of the war and subsequent victory celebrations. The entire Weimar right wing had its recurrent flag-festooned German Days, when all the patriotic organizations would congregate in one particular town. Big veterans' organizations such as the militant Steel Helmet had annual monster rallies, with 100,000 and more uniformed marchers.[24] They also had frequent, uniformed nationalist demonstration marches to rival the heretic trade union and Socialist or Communist demonstrations of the left. The youth organizations had their own massive rallies to celebrate their sense of youthful community and solidarity in an inspirational style all their own.

But none of these came even close to the consummate mastery of Hitler in weaving his own myth. Legends and images worthy of any religious cult soon developed around his appearances. In the movie, *Triumph of the Will,* Hitler flies through the clouds (airplanes still being rather unusual transportation in those days) to the party rally against a background of pompous Wagnerian music. During the hectic "fighting years," 1929–1932, many people believed that the weather would turn balmy whenever he came to town for a rally. This myth of "Hitler weather" must have been difficult to maintain against the odds in rainy Germany. Hitler always arrived after a judicious delay to build up the expectations of the audience, and he always wore just the right kind of rather modest and respectable clothing so as not to alienate his particular audience. His speeches were also carefully tailored to the sensibilities of particular audiences and adjusted in tenor according to audience reactions.

Listeners rarely could recall his particular messages or formulations but only the inspiring emotions of the occasion. Here is an account of such a rally by a German-Russian emigré:

My heart pounding with curiosity and anticipation, I was awaiting the appearance of our Hitler from my seat in the crowded auditorium. A storm of jubilation rising from afar, from the street and moving into the lobby, announced the coming of the *Fuehrer*. And then suddenly the auditorium went wild, as he strode resolutely, in his rain coat and without a hat, to the rostrum. When the speech came to an end, I could not see out of my eyes any more. There were tears in my eyes, my throat was all tight from crying. A liberating scream of the purest enthusiasm discharged the unbearable tension as the auditorium rocked with applause.

I looked around discreetly and noticed that others, too, men and women and young fellows, were as deeply moved as I. They also wiped tears from their eyes. Deafened and with a sense of enormous joy I stormed into the street. At last I was no longer alone. There were people around me who felt the same as I, who were looking at each other in joyful rapture, as if they were all one family or a brotherhood (*Bund*), or a new, firm, and happy community where everyone could read in the others' eyes a solemn oath of loyalty. . . . This experience I had again and again during the course of the following years, and my feeling became ever stronger and deeper.

It is worth noting that this enthusiastic description contains not a word about the content of the speech. The man's personal isolation and the momentous confrontations of the Russian revolution and civil war eased his way from militant anti-Bolshevism in Moscow or Riga to militant anti-Marxism in Berlin or Halberstadt.

IV

Joseph Goebbels, the *Gauleiter* of Berlin during the fighting years and later the Minister of Propaganda of the Third Reich, was nearly Hitler's equal when it came to staging monster rallies and orchestrating propaganda. One of his master performances shall serve to illustrate the effectiveness of the Nazi appeal to the entire nationalistic audience in Germany in the crucial year 1932/1933. The ability of the NSDAP to broaden its allure in such a short time from a fringe position indeed begs for an explanation: Why were the voters of respectable bourgeois conservative (DNVP) and liberal (DDP, DVP) parties in 1932 suddenly no longer satisfied with the nationalism that all of these parties shared with the Nazis? Why did many of the Weimar parties practically give up their existence voluntarily before the new dictator suppressed them in July of 1933?[25]

To be sure, the Nazis had some distinctive attractions over their bourgeois competitors, most of all their cocky self-assurance and the storm troopers marching and battling all over the country. They also had the extremist's advantage of outbidding and outpromising their rivals. But on the other hand, they had some conspicuous faults in the eyes of the respectable bourgeoisie, especially their street brawls and quite a few of their uncouth leaders, whose violent, quasi-revolutionary language must have frightened the bourgeoisie. Their breakthrough into respectable bourgeois groups and their repeated alliances with the conservative right since 1929 could not completely have expunged their earlier, rough image.[26] Their open and strident anti-Semitism also was not much of an attraction with the bourgeoisie, which preferred more discreet forms of the same prejudice. The turning point must have been the emotional momentum of the carefully staged "national revolution" with which the Nazis swept the German bourgeoisie off its feet. Secondly, the barely hidden Nazi appeals to the workers, the little people and the unemployed, and the anti-establishment tenor of Nazi propaganda (even though in conflict with the Nazi breakthrough to bourgeois acceptability) gave the party an invaluable strategic advantage in the trough of the Great Depression. All the other bourgeois parties, one by one, had emphatically turned to the right in the late 1920s, leaving their large lower middle class and "Tory worker" following behind.[27] Under the pressure of the economic crisis (especially its psychological effect) and unable to see their way to the Socialists or Communists, these voters must have found the Nazis to their liking.

As for the "national revolution," this was a potent tactical policy line adopted by the Nazis to ease their way into power. It was at once a propaganda campaign and an alignment with von Papen, the Conservatives, and the Steel Helmet veterans in juxtaposition to the socialist coalition proposed by Hitler's last predecessor and antagonist, General Kurt von Schleicher.[28] As a propaganda and political mobilization campaign it loosed a veritable avalanche of nationalistic storm trooper and Steel Helmet ostentation that in the course of 1933 swelled the storm trooper ranks with millions of new members, especially from the veterans' groups. It also aroused millions of other opportunists to volunteer other kinds of support and cooperation with the Nazi takeover. After all, anybody could claim that his (her) patriotism had suddenly been awakened to a fever pitch.

The resultant tidal wave of both false and genuine nationalistic mass enthusiasm in early 1933 drowned out all resistance and made it easy for Hitler to overpower and push aside all rivals, including his Conservative allies. The rumors of an impending Communist coup[29] only intensified the desire to replace any influential persons wanting in zeal with a Nazi or a convincingly nationalistic opportunist. The mass hysteria engendered by the Reichstag fire and the subsequent election campaign further served to heighten the hectic climate of opinion in which the Communist party—quite innocent of the Reichstag fire—was suppressed. This climate in turn gave legitimacy to the persecutions and terrorism campaigns of the storm troopers, who had already been sworn in as auxiliary police and now established the first concentration camps for the Marxist heretics and other political enemies. With the blessing of President von Hindenburg, Hitler received emergency powers, basic rights were repealed, and all state governments had to accept governments that corresponded to the Nazi and nationalist majority garnered at the March elections.[30] This then was the atmosphere in which Goebbels, the new Propaganda Minister, staged his nationalistic master performance to overcome the last reluctance among nationalistic conservatives to ride the Nazi tiger all the way into the Third Reich.

Goebbels' masterly nationalistic show was the convening of

the newly elected Reichstag on March 21, 1933, the anniversary of the founding of the Bismarckian Empire in 1871. The event took place, after Protestant and Catholic church services, in the Potsdam Garrison Church, at the tomb of Frederick the Great and before the regimental flags of Prussian military glory. The Protestant deputies marched into the Garrison Church led by Goering, the Catholics by Chancellor Hitler himself. President von Hindenburg, the great war hero, gave a brief speech before the assembled dignitaries, including other distinguished old German generals, followed by a speech of Hitler who had always advertised himself as a simple German soldier of the great patriotic war. From all accounts everyone was deeply moved by the skillful invocation of the glories of the nation in this national shrine.[31] Two days after this nationalistic revival meeting, the Reichstag was induced to pass the infamous Enabling Act, which gave Hitler complete governmental powers for four years. Only the Socialist heretics of the Reichstag had the backbone to stand up and argue against this sell-out of parliamentary power to the dictator.[32] A month later, the trade unions were similarly overwhelmed with flattery and nationalistic revivalism. The Nazi government declared the first of May the National Day of Labor, a paid holiday, and showered the trade unionists with flattering speeches, rallies, and nationalistic tributes to the German working man. The next day, the storm troopers took over all trade union buildings and offices and sealed the fate of this last powerful, but already demoralized, fortress of Weimar republicanism.

In this fashion, the first German democracy, the Weimar Republic, was carried away on an emotional tidal wave of quasi-religious nationalistic fervor. Carefully stage-managed and directed, but obviously relying on an extremely susceptible public, the uplifting enthusiasm of a "national renaissance" thus ushered in the grim reality of Nazi dictatorship and its pursuit of war and genocide. The religious ecstasy of the moment must have obscured for most nationalistic Germans the horrible policies to which their transport of emotion in the long run gave the authority.

NOTES

1. Examples of such nonreligious connotations are the shift from local to national identification and the concept of nationalism underlying Karl W. Deutsch's model of social mobilization. See Deutsch, *Nationalism and Social Communication,* (Cambridge: MIT Press, 1953).

2. Our concept has much in common with those of ideology or "political religion" used in David E. Apter, ed., *Ideology and Discontent* (New York: Free Press, 1964), esp. pp. 18–30; and William T. Bluhm, *Ideologies and Attitudes: Modern Political Culture* (Englewood Cliffs, NJ: Prentice-Hall, 1974), pp. 10–16, 27–30.

3. See, for example, Hermann Rauschning, *The Voice of Destruction* (New York: Putnam, 1940), pp. 231–232. The ulterior motive of Hitler and the Nazi leadership, in any case, was their own glory and success.

4. See, for example, the quotations from the Abel file of Germans who later joined the NSDAP, Merkl, *Political Violence Under the Swastika: 581 Early Nazis* (Princeton University Press, 1975), pp. 53, 55, 154–158.

5. The issue of Prussian-dominated "Smaller Germany" versus a "Greater Germany" inclusive of Austria also involved the question of including the large non-German populations of the Hapsburg empire.

6. Popular parlance quickly coined phrases such as that of the *Speckdänen* (bacon Danes), Germans who would become Danes when such a switch promised a better food supply for themselves. In reality, of course, any ethnic border is likely to produce also large numbers of people of mixed or uncertain ethnic parentage, bicultural and transcultural people who refuse to be cast as members of only one ethnicity.

7. One of the worst cases of such terrorism was the brutal slaying by storm troopers of a young worker of slight involvement with the Communists in Potempa (Silesia) in 1932. The victim also happened to be an ethnic Pole who had been involved in the earlier Polish agitation for turning over parts of Silesia to the new Polish nation-state.

8. See the many telling stories and quotations in Merkl, *Political Violence Under the Swastika,* pp. 104–118 and 189–206.

9. By spring of 1918, the eastern territories occupied by German and Austrian armies extended deeply into the Ukraine and Southern Russia along a line not exceeded by far in World War II.

10. The Pan German League, according to Koppel Pinson, "acted as a sort of general staff for the various nationalist organizations. . . ." and had influence in the highest circles of government, including the Agrarian League and the navy. *Modern Germany, Its History and Civilization,* 2nd ed. (New York: Macmillan, 1966), p. 310.

11. On the *voelkisch* writers, see esp. George Mosse, *The Crisis of German Ideology* (New York: Grosset & Dunlap, 1964). Writers like Paul A. de La-

garde and Julius Langbehn typically called for an intensification of German culture and sentiment into a source of morality and a new religion.

12. For an excellent review of the *voelkisch* literature and discussion of *voelkisch* groups at the end of the war and the beginning of the Weimar Republic, see also Martin Broszat, *German National Socialism 1919–1945* (Santa Barbara: Clio Press, 1966), chap. 3, esp. pp. 33–36.

13. The *voelkisch* founder of the Fatherland party was Wolfgang Kapp, who later in 1920 organized the initially successful Kapp putsch against the Weimar government.

14. See esp. Uwe Lohalm, *Voelkischer Radikalismus* (Hamburg: Leibniz, 1970).

15. See, for example, Pinson, op. cit., p. 480. The early Nazi party was linked with the Sudeten German Workers party and the Austrian National Socialists. The Sudeten German Rudolf Jung and the Austrian Walter Riehl were very influential in it. Jung's book *Der nationale Sozialismus* (Munich, 1920) was a Pan-German diatribe against the Jews and the Old Testament.

16. See also Ernst Nolte, *Three Faces of Fascism* (New York: Holt,Rinehart & Winston, 1966), pp. 295–297, and Bradley F. Smith, *Adolf Hitler: His Family, Childhood, and Youth* (Stanford: Hoover Institution, 1967), pp. 138–150.

17. See, for example, Andreas Hillgruber, *Deutsche Grossmacht und Weltpolitik* (Duesseldorf: Droste, 1977), pp. 252–275, and Peter H. Merkl, *German Foreign Policies, West and East* (Santa Barbara: Clio Press, 1974), pp. 74–81.

18. A *Reich* Committee on Organized Youth in 1927 estimated a total youth group membership of nearly five million in Germany. Most of the veterans' organizations also professed a profound distrust for political parties, including the Nationalists (DNVP) to which they were the closest in attitudes.

19. Several psychohistorians have sought to derive Hitler's terrible anti-Semitism from his anguish about his mother's painful death under his care. However, the record shows that Hitler continued to treat the doctor with affectionate respect and even gave orders to spare him the fate visited on many Austrian Jews after the *Anschluss*. See especially the critical discussion by Helm Stierlin, *Adolf Hitler: A Family Perspective* (New York: Psycho-history Press, 1976), pp. 30–42.

20. Quoted by Joachim Fest, *The Face of the Third Reich* (New York: Pantheon, 1970), pp. 142–143.

21. The period is calculated from the September 1930 elections, the first Nazi landslide, when the party had 130,000 and the SA 70,000 members, to January, 1933, when there were 900,000 and 700,000, respectively. See Fest, op. cit., pp. 143–145, and Andreas Werner, *SA und NSDAP*, unpublished dissertation at Erlangen University, 1964, pp. 544–552.

22. The latter vote still amounted only to 43.9 percent of the popular vote.

By April, 1932, Hitler had already drawn 13.4 million votes (37.0 percent) as a presidential candidate running against the incumbent, Paul von Hindenburg.

23. See, for example, the extravagant language used by the membership regarding Hitler, Merkl, *Political Violence,* pp. 130, 167, 349, 354, 396–399, 469–471, 642, and 663.

24. See Merkl, *The Making of a Stormtrooper* (Princeton: Princeton University Press, 1980), chapter 2.

25. See esp. the essays on each party in Erich Matthias and Rudolf Morsey, *Das Ende der Parteien* (Duesseldorf: Droste, 1960). Only the Socialists and Communists had to be outlawed.

26. Their alliances with the Steel Helmet and DNVP in the Young Plan campaign of the 1929, in the Harzburg Front of 1931, and in the Hitler cabinet of 1933 obviously helped, and yet there was a noticeable turning away of the upper middle class voters from the Nazis over the Potempa murder of August 1932, when Hitler went out of his way to give his moral support to the murderers.

27. According to Richard F. Hamilton, *Who Voted for Hitler?* (Princeton: Princeton University Press, 1982), this along with the rural landslide was the crucial electoral movement toward the NSDAP. The German equivalent of the Tory workers may have been largely of rural origin themselves.

28. Schleicher had proposed to bring together the trade unions and Social Democrats with the left (Strasser) wing of the NSDAP, but the coalition never came off. Hitler took brutal revenge on Schleicher by having him assassinated at the time of the Roehm purge of 1934.

29. There were also rumors of a military coup attributed to the deposed Chancellor von Schleicher which had likewise no basis in fact.

30. There were also systematic purges of the civil service and courts as well as of associations of all kinds to remove oppositional elements. Eventually, even local governments fell victim to the Nazi *Gleichschaltung.*

31. Among those deeply stirred by the uplifting spirit of the "national revolution" of those days was an enthusiastic young cavalry lieutenant by the name of Claus Schenk von Stauffenberg. Eleven years later he felt morally compelled to attempt an abortive assassination of his fallen idol, Hitler.

32. The other parties also were given assurances and promises of various sorts to obtain their assent. The Communists had already been suppressed at the time.

SIX

Catholicism and Irish National Identity

Michael J. Carey

In few countries is there so close a relationship between a particular religion and national identity as there is in the case of the Republic of Ireland. Irish and Catholic are nearly synonomous. Ninety-five percent of the population in the Republic is Catholic and, more remarkably, most are active Catholics who practice their faith by attending mass. The link between Irish national identity and Catholicism is so strong that society, the political system, and even the Constitution profoundly reflect church influences. Ireland is neither secular nor truly plural, but is rather a society penetrated—willingly—by clericalism. Unlike most other Western European nations, political and economic development in Ireland resulted not in secularist values and pluralistic tendencies which are common to modern nations; rather Ireland retained its bonds to Catholic orthodoxy, retained a very special political place for the Church, and even received recognition of this status by Vatican diplomacy. Pope John Paul II's visit in August 1979 to Ireland served the triple purpose of bestowing a favor upon a conservatively Catholic nation, reinforcing devotional aspects of the faith at a Marian shrine, and without contradicting the former goals, seeking to disarm religious bigots with an ecumenical appeal to Christians to solve political problems without political violence. On the one hand Vatican diplomacy had never included a papal visit to Ireland; on the other hand papal visits abroad constitute rare tools of Vatican diplomacy.

The close identification of Catholicism and nationalism is further indicated by recent political controversies in Ireland. In few Western nations would it be necessary for a national political leader, in this case an Irish senator, to call for a secular nationalism to replace a faith and fatherland conception of nationalism.[1] Faith and fatherland does more accurately describe Irish nationalism, that is, to be Irish is to be Catholic. Other controversial political issues today in Ireland are liberalization of anti-contraceptives law and legalizing divorce—issues that reflect predominant Catholic values and the role of the Church in society and politics. Another example of the intensity of Catholic identification is found in a recent survey by the Bishop's Research and Development Commission of students at Ireland's five universities, which discovered that there is a rise in the number of students who have lapsed or left the Church. Fourteen percent of the university population are ex-Catholics, a figure much higher than that for the general population. More interestingly, among those who consider themselves Catholics, 80 percent go to Sunday mass.[2] This last figure would gladden the heart of many a Catholic chaplain at universities in other countries!

Irish Catholicism, described as austere, puritanical, cold, and authoritarian, and as a folk church "geared to its own idea of the needs and the limitations of a peasant people"[3] managed by default and sometimes in spite of itself to assume the cultural and political leadership role in a potentially revolutionary nation. Especially in the modern era from 1800 to the present, the Church achieved its position by default; no alternative institution existed much of the time. In spite of itself, because of the often negative role of the Church hierarchy vis-à-vis nationalistic revolutionaries, the Church became more influential. Locally and despite the hierarchy, priests were leaders of communities and sometimes identified with local agrarian causes and even nationalist aims. The Church was also not a great landowner and hence not a source of envy to peasants thrown off their land, or forced to pay rack rents. While it was the Catholic bourgeoisie cut out of the political process in their own country by the English Ascendency that truly created modern Irish nationalism in the nineteenth century, these middle-class forces worked in conjunction with the tenant-agrarian-local forces. Catholic, national, and tenant became interchangeable terms.

Even before the modern era of Irish nationalism the conjoining of Catholicism and Irish cultural identity took place, first by early Christian missionaries who succeeded in converting Gaelic pagans into Gaelic Christians throughout the Island. The introduction of religious differences came with colonization by England and a policy aimed specifically at converting the Irish when Henry VIII broke with Rome. Eventually, force of arms, the plantation system, and Penal Laws made most of the population (the Catholics) virtual outlaws.[4]

Catholicism in Ireland (past and present) provides individuals with a *Weltanschauung,* as does any religion that helps orient or influence political values. Religious values can promote acceptance or rejection of both governments and their policies. Religious activities are also social insofar as they bring together people with shared views. Besides providing community and values, a religion also socializes members by providing continuity of the community, and in some cases a sense of national identity.

From this brief introduction it can be seen that Ireland, with its virtually total connection of Catholicism and Irish national identity, is an unusual case among Western nations. A comprehensive analysis of this connection is called for. First, a brief overview of the early identification of Catholicism with Irishness is presented. Next, an analysis of the modern period (1800 to the present) is divided into two sections: first, dealing with the socio-political role of Catholicism, i.e., with identification of Catholicism with Irish nationalism; second, analyzing the political or action role of the Church in nationalistic politics. Finally, conclusions from this exceptional case of the nexus between religion and nationalism are presented.

EARLY IRISH NATIONAL IDENTITY

Christianity was introduced at an early date to Ireland (perhaps as early as 390 A.D.), and eliminated paganism without overturning the Gaelic feudal political system on the Island. Challenges to the religious and political system came from marauding (and settling) Scandinavians. However, the feudal system survived until well into the medieval era when the Anglo-Norman invasion of the twelfth century occurred. Gaelic society, disrupted but not destroyed, adapted to and adopted the invaders. Many of these colonials were Hibernicized, taking up the Irish language, customs, etc. The eastern section of Ireland closest to England, referred to as the Pale, developed a distinctly English upper-class culture with an elite of Englishmen. In general, the medieval era is marked by a basic duality between two nations or cultures. Distrust and tension between the two nations that formed the Church increased. Generally two national churches evolved, one for each community: the Irish and the English Ascendency. Moreover, Protestantism was never a decisive factor, as the Irish were not dissatisfied with the papacy,[5] in contrast to continental Europe, where political-religious conflict with the papacy occurred.

Henry VIII's own reformation created a profound religious breach between the colonizer and the colonized, who remained faithful to their religious traditions. Unwittingly, the English colonizers provided a very clear point for Irish cultural identity, the identification with Roman Catholicism by the native population. The English Ascendency, with its own church, then proceeded to define political loyalty as religious loyalty too, and aggravated this split with specific policies to promote the English Church and denigrate and suppress the Irish Church.

The seventeenth century was decisive for the Gaelic feudal system or what remained of it, as the Catholic Gaelic aristocracy tried to overthrow the colonizers, and failed. English law was extended to the whole country at this time, and Irish civilization itself was overthrown; the Irish language and religion were all that remained.[6]

The English tried to force conformity to their church by arms, by missionary campaigns, and by introducing Protestants (e.g., Scottish Presbyterians) into the country. None of these methods succeeding in changing the Irish identification with Catholicism. English *realpolitik* dictated English policy as much as (or perhaps more than) did domestic considerations. Ireland's sympathy for and cooperation with Catholic Spain and France in their wars with England in the sixteenth and seventeenth centuries caused the English to fully subjugate Ireland for their own security purposes.[7]

Ulster, the northern province of old Gaelic Ireland, was a source of domestic trouble, as Irish chieftains offered the most effective resistance to religious and political Anglicanization. The British singled out Ulster as a special problem province. Land was seized for treason and given to English and Scottish settlers,[8] a policy that led to today's Protestant enclave in Northern Ireland. English administration completely supplanted the Gaelic system. For example, the practice of electing a ruler was declared illegal, and justice was dispensed only in English courts.[9] In 1641 reaction to oppression by the Irish led to further repression and confiscation of land and led to Cromwell's turning on Ireland with his Puritan army after defeating the Stuart forces. Wealthy Catholics who supported the rebellion lost all property and all rights to it. Other wealthy Catholics who did not support the rebellion were forced to move to a barren western district (Connaught) and were allowed to retain property. All their seized holdings were distributed to Cromwell's men, which effectively put an end to the Irish Catholic gentry.[10] Later in the century the Catholic–English ruler conflict emerged again in the James II's fight in Ireland for his throne of England. All of Ireland except Ulster was Jacobite. The ensuing Battle of the Boyne and the siege of Londonderry entered the Protestant Ulsterman's mythology and guaranteed the future of Protestants in Ireland,[11] (in the North, that is).

One of the most important results of the destruction of the Gaelic culture and resultant identification of the people with Catholicism was the virtual elimination of social conflicts between Catholics.[12] Especially in the region where the Irish language was still spoken, life was very homogeneous. At the same time the power of priests over their communities increased. Education of Catholics, proscribed by the colonizers, could not weaken this form of clericalism. Priests were spiritual, intellectual, and to an extent political leaders of their parishes.[13] The dominated population was left with only one organized force, the Church. They centered their lives around it, and accepted its power. In short, "Irishness" became identified with Catholicism.

In summary, the early era prior to development of revolutionary nationalism, was dominated by colonization and religious conflict, and actually reinforced Irish cultural identification with Catholicism. The mass of the people, the peasantry, and townspeople throughout the country (with the exception of the North) remained Catholic and self-identified as Irish. The Established Church of the English, the official church (supported by administrators, the landed aristocracy, and the elite townspeople) never truly became the "Church of Ireland," as it was named. The Presbyterian Church retained the allegiance of the Scottish settlers and merchants in the North and, to the extent they existed, elsewhere in the country.[14]

THE MODERN ERA

Whether described in sympathetic or unsympathetic terms,[15] the role of the Church and religion in the daily lives of the Irish is depicted as dominant, more so than in any other country. The people are said to put more trust in their bishops than in their elected deputies in the Parliament. Since the 1800s, especially during the union with England, the clergy actively engaged directly in politics, and occasionally the lower clergy

played roles in revolutionary organizations. The hierarchy made
political pronouncements then, and continues to do so. Open
involvement in politics decreased after independence, although
parish priests continued to play important roles locally. Today,
the pervasiveness of the Church continues and since independence it plays a more subtle role. The modern era is marked
by a continued infusing of Irish life with an authoritarian manner; however, this role of the Church is generally viewed as
legitimate. For example, most schools today are run by the
Church in an authoritarian fashion. It is important to note of
course that the Church encouraged support of the new democratic state after independence. To the extent that the newly
independent Ireland was a developing nation the Church helped
provide support for it. Priests in their communities provided
important organizing capabilities, and peasant organizations
promoted political change. The last two roles were most important in the revolutionary era of the nineteenth century.[16]

It would be mistaken to conclude that the national identification with Catholicism made the Church revolutionary
nationalist in spirit or policy. Indeed, the Church has been described as a non-nationalistic church, a conservative, anti-
revolutionary, anti-Protestant church that was willing to
cooperate with the English rulers.[17] Important elements in the
Church supported union with England, condemned Fenianism
(revolutionary nationalism), stood by the powerful landlords in
time of famine, suspected the Irish national leader Parnell, and
did this in return for control over primary education in Ireland.[18] At times the papacy, of course, worked against the desires of Irish nationalists and in favor of the upholders of law
and order too. As mentioned before, the Church retained its
support and the close identification of Irish national identity
with Catholicism despite itself.

The role of the Church in, and identification of Catholicism
with, Irish nationalism is, then, not explained only by the political roles the Church played, nor by the conjunction of Catholic grievances and reform movements and rebellions alone.
Before those roles are identified, a deeper socio-political signif-

icance of Catholicism must be examined to understand fully
the issue at hand. In other words, the special case of clericalism and its role in Irish society must be examined to explain
the special attachment to Catholicism.

Secularism came late to Ireland and certainly is not pervasive today. By the 1950s perhaps, the modern, individualistic,
empiricist viewpoint of life existed only among the modern
population of Dublin. Most of the population held a traditional—sacred—view of life. The extent to which changes have
taken place is not altogether clear, although the statistics on
mass attendance and prevalence of Catholic values today suggest secularism is gaining very slowly. The absence of a secularist value system is one gauge of the strength of Catholicism.
Catholicism at its core maintains not only a belief in the supernatural and God, but that God destined man for a special end
that requires supernatural assistance to attain. Indeed, the
supernatural side of human existence is the most important.
This conception of the cosmos affects a Catholic society. It is
the antithesis of secularism.

This Catholic outlook affects the way the Irish view the family, society, and politics. The value system is based on this
outlook. According to sociological research this belief system
still clearly predominated in the 1950s; it is eroding only
slowly.[19] The most profoundly Catholic outlook is that of the
county man, while the city dwellers (e.g., in Dublin) reflect the
changed perspective—but one that is only modified slightly.
Basically certain aspects of family patterns have been altered,
yet fundamental values and beliefs remained. It is doubtful that
values and beliefs will not be changed more in the future, due
to cosmopolitan European influences. Joining the Common
Market in 1972 opened the door for secularization, yet the
transformation probably will be slow.

The traditional belief pattern is Jansenistic, with a strong
emphasis on the weaknesses of human nature and man's inability to act and think. With great distrust of human reason,
God's grace is needed even more. Puritanism and fatalism tend
to be characteristic of this Catholic tradition. This outlook,

combined with other factors already mentioned, leads the Irish to "an intensified reliance upon the teaching power of the church as voiced by the clergy."[20] When the role of the Church and priests is extended to the social and political realms of life, as in Ireland, the outcome is clericalism. This is not the clericalism of nineteenth-century France, with excessive hostility to republican forms of government, etc., but rather a peculiarly Irish clericalism, the conservative, traditional, pervasive influence of the clergy over a Catholic population. No realm of human activity is immune. The point is that while Ireland today is undergoing slow secularization as the society is transformed from a rural one into an urban industrial one, clericalism was a dominant political feature until recently. This form of clericalism, especially in the nineteenth and early twentieth century, accounts to a large degree for the pervasive identification of Catholicism with Irish nationalism. The nationalism was not a secular nationalism; it was unlike what happened in some other European nations. The peasantry did not even in part divorce itself from Catholicism and the clergy.

CATHOLICISM AND NATIONALIST POLITICS

This discussion of Catholicism and nationalist politics needs to be qualified by the following distinctions between levels of the Church and its followers. The Vatican in the nineteenth century, generally allied with the forces of reaction in Europe, often followed policies at the expense of Irish nationalists. The Catholic hierarchy in Ireland, generally antinationalist, feared and opposed the revolutionaries and their republican aims. The few revolutionaries who suggested religion was a matter of conscience appeared dangerously anticlerical and "continental" to the hierarchy. In the mid- and late nineteenth century, some of the hierarchy became nationalists and supported the various movements. The local clergy was most likely of all levels in the Church to be nationalist. If these clergy were not ardent nationalists they occasionally ignored the secret society activities of their parishioners. Thus, differentiation in Church support confuses the issue of Catholicism and nationalistic politics. At times the source of conflict was over means (e.g., nonviolent versus illegal means) and at other times over goals (e.g., a republican form of government).

In the late 1700s, a nonsectarian movement called the United Irishmen pushed Irish nationalism to the left with their republican ideals from revolutionary France. Protestant and Catholic middle-class revolutionaries joined with Catholic peasants in fomenting small rebellions throughout Ireland. Some local clergy were regarded as local leaders. These rebellions failed due to lack of support and superior English might. The Protestant element in national agitation disappeared as an organized force while later a few individual Protestants participated. Most of that group supported union with England to protect themselves and their own religion.

Catholic and nationalist agitation on an organized countrywide basis did not occur until the early nineteenth century, when the Catholic rights movement developed. The goal was to achieve Catholic emancipation and full civil rights, and to press the claims of the lower classes. Its famous leader was a middle-class Catholic barrister, Daniel O'Connell. The Catholic Association created around this national cause has been called the first parliamentary party of the modern era; it was at least one of the first mass movements in Europe. Once emancipation was granted after the English prime minister gave in to the Irish (against the wishes of the king), the political machine could be used fully. Clerical support and development of the tenant vote created a party machine that could win one-third of the constituencies in Ireland. Representatives went to the English Parliament. The machine was centrally organized. It approved candidates, had a large income "from the network of parishes through the penny rent. The clergy acted as local and constituency organizers, passed down directives, and above all, gathered, led, and steadied the voters on the day of polling."[21] The party was actually two-tiered, with a middle-class club of the traditional type and an army of humble supporters who gave the party its mass base. Cooperation with the Church was guaranteed by making all Catholic priests ex-officio members. This gave the Catholic Association higher standing with the people and forestalled clerical criticism of a laymens' organization that rivaled the Church.[22] It is ironic that national aspirations were fed by these relatively constitutional or legal means and later strained that approach to political change to the breaking point. It should be noted that this tension between nonviolent and revolutionary means continued in the nationalist movement until independence was gained (by political violence).

A group of young Turks helped O'Connell in the repeal of Union efforts. These constitutional and revolutionary separatists were split by religious issues; some of these Young Irelanders believed religion to be a matter of conscience, and thus supported plans for several nonsectarian colleges. The Archbishop of Tuam led the Catholic hierarchy in "condemning these godless schools because they provided for the secular education of Irishmen of different religious persuasions at the same institution."[23] A secret society of revolutionaries, the Fenian Brotherhood, which repudiated constitutional methods, supported the separation of church and state. Again the hierarchy condemned the groups of nationalists because they disapproved of all oath-bound secret societies. In 1861 the hierarchy issued letters warning that excommunication from the Church was automatic for those taking the Fenian oath. The organization that existed in both Ireland and the U.S.A. grew slowly, due to opposition by the Church. The English government in Ireland tried to influence the Vatican to limit priests, who the government feared were supporters of the Fenians.[24]

Another nationalist agitational organization, the Land League, flowered in the 1870s and '80s with approval by a number of bishops and most of the parish clergy. The Archbishop of Cashel committed himself to the League, kept the clergy in the forefront of the nationalist organization, preserved Church power, and prevented alienation of the people. The local clergy especially supported these later nationalists movements: they came from the local areas and were well acquainted with the problems in the countryside. Movements could not be started and certainly could not succeed without assistance from local priests.[25] In most cases, these were political movements utilizing legitimate means, not political violence.

Irish nationalism, channeled into legal party politics in the late nineteenth century, focused on the Home Rule issue. Charles Stewart Parnell, leader of the Parliamentary Party, had a stormy career in Irish nationalist politics. The Church role is most remarkable not for its support of him but rather for its attack on him and the near collapse of his party when Parnell was victimized in the English press and by the government for a romantic liaison. His conduct violated the puritanical norms of the Catholic hierarchy in Ireland. When Parnell tried a speaking tour to save his party it "was lost before it began since the Catholic bishops and parish priests immediately threw their weight against the tainted leader."[26] In the same time period, a second strand of Irish nationalism blossomed: a romantic nationalism glorifying Irish culture, language, traditions—the Irish soul. The fanaticism and political violence to come was in part a result of the growth of this second strand. The violence it helped promote appears to violate the hierarchy's norms even more than the more peaceable Parnell's private behavior.

The Parliamentary Party, reunited under John Redmond in 1900, tried to recapture its position of power and nationalism without sectarianism. Redmond let national interests transcend his sectarian interests and maintained political ties with the Liberals in England. Both parties sought Home Rule. Redmond, his party, and his ties to the Liberals were suspect, since the Liberals had anticlerical, freethinking, materialistic values, according to the Irish hierarchy.[27]

In the modern era it is the romantic nationalists who most fully identified Catholicism with Irish nationalism. It was they who injected Catholicism most completely into nationalistic politics, in this case revolutionary violence. In earlier eras certainly the blindly sectarian uprisings accomplished much the same thing, but on a local basis. Some of the best examples are the rebellions of the 1640s, and the Jacqueries of the 1700s; even the Rebellion in 1798 was marred by blind sectarian bloodletting. [28]

The origins of the romantic nationalists are found in Gaelic sports groups, Irish language enthusiasts, and Anglo-Irish intellectuals who helped promote a literary renaissance. Estrangement of the Anglo-Irish intellectuals from the Catholic middle-class revolutionary forces was probably inevitable, given their differences. Yet together, a mythical and mystical modern nationalism replete with a national soul and character was forged out of the combination of romantics. Several Catholic poet-revolutionaries made up part of the leadership cadre in the Irish Republican Brotherhood, a leading illegal organization that helped plan and carry out the Easter Rebellion.

Patrick Pearse, Thomas McDonagh, and Joseph Plunkett were language enthusiasts, poets, violent revolutionaries, and deeply religious Catholics. Their doctrine was messianic and preached sacrifice; it was mystical, apocalyptic, and a religion of retribution. [29] Two other strands of their ideal nationalism were the peasant tradition and heroic ideal (e.g., of the mythical Gaelic warriors). These two strands were subordinated to the third, the religious element, which was to them the most significant "to the integrity of the Irish national character—the Roman Catholic religious tradition that had survived despite centuries of persecution." [30] The sense of religious conviction was the strength of their poetry and nationalism. Peasant customs and literature were reinterpreted via their Christian sentiment; even the old pre-Christian sagas were interpreted as having religious significance. Religious persecution of the Irish was compared to that of the early Christians.

The Easter Rising in 1916 was in itself symbolic within the Christian context as a resurrection, as is the symbol of the-Rising—the Easter lily. The rebellion was crushed and some of its principal leaders were executed; the Irish masses did not rise up in support of it. It was, indeed, the execution of the leaders that truly struck a cord in the populace. An important consequence of increased popular sympathy was the Conscription Crisis of 1918. Opposition to conscription in Ireland, a sentiment nearly universal everywhere except Ulster, was unanimously upheld by the hierarchy. The bishops called the government's conscription bill oppressive and inhuman, and claimed the Irish had a right "to resist by every means that are consonant with the laws of God."[31]

Independence, gained in 1922, created the Free State of Ireland, a parliamentary democracy whose constitution reflected liberalism due to its English inspiration. The state was not a self-declared Catholic state, yet in fact it was and is. Leaving six relatively Protestant counties attached to the United Kingdom helped guarantee that the Free State would be Catholic. The power of the Church and acquiescence of the Catholic population helped perpetuate a relatively sectarian state. Pluralism has not flourished because it need not—a tiny Protestant population in Ireland makes no successful claims for pluralism, nor does a secular political party of any sort make the same claims. After independence, Irish political culture was able to take on fully the "Catholicness" of the population, in part because of social legislation that reflected Catholic values, e.g., in the censorship law, proscription of divorce, educational policies that guaranted in most cases sectarian control of schools, etc. In a large sense, the Church has been able to "withdraw" from politics since its position and values are relatively secure, and the population generally upholds its values. Hence, Ireland's political culture reflects these values—and when the Church needs to intervene it can subtly do so by influencing the regime in office.[32]

What conclusions can be drawn from this necessarily brief analysis of Catholicism and Irish national identity? One point is obvious and yet bears reiteration. A national political culture reflects society's dominant values, and in a homogenous society religious identification is likely to be paramount. In particular, the self-definition of what the Irish are automatically and necessarily includes Catholicism. Second, a national revolution will also reflect religious values from the political culture. Certainly nationalism and religion are not synonymous, and the political values and purposes of the clergy and hierarchy may diverge from the interests of nationalists. Yet the role of religion in Ireland over time guaranteed a close connection between religious identification, values, and nationalism. The cultural connection between religion and Irish identity preceded modern nationalism by many centuries. This conjunction of religion and identity was reinforced by colonialism, and the eventual evolution of modern nationalism in Ireland fully reflected this Catholic identity as well.

Important questions that can only be partially explained are raised by this examination of Catholicism and Irish national identity. For example, why are Catholicism and nationalism in Ireland more closely identified than in other Catholic European countries? The most fruitful areas of further research to elucidate this question should concentrate (to start with) on the colonial political circumstances of Ireland, where a separate culture, language, and religion existed among the masses of the people, partitioning them from the colonizers.[33]

Another subtopic vital to this question is the role of clericalism in a peasant society. Here the role of authority and political organization needs further exploration to describe how Irish peasant society's hierarchical order and integration of religious, social, and political values contributes to the political role of the Church.

NOTES

A special thanks to Mary Robinson for her research assistance and especially to my colleague, David Williams, for his help with the manuscript. The author assumes all responsibilities.

1. *The Irish Times,* 13 August, 1978, and 14 August, 1978. 1.3 million people filled Phoenix Park to hear a Papal Mass. The population of the Republic is about 3.5 million, of the North about 1.5 million. See *Ireland Today,* #958, 15 October, 1979, pp. 4–7, describing the Pope's visit to Ireland.

2. *The Irish Times,* 3 August, 1978.

3. Basil Chubb, *The Government and Politics of Ireland* (London: Oxford University Press, 1974), p. 53. A short story by Irish author George Moore, "Home Sickness," (1903) bears out these characterizations of Irish Catholic-

ism. The protagonist returns to his village after emigrating to America. In his village the obedience of these people to their priest surprised him; and he listened in anger and wonderment as the priest scolded parishioners about dancing going on in their homes and about boys and girls loitering along the roads. Liam O'Flaherty's "The Fairy Goose" (1927), provides a good example of the peasant society, with superstitions from pre-Christian times still alive and the peasants' propensity to believe in such, intermingled with their Catholic faith. Both short stories are found in Frank O'Connor, ed. *Modern Irish Short Stories* (London: Oxford University Press, 1974).

4. Richard Rose, *Governing Without Consensus* (Boston: Beacon Press, 1971) p. 247.

5. This section is largely informed by John Watt, *The Church in Medieval Ireland* (Dublin: Gill and Macmillan, 1972), pp. 215–216.

6. See Robert Dudley Edwards, *Church and State in Tudor Ireland* (New York, Russell, 1935), Chapter XXI, for a summary of the Tudor period. In regard to the Irish language and national identity see Michael J. Carey and William Neeley, "Implementing Bilingualism in the Irish Republic," forthcoming.

7. See Thomas Hachey, *Britain and Irish Separatism* (Chicago: Rand McNally, 1977), p. 1.

8. Ibid.

9. Patrick Buckland, *Ulster Unionism and the Origin of Northern Ireland 1886–1922,* (Dublin: Gill and Macmillan, 1973), p. xvii.

10. Hachey, op. cit., pp. 2–3.

11. Buckland, op. cit., pp. xvii–xix.

12. See for example, Eric Strauss, *Irish Nationalism and British Democracy* (New York: Columbia University Press, 1951), pp. 15–16.

13. Ibid.

14. See, for example, Robert Dudley Edwards, op. cit., p. 307.

15. Sympathetic treatments of the role of Church and religion in Ireland are found in: John Watt, op. cit., Robert Dudley Edwards, op. cit.; less sympathetic or unsympathetic treatments are found in Felecian Prill, *Ireland, Britain, and Germany, 1871–1914* (Dublin: Gill and Macmillan, 1975), and Eric Strauss, op. cit. Perhaps the most balanced treatments are found in Conor Cruise O'Brien, *States of Ireland* (London: Hutchinson, 1973), Garret Fitzgerald, *Towards A New Ireland* (Dublin: Gill and Macmillan, 1972), and Owen Dudley Edwards, et al., *Celtic Nationalism* (New York: Barnes & Noble, 1968).

16. Much of this is summarized in David E. Schmitt, *The Irony of Irish Democracy* (Lexington: Lexington Books, 1973), pp. 48–53.

17. For example, see Liam de Paor, *Divided Ulster* (Harmondsworth: Penguin, 1971), pp. 38–39.

18. Francis Hachett, *Ireland: A Study in Nationalism* (New York: Huebsch, 1918), pp. 144–145.

19. This section is largely informed by the extensive research of Alex Humphreys, in his *New Dubliners* (New York: Fordham University Press, 1966), pp. 22–39.

20. Ibid., p. 26.

21. Paul Martin Sack, *The Donegal Mafia* (New Haven: Yale University Press, 1976), p. 29. See also James Bryce, *Two Centuries of Irish History* (London: Kegan Paul, 1888), pp. 273–275.

22. Strauss, op. cit., pp. 92–93.

23. Hachey, op. cit., p. 7.

24. Leon O'Broin, *Fenian Fever* (New York: New York University Press, 1971), p. 45.

25. Felecian Prill, op. cit., p. 68.

26. Hachey, op. cit., p. 31.

27. George Dangerfield, *The Damnable Question* (Boston: Little Brown, 1976), pp. 12 and 28.

28. A recent historical novel depicts the sectarianism of the 1798 uprising, in this case in Killala. See Thomas Flanagan, *The Year of the French* (New York: Holt Rinehart, Winston, 1979).

29. Hachey, op. cit., p. 141.

30. Richard Loftus, *Nationalism in Modern Anglo-Irish Poetry* (Madison: University of Wisconsin Press, 1964), p. 133.

31. Hachey, op. cit., p. 197.

32. For examples of this relationship, see J.H. Whyte, *Church and State in Modern Ireland, 1923–1970.* (Dublin: Gill and Macmillan, 1971), ch. 1, although its author might disagree with this general description of church–state relations.

33. See Carey and Neeley, op. cit.

SEVEN

Church and Nation in Socialist Poland

Michael D. Kennedy and Maurice D. Simon

NATIONALISM AND CATHOLICISM

The image of Poland in the modern world is closely associated with Roman Catholicism and nationalism. The partition experiences of the eighteenth through the twentieth centuries produced an acute awareness that the very existence of the Polish nation was in jeopardy. As a result, intense national loyalty and deep Catholic identification have been reinforcing elements in the shared political and moral values of Poles. Neither the tragic experiences of the Nazi occupation nor the imposition of an undesired post-World War II communist regime have weakened powerful national and Catholic feelings. On the contrary, the period from summer 1980 through mid-1982 witnessed an outburst of strong national and religious emotions throughout the country as the Solidarity movement mobilized and activated the population toward profound transformations of the socioeconomic and political systems. Although the full emergence of what Solidarity intellectuals have termed the "civil society" has been blocked by a tough reign of martial law, there can be little doubt that "national accord" requires the cooperation of the Catholic Church because it is the integral embodiment of contemporary Polish nationalism.

The official ideology of the postwar socialist state stands opposed to a nationalism that is associated with Polish-chauvinism (glorification of the Polish national character, preoccupation with the past, self-assertiveness versus othernations—particularly anti-Russianism). Instead, an internationalism that incorporates a favorable orientation toward other socialist states has been deemed a superior value and in doctrine is seen as eventually supplanting the traditionally negative forms of nationalism cited above. This nationalism/internationalism dichotomy is, in essence, a manifestation of the long-standing political debate in Poland over romanticist "idealism" versus positivist "realism," a controversy generated by the vulnerable geopolitical location of the country. As the writings of Adam Bromke so effectively illustrate, socialist Poland has had to wrestle continuously with the choice between the idealists' policy of unremitting efforts to maximize Polish autonomy and the realists' position of accepting limited independence as a bearable political necessity.[1] The idealists have sought to foster national consciousness by emphasizing Poland's uniqueness historically and culturally, while the realists have played down its distinctiveness.

While the socialist state has favored the realist/internationalist view in official doctrine, practical politics has dictated that national feelings be acknowledged. A compromise formulation that stresses Poland's emergence as a "new socialist nation" has been employed by the authorities in a bid to strengthen and legitimize citizens' support for the state.[2] "National consciousness," "patriotism," and "pride in the nation" have been endorsed as substitute terms for nationalism. In its political socialization programs the socialist state has attempted to portray itself as "the continuator of a 'national idea' of what is 'best' and 'progressive' in the national tradition" and has displayed "pride in national purity, Polonism, almost parochial in its stress on national distinctiveness, past and present."[3] Thus, in 1975 the Polish United Workers' Party (Communist Party) declared:

Socialism embodies a heart-felt attachment to the homeland. Patriotism is a valuable trait of our nation, and it has been manifested by immense sacrifice; patriotism is deeply ingrained in our tradition. Today it is love of the socialist homeland, the one which has changed the lot of the nation, that has ensured a new, respectable life for the people and has opened up broad prospects. We should constantly invigorate this kind of patriotism, and cultivate pride in its record, standing, and advancement.[4]

Most analysts would agree, however, that the state's campaign to gain acceptance by wrapping itself in the cloak of nationalism has been only partially successful.

The explanation for the limited success of such a campaign is rather evident. Popular conceptions hold that the socialist state is a foreign implant, the creation of a Soviet-dominated communist party. Some of the reasons for these attitudes are derived from the history of the communist party: its anti-independence internationalist program from the late nineteenth century until 1917, its opposition to the existence of the post-1918 Polish state and its subservience to Soviet goals until its dissolution by the Comintern in 1938, and the rejection of Wladyslaw Gomulka's nationally oriented communist course from 1948–1955. Nationalism within the party has been existent intermittently (it has been associated with Gomulka's position of 1944–1948 and 1956–1957, Mieczyslaw Moczar's faction of 1968–1970, and the Grunwald Patriotic Organization of 1981), but generally speaking these orientations have failed to prevail on a long-term basis.[5] Therefore, we cannot know whether a nationalist emphasis by the party would have yielded greater mass support for the organization. The party's constant praise of "proletarian internationalism" and fraternal support for the Soviet Union grate on the population, whose anti-Soviet feelings are quite obvious. For example, in a national survey that asked Poles in what country other than Poland would they most like to live, only 5.8 percent named the Soviet Union as opposed to the 55.3 percent who identified Western democracies.[6] As we shall see, nationalism in the contemporary period has functioned primarily to boost the standing of the Church and opposition groups.

Since the term nationalism conveys a constellation of the romantic idealist values that have been officially disavowed, especially anti-Russian sentiments, empirical investigations have focused on less sensitive, less politically volatile subjects. These studies of attitudes toward the nation and patriotism have been limited in number and cautious in approach. The overall impression, however, is that contemporary Poland manifests both elements of the romantic idealist national dispositions and the state sponsored "socialist nation" orientations. This mixture of attitudes is illustrated by responses in a nationwide survey of the urban population to the question, "What, primarily, does patriotism depend upon?"[7] Table 1 presents the results:

TABLE 1
Understanding of the Term "Patriotism" *

"What, primarily, does patriotism depend upon?"	*Respondents (in percentages)*
1. Fulfillment of one's daily responsibilities	43.3
2. Striving for social justice	41.9
3. Readiness to give up one's life in times of war	38.6
4. Working to raise the well-being of society	35.1
5. Speaking well of Poland and of Poles	30.5
6. Familiarity with the native culture and history	26.5
7. Always preferring Polish things over foreign things	23.9
8. Conscientious observance of all authoritative rules	18.8
9. Other (a variety of answers)	1.5
10. It's difficult to say	2.1

N = 1,907

SOURCE: Jerzy Szacki, *Polacy o sobie i innych narodych,* (Warsaw: Osrodek Badania Publicznej i Studiow Programowych, 1969), p. 16

* Percentages exceed a total of 100% because respondents could mention three items.

As can be seen, attitudes propagated by the socialist industrial state, especially responsibility, a sense of social justice, and a positive work ethic (items 1, 2, and 4) received considerable support. There is nearly as much support for the more traditional patriotic responses of self-sacrifice in times of peril, loyalty, and historical consciousness (items 3, 5, and 6).

Other studies show that the term patriotism continues to evoke a positive response from Poles. When a representative sample of Warsaw youth was asked whether they agreed that in the second half of this century the concept of patriotism had become "obsolete," 54 percent replied "decidedly no," 27 percent "rather no," 8 percent "rather yes," and only 3 percent "decidedly yes"—virtually replicating the answers given by their parents to the same question.[8] A more complex picture of nationalist tendencies emerged when parents and children were asked "Do you agree with those who state that Poles have more valued characteristics than other nationalities?" On the one hand, more parents (36 percent) displayed this type of national pride than did their children (22 percent). On the other hand, perhaps reflecting a national inferiority complex stemming from their tragic twentieth-century memories, 42 percent of the parents stated that Poles have less valued characteristics than other nationalities. Only 5 percent of their children took this position. The majority of youth (54 percent) maintained that Poles are not essentially different in terms of valued characteristics than other nationalities, as contrasted to a small minority (8 percent) of the adults.[9] In sum, adults seem to view Poland as being more nationally distinctive in either a positive or negative way. Their offspring seem to have absorbed the more internationalist or realist perspective that has been basic to the political socialization strategy of the party.

Virtually all observers of Poland agree that the population has an extremely well-developed historical consciousness. This keen awareness of a common history is illustrated by a recent survey of Polish youth, ages fifteen to sixteen. Asked to identify the national heroes of the pre-World War II period, the youth were able to provide lengthy lists with cultural and scientific figures receiving the most frequent citations: Marie Curie-Sklodowska (64.0 percent), Adam Mickiewicz (60.5 percent), Mikolaj Kopernik (53.5 percent), Fryderyk Chopin (45.5 percent), and Henryk Sienkiewicz (40.5 percent). Madame

Curie and Copernicus, of course, brought world attention to the scientific talents of the Poles, just as Chopin drew acclaim for their accomplishments in music. Mickiewicz and Sienkiewicz, nationalist writers who romanticized the Polish struggles for freedom and independence, remain massively popular figures even under socialism. Interestingly enough, the major political figure cited as a national hero was Tadeusz Kosciuszko, who led the uprising of 1794 against Poland's partition. When the listed national heroes are categorized, it becomes clear that youth are primarily interested in the cultural and scientific personalities of world renown or the figures who engaged in liberation struggles during the partitions and World War II. The revolutionaries connected with Poland's socialist history inspired only slight interest.[10] The public has also shown a strong familiarity with the military campaigns of the past, an indication of its sensitivity to geopolitics. Here, one study revealed implicit anti-Soviet sentiment by finding that the achievements of the Polish non-communist Home Army during World War II were better known and more highly valued than those of the Polish People's Army, which operated under Soviet general command.[11]

Journalistic accounts of Poland during the Solidarity period confirm that nationalism remains a strong force in political life. During the crisis of 1980 to the present, national symbols have flourished in the form of banners, buttons, and slogans. Among those figures and events most frequently encountered are "May Third" (the date of the enactment of the liberal constitution of 1791), Tadeusz Kosciuszko (independence leader of 1794), Adam Mickiewicz (the great nationalist poet of the nineteenth century), and Marshal Jozef Pilsudski (the leader of the war against Russia in 1920). All of these represent the Polish desire for expanded freedom and independence. In the pre-Solidarity period, the opposition set up the "flying university" (Association for Scientific Courses) designed to supplement and correct the historical record supplied by the regime. Following the formation of Solidarity, national emotions were stirred by calls for telling the truth about the Katyn Forest massacre of Polish military officers during World War II (an atrocity probably committed by the Soviets in 1940) and by exhibitions commemorating the political disturbances of 1956, 1968, 1970, 1976, and 1980.[12] Solidarity incorporated nationalism into its political strategy by adopting the slogan of "Let Poland be Poland" and by taking special care to close its meetings with the singing of the national anthem, which is emotionally spellbinding. While it is most certainly an exaggeration to state that the crisis of 1980–1982 is a product of Polish nationalism, the traditional idealist disposition did gain strength and played a crucial role in the unfolding events.[13]

Despite thirty-five years of socialism, the Catholic Church remains the preeminent institution in Poland in terms of commanding allegiance. Exact figures are not available, but most analysts estimate that nearly ninety percent of the thirty-six million Poles are Catholics. Religious practice in Poland is widespread. On Sundays, it is believed that nearly half of the population attends mass. Adherence to Catholic rituals—baptism, confession, communion, and church weddings—is almost universal.[14] A recent study of secondary school youths in their final year of study provides the following declarations of belief: 12.8 percent saw themselves as "deep believers," 4.37 percent as "believers," 20.9 percent as "believers, but having certain reservations," 5.0 percent as "non-believers, but linked by tradition," 7.3 percent "non-believers," 1.1 percent "decided opponents of religion," 4.5 percent "undecided," and 4.6 percent "indifferent." The frequency of church attendance was indicated as: several times a week—6.8 percent, once a week—50.4 percent, at least once or twice a month—13.1 percent, at least once or twice each quarter—5.0 percent, only on major church holidays—11.0 percent, and not attending—12.8 percent.[15] These responses would seem to confirm the typical image of Poland as a devout Catholic nation.

The reality is somewhat more complex. These same students, when asked to define the motives for their religious beliefs and given three choices, offered the following choices most frequently: "Religion helps me in difficult life situations"—50.2

percent; "I believe because I was brought up in the spirit of
religion"—46.4 percent; "Religion affords me the certainty that
in my daily life God is watching over me"—44.7 percent; "Religion permits me to improve the attributes of my character"—
40.9 percent; and "Religion provides me with a deeper sense of
my own life"—40.2 percent.[16] These responses suggest that for
some students the Church is an integral part of their family
tradition, for others it provides emotional security, and for others it is a moral and ethical guide. Additional insights are provided by responses to a question asking what decides why they
attend church services. Given three choices, the three most frequent answers were: "I go because services support me in my
daily life"—53.5 percent; "In this way I wish to emphasize my
connections with the Church as a religious community"—45.7
percent; and "I go in order to deserve salvation"—27.0 percent.[17] Again, these attitudes convey a variety of motiva-
tions—a blend of traditional, religious, and emotional considerations. Perhaps this is why the Catholic Church has become
so powerful in Poland. It meets a wide spectrum of human
needs and since it is embedded deeply in Polish history it has
been a familiar source of support.

Socialism and industrialization have brought forth processes
of secularization that have altered the role of the Church. The
Polish Catholic Church has maintained a quite conservative
position on many social matters. It is common knowledge that
a sizeable portion of Poles ignore Church positions on birth
control, sexual mores, and even abortion. The existence of a
public system of education largely independent of Church control has strengthened secularization. Urban industrial patterns
of living have shifted many daily values and practices. A brief
illustration of the secondary students' attitudes on some selected questions demonstrates this point. Asked how they evaluate the view that only a Catholic can be a good Pole, 31.5
percent of the students responded very negatively, 31.4 percent
rather negatively, 18.3 percent rather positively, and only 8.7
percent very positively. In a similar vein, asked whether the
Church should decide what is moral and immoral in society,

15.5 percent were strongly negative, 26.3 percent rather negative, 30.1 percent rather positive, and 15.9 percent very positive. The statement that only a religious man can live and behave honestly was soundly rejected, 38.8 percent replying very negatively, 32.0 percent rather negatively, 13.6 percent rather positively, and 9.1 percent very positively. The viewpoint that the education of youth should be based on a religious world outlook divided the students nearly in half, with 15.2 percent expressing strong agreement, 29.6 percent moderate agreement, 23.6 percent moderate disagreement, and 15.2 percent strong disagreement.[18] These attitudes suggest that a substantial proportion of Polish youth are not submissive to the Church's moral teachings, especially when it comes to guidelines for social behavior.

Even when the secularization of beliefs is noted, it is clear that the grip of the Church over the Polish population remains quite firm. The explanation for this is found in the role of the Church as the guardian of national values. As one observer has noted, "In the battle between Catholicism and Communism for the hearts of the Polish people, only the former has been able to tap into and express Polish nationalism, while the latter's inability to do so accounts in part for its inability to rule." He quotes a young student's position: "For us, the Church signifies patriotism, tradition, continuity, and stability."[19] From 1980–1982, the Solidarity movement drew on this reality by integrating strong national sentiments and religious symbolism. During the Gdansk strike, photographs of Pope John Paul II were displayed everywhere. Walesa decorated his lapel with a badge with the picture of the Black Madonna of Czestochowa. Crucifixes were prominent in the conference hall during negotiations. Priests conducted mass in the occupied shipyard. This set the pattern for the whole 1980–1982 period, as Solidarity sought the approval and protection of the Church by including it in its own deliberations and activities and by supporting policies that would widen the freedom of the Church. While denying its affiliation with the Church, Solidarity has stated, "It is true that among the union symbols those of the Catholic religion are of great consequence. This reflects the respect which society, most of the people being Catholic, has for the moral authority of the Church."[20]

Solidarity as an organization and the Catholic Church as an institution were mutual beneficiaries of this relationship. This is best illustrated by a now famous public opinion poll conducted in May of 1981. In this nationally representative survey, respondents were asked to rank organizations and institutions in terms of the degree of trust and confidence they had in them. Among the fifteen listed organizations, the Catholic Church ranked first with 94 percent of the respondents declaring confidence in it. Solidarity was a close second with a 90 percent confidence rating. Interestingly enough, the military was third with an 89 percent rating, perhaps reflecting national pride prior to the imposition of martial law. Most significantly, the Communist Party ranked fifteenth, or dead last, with a 32 percent rating.[21] In the sections that follow, we will analyze how the Church and national feelings have become so interrelated and how this relationship played a role in the unfolding crisis of 1975–1982.

HISTORICAL OVERVIEW: 966–1975

The immensely important institutional role of the Catholic Church in Poland can best be explained by a brief historical review. The history of the Polish state itself coincides with the acceptance by Mieszko I and his court of Christianity in 966. In the centuries that followed, Poland came to be a regional power in East Central Europe, dominating regions that were not ethnically Polish, and even attempting to "Catholicize" Orthodox believers in the East in the sixteenth and seventeenth centuries.[22] Poland failed, however, to develop a state sufficiently strong to guarantee its continued existence and to overcome threats from its neighbors.[23] In 1795, Poland was partitioned between Prussia, Russia, and Austria and ceased to exist as a state.

As a state, Poland did not regain its existence until 1918, but when it did emerge it did so quite conscious of its national identity. Catholicism played a complex but significant role in preserving Polish nationalism and preventing the full assimilation of the nation into its neighbors' societies. Of particular importance was the Church's role in maintaining the Polish language. As the only public national institution where Polish could be freely spoken during the partitions, the Church became permanently identified with the protection of the Polish language and culture.[24] Since two of Poland's occupiers, Protestant Prussia and Orthodox Russia, were of different faiths, the Polish gentry and intelligentsia came increasingly to equate "Polishness" with Catholicism.[25] These dispositions were restricted mainly to the upper classes, for prior to the 1870s there was a deep gulf between the nobles and the peasantry. In fact, the partitioning powers tried to form alliances with the peasantry against the Polish nationalistic nobility, which has been cited as one key reason for the failure of the 1846–1848 independence struggles.[26]

From this point forward, the role played by Catholicism in fomenting nationalism grew progressively important. Initially, the Vatican and upper levels of the Church hierarchy in Poland failed to give support to the successive Polish uprisings and to Poles' national aspirations.[27] Catholicism was, however, more than an institutional factor in Polish history. The common Catholicism of many ethnic Poles ultimately proved to be a decisive factor in developing a nationalism that cut across social classes.

The struggles against the Protestant Prussians and the Orthodox Russians helped to end the peasants' isolation from the nationalism of the nobles and the intellectuals. In fact, it was religious and cultural suppression that drew workers and peasants to Polish nationalism.[28] In Bismarck's Kulturkampf of the 1870s, the German threat to the peasants' language and religion drew them into the Polish nationalist cause.[29] Essentially, Catholicism played a major role in developing Polish nationalism by serving as principal barrier to extranational cultural and religious infringements on the Polish identity. Otherwise, within

the Polish community during the nineteenth century, the nationalist impulses "came from sources that stood aloof from or
opposed orthodox Catholicism."[30]

With the establishment of the Second Republic in 1918, most
of the doubts about the patriotism of the Church were eliminated.[31] Polish priests were very active in liberation struggles
and Catholicism came to have a special place in the newly independent Poland.[32] Although the Constitution of 1921 granted
religious tolerance, it mentioned the Roman Catholic Church
as having "a preeminent position in the state among legally
equal religions."[33] In fact, the Holy Virgin of Czestochowa, a
Catholic shrine and object of pilgrimage for Polish Catholics,
was considered the Queen of Poland during the Second Republic.[34]

World War II and its outcome only served to strengthen the
position of the Church in Polish society. Catholic priests were
accorded the same gruesome treatment as the rest of Polish
society under the occupation. About twenty percent of all Polish clergy were executed.[35] Also, the Catholic hierarchy was
quite involved in the Polish resistance movement. Its special
and heroic role during the occupation virtually guaranteed the
importance of the Catholic Church in postwar Poland. Another
factor that assured an important role for the Church was the
new religious demographic composition. By shifting the boundaries westward, Poland lost a large non-ethnically Polish population in the east. Moreover, most Protestant Germans left
Poland, and with the genocidal extermination of about three
million Polish Jews by the Nazis, Poland wound up being almost religiously homogeneous, a condition that Poland never
previously experienced. In 1791, before the partitions, it was
only 54 percent Roman Catholic; in the Second Republic it was
65 percent Catholic (1931); but in 1946 it was 96.6 percent
Catholic.[36]

The Catholic Church's position in postwar Poland is indeed
important, and unusual for a country with a Soviet-type communist government. This importance can best be explained by

its role as the only genuine national alternative to the state during this period. The lack of legitimacy of the communist party in Polish society is a crucial factor contributing to the Church's status. As we pointed out earlier, the communist party had traditionally been regarded as being an antinationalist force. Historically, the communists failed to support Polish independence struggles: until 1918 they were opposed to Polish independence; subsequently, they supported the Russians in the Polish–Soviet war of 1920; and they had ties with the Soviet-dominated Third International, the Comintern. Only during World War II did the communists emerge as a nationalist force, operating in the underground resistance movement with future First Secretary Wladyslaw Gomulka as one of their leaders. But that nationalist faction of the communist party was purged from the party in 1948 during the period of Polish Stalinism. With this purge of the more independent communist faction, the party's close links with the Soviet Union were assured.[37]

At this point, Poland embarked on the road to socialism, Soviet style. Part of that campaign for socialist transformation was the attempt to undermine the ideological and institutional authority of the Catholic Church. Through 1956, the communist party endeavored to destroy the Church as an independent institution. Slander, the establishment of alternative "patriotic" Catholic groups, elimination of Church relief agencies, and individual cases of political and legal repression were all employed by the regime against the Church.[38] The Primate, Cardinal Stefan Wyszynski, was himself arrested in 1953. All of this served to bolster mass support for the Church, given the prevailing anti-Stalinist sentiments. The Church managed to survive, and after the installation of the more nationally conscious Gomulka as party chief in October 1956, Wyszynski was released and a new era of Church-state relations began.

During Gomulka's tenure as party leader, Church-state relations were uneven. The Church was definitely not repressed as it had been in the previous era, but it was also not entirely free. The state continually tried to restrict the Church's influence by circumscribing its activities in religious education and social affairs. In many cases, however, the Church successfully resisted these government efforts.[39]

Another turning point in Church-state relations began in 1968 and 1970 when students' and workers' riots, respectively, broke out, resulting in severe police brutality, death, and political repression. The Church was outspoken on both of these occasions. These Church reactions were harbingers of the role the Church was to play from 1975 on: that of the defender of human rights in the nation. Once again, the Church became the repository of Polish national values.

CHURCH AND NATION IN CRISIS: 1975–1982

Events during the 1975–1982 period placed the Church in a pivotal political position where its status as a repository of national values became even more obvious. Since 1975, Poland has experienced severe political, economic, and social instability: from the controversy over constitutional revisions to the violence of workers' riots in 1976; from the elation over the election of a Polish pope and the beginnings of the "self-organization" of society to the trauma of martial law.[40] In the brief account of the most recent period of Polish history that is to follow, two major themes on religion and nation in Poland will be emphasized: (1) the institutional significance of the Catholic Church in this period of instability; and (2) the interaction of religious and national sentiments in the self-organization of Polish society.

At the Seventh Party Congress of the PUWP in December 1975, amendments to the 1952 Polish constitution were introduced. Among the proposed changes, the two most objectionable to many sectors of Polish society were references to the "unshakeable and fraternal bonds with the Soviet Union" and "the leading role of the Polish United Workers' Party."[41] Both amendments were perceived as breaches of national sovereignty and as violations of the Helsinki Human Rights Agreement to which Poland had subscribed. Various protest letters

were sent to the Sejm, the Polish parliament, but more significantly than that the Catholic Church also entered the fray. Primate Stefan Wyszynski and Cardinal Karol Wojtyla (the future
Pope John Paul II) denounced the amendments in widely known
sermons. The significance of these actions was twofold: (1) The
Church moved from its normal stance of almost exclusively defending church interests to the broader position of defending
human rights; and (2) it signalled the beginning of cooperation
between the Church and various opposition forces.[42] This constitutional controversy also produced a split in the principal
Catholic parliamentary opposition group "Znak." This split was
not significant, however, as Znak's importance as an opposition group came to be supplanted by various dissident groups
later in the 1970s.[43]

Similar to the events of December 1970, an announcement
of increases in basic food prices on June 24, 1976 provoked
workers to strike and to take to the streets. For two days,
workers launched violent protests, including setting fire to the
party headquarters in Radom. On the night of June 25, the
price increases were rescinded by the authorities. Despite the
withdrawal of the price hike, repressive measures were introduced against those workers who were involved in the strikes,
including dismissals, arrests, and internments. This repression
generated protests from the working class and, most importantly, marked the beginning of an alliance between dissident
intellectuals and workers. One of the most important dissident
groups to emerge at this time was the Committee for the Defense of Workers (KOR), which publicized and protested the
repression, and sought financial and legal assistance for those
workers and their families who were victimized.

The response of the Church to the riots and subsequent
repression was a sign of the future relationship that was to be
forged between the Church and the opposition. Initially, the
Church was quiet, but after the suspicious death of a dissident
student in May 1977, both Wyszynski and Wojtyla voiced public criticisms of government repression.[44] Nevertheless, their
criticism was typically moderated by calls to the population for

caution and restraint. Gradually, the nature of Church criticism and action came to take on a more supportive role for the opposition. Although the Church would not explicitly ally itself within any specific movement, official statements by the Polish Episcopate commended the actual activities undertaken by the various opposition groups without naming names. In the instance of KOR, the Church acknowledged its support for KOR's activities by doing as KOR suggested: taking up a collection for victimized workers and their families.[45]

During this period, the Church continued to press for its own specific demands: a relaxation of restrictions for permits to construct churches, greater opportunities for pastoral work, the relaxation of censorship, and the observance of full human and civil rights by the state. Although there may have been differences between the Church and the growing secular opposition, the Church's attempts at defending its own interests provided indirect support for the broad opposition. In fact, both sides recognized the coincidence of interests between the Church and opposition. Priests became members of both KOR and the Movement for the Defense of Human and Civil Rights (ROPCiO).[46] KOR democratic socialists reconsidered the role played by the Catholic Church in Polish society, emphasizing the importance of Catholic support in building the democratic opposition movement.[47]

Although the Church was clearly supportive of the opposition forces, even in the early stages of the self-organization of society its role as a mediator between the authorities and opposition was evident in an embryonic form. The state, recognizing the influential and potentially moderating role the Church could play in the volatile circumstance of the late 1970s, often appealed to the Church for cooperation. Mieczyslaw Rakowski, the editor of the liberal party periodical *Polityka,* called on the Church to help the authorities maintain social peace and order, to help overcome the spiritual malaise affecting all parts of society, and to avoid any conflicts or tensions.[48] There was an evolution in Church-state relations in a relatively short pe-

riod from a relationship of dialogue to an attempt at cooperation.[49]

The election of Karol Wojtyla, Archbishop of Krakow, to
the Papacy of the Roman Catholic Church in October of 1978
made that cooperation all the more important. The election of
a Polish pope, the first non-Italian pope in 455 years, enhanced
Polish national pride and self-esteem, considerably elevating the
prestige of the Church and Catholicism in Poland itself. This
increase in prestige was evidenced by the increases in attendance at churches in Poland and the closer attention given to
Church dignitaries by foreign officials.[50]

This surge in national pride over the election of a Polish pope
did not go unnoticed by the communist party. Seeking to benefit from these national sentiments, the Party sponsored the six-
tieth anniversary celebration of Polish independence. However, it extended the commemoration through the week of
November 6 to 11, 1979 in order to combine it with the hon-
oring of the Russian October Revolution. This seemingly triv-
ial matter—the date for recognizing Polish independence—
spawned another controversy that was itself an expression of
strong Polish national feelings and pitted society against the
communist party. November 11 had been the traditional date
for celebrating Polish independence: the diminution of its importance by the party provoked widespread protest from both
dissident groups and the Catholic Church. The Church showed
its reverence for patriotic obligations and its opposition to the
party in a pastoral letter from Cardinal Wyszynski in which he
called for the recognition of November 11 and also stated emphatically that:

People who are in power in our fatherland bear the responsibility for Poland's
freedom and dignity. Conditions of social life must be created in which the
people can fully feel that they are the masters of their own land, which was
given to us, centuries ago, by the father of all peoples.[51]

This incident was yet another example of the implicit support
given by the Church to the opposition, but it was a support

that was couched in language that assured the Church's organizational and conceptual separation from the dissident movement. It also served to show how strong national feelings were often expressed in terms of opposition to the communist party and the state. The opposition movements themselves were imbued with a strong national consciousness.

The strength of the democratic opposition was considerably augmented by the visit of Pope John Paul II to Poland. After a series of negotiations between Polish Church officials and state authorities, the pope visited his homeland from June 2 to 10, 1979. The significance of this visit for later events has been consistently noted by all sectors of Polish society—Catholics, government officials, and opposition groups.[52] Beyond providing a moral impetus, that the entire Papal visit was organized without the substantial help of official and state agencies gave Polish society a deepened confidence in its own organizational capabilities and a recognition of the potential for establishing extensive nonofficial networks of communication.[53]

Between the visit of the pope in June of 1979 and the creation of Solidarity in August of 1980, there was no obvious improvement in Church-state relations. The Church continued to grow stronger while the party and the government continued to grow weaker. The Church tried to maintain its separateness from the opposition movement although its implicit support became more and more obvious. Church services were used by the dissidents to commemorate the workers slain in December of 1970;[54] Church facilities were used by hunger strikers in May 1980, as had been done in May 1977 and October 1979; and the Church made public statements that called for the respect of human rights and an end to the reprisals against individuals with nonconformist political views.[55]

On July 1, 1980 the government announced meat price hikes of as much as one hundred percent. Almost immediately and for a month thereafter strikes broke out at factories throughout the country, with KOR (now renamed KSS–KOR or the Social Self-Defense Committee–KOR) acting as a communications center for strike information. On August 14, events in Gdansk began to take center stage, with sixteen thousand workers at the Lenin shipyards demanding: (1) a memorial to the workers who died in the 1970 protests; (2) the rehiring of three recently fired workers; (3) a raise in wages; and (4) the right to an independent union. The workers in Gdansk maintained their position until after the negotiations of August 23–31, which provided for the right of establishing an independent trade union, later called Solidarity.

During this period, the adoption of a cautious yet mediating role by the Catholic Church began to crystallize. Until mid-August, the Church seemed to have deliberately avoided commenting on the strikes.[56] The first remarks on the situation were made on Assumption Day, August 15, when in a sermon at the Jasna Gora shrine in Czestochowa Cardinal Wyszynski said that "bread is the property of the whole nation" and that Poles were asking for it in a "very tactful way, a way full of dignity."[57] This rather oblique statement of support for the striking workers was followed by more moderate, but direct references.

The next major statement by the Church was in another sermon by Wyszynski on August 27. The speech itself appealed to both sides in the dispute by calling for mutual restraint and responsible behavior. Portions of the sermon criticizing the atheistic government were deleted in the edited version that was broadcast over Polish television, so that it appeared as if Wyszynski was actually calling on the workers to end the strike without any sharp criticism of the government. The Church, obviously disturbed, amplified its position and attempted to link itself to national feelings by asserting that a precondition for the return of social peace and order was a recognition on the part of the authorities of the "inalienable rights of the nation."[58]

In the agreement finally reached on August 31, the Church played a considerable role. Under Wyszynski's direction, his aide Romuald Kukolowicz and two Catholic lawyers flew to Gdansk, where they were able to assist in the breaking of the negotiations deadlock.[59] Significantly, these negotiations in-

cluded the workers' demand for the provision of television and
radio air time for Catholic Church services. It should be added
that various important Catholic lay figures like Tadeusz Ma-
zowiecki, the editor of the liberal Catholic periodical *Wiez,*
served as advisors to Solidarity both during and after the strike
period.

As we noted earlier, the protesting workers and Solidarity
came to embody a profound sense of Catholicism. This was
quite evident in Gdansk where on August 17, 1980 the Gdansk
bishop Kaczmarek sent medals of the pope to members of the
strike committee. On that same Sunday, a local priest celebrated a mass near one of the shipyard gates in front of five
thousand workers inside the gate and another two thousand
people outside. A large wooden cross commemorating the martyred workers of 1970 stood nearby, covered with flowers.[60]
The mass on the following Sunday drew almost twenty thousand people.[61]

Just as the Catholic Church had always been prominent in
demonstrating its ties to Polish history, Solidarity spontaneously displayed its Catholic religiosity and consequently
deepened its national identification. The commemorations held
by the union for the martyrs of previous protests were characteristically marked by a great deal of religious symbolism. For
example, in ceremonies held on December 16 and 17, 1980, a
monument was dedicated to those workers killed by government troops in that city exactly ten years before. The monument was an intentional blend of Catholic and national symbols, composed of three crosses marking faith and on them three
anchors evoking Polish national feelings. Although no sermons
were delivered there, Church dignitaries were present and in
the workers' speeches there were frequent religious references;
letters from the pope were read to the crowd.[62] At the Solidarity National Congress in the fall of 1981, the new primate Jozef
Glemp celebrated mass before the beginning of the congress.
The Catholic aura of the movement was evidenced by a large
cross which hung next to the national emblem—the Polish ea-

gle—just above the podium. Frequent references were also made to church and religion in the congress speeches.[63]

Some analysts of the 1980–1982 period have argued that this religious symbolism of the movement became the language of social liberation in that it represented "the continuity of the Polish cultural heritage, the ancient struggle for national independence, and the self identity of the individual in a world of social relations dominated by the state."[64] Thus, in addition to the protective role offered by the powerful, institutionalized Catholic Church, the very Catholicism of the workers provided a means of identification with each other, an allegiance to the Polish nation, and a clear opposition to the officially atheistic communist party.

At all times, however, both Solidarity and the Church sought to maintain their separate and distinct identities. Lech Walesa, the Solidarity leader, stated in an interview that there was a conceptual and institutional separateness between the union and the church. He consistently maintained that there were both believers and non-believers in the union and that it would remain pluralistic in its world views. Nevertheless, he stressed that all union members recognized that the Church provided a "moral foundation" essential for the resolution of the ongoing crisis.[65] The Church also emphasized its separateness and in fact acquired a new role, embryonic from 1976 on, but born only after the establishment of Solidarity: the role of mediator between the communist authorities and the opposition.

Before the emergence of a third force in Polish society, the Church, by defending its own interests and identity, had been the only major effective opposition to the government. Now it sought to have a calming influence on the more radical sectors of the opposition. The emergence of a very popular and legally institutionalized movement in the form of Solidarity posed certain risks: destabilization and disruption might erase the mutual gains achieved by both the Church and the union during the crisis. The Church astutely maintained its separateness from the Solidarity union while voicing sympathy with its goals and gratitude for Solidarity's influence in obtaining concessions from the state on religious matters. Archbishop Glemp carefully expressed these themes when he said:

> The Church is supporting Solidarity not as an ally but as a defender of human rights in the spirit of the Gospel. . . . We do not want to dominate Solidarity, but we are ready to defend it if human rights are violated. . . . The Church will counsel moderation and restraint in any conflict situation.[66]

This intermediary role of the Church became evident in several settings: in Church-state meetings, Church-opposition meetings, and in Church presence at negotiations between the authorities and the opposition. In the Church-state relationship, the Joint Committee of the Episcopate and Government (inactive since 1977) met on September 24, 1981, and after ten sessions of negotiations with the government they achieved several of their long-standing goals, most of these associated with strictly Church interests.[67]

In its relationship with Solidarity, the Church played a moderating role as the party had hoped. Bishops continually emphasized the need for social peace and internal stability, with the pope even issuing pleas to Solidarity through Wyszynski that it should exercise "great patience and understanding."[68] On December 12, 1980 the Bishop's Conference warned against activities that could endanger Polish sovereignty. When the Director of the Press Office of the Polish Episcopate, Father Alojzy Orszulik, subsequently denounced the fiery rhetoric of Jacek Kuron, a prominent KOR advisor to Solidarity, that action created such a controversy within the union movement and in the entire Catholic community that it necessitated a clarification by Wyszynski. Wyszynski, recognizing that the Church had been a major beneficiary of Solidarity's boldness, asserted that there was no Church opposition to the dissidents, but that moderation was the wisest course.[69] He was reputedly anxious about possible Soviet intervention and is quoted as advising a delegation of Polish workers, "Beware of getting too near the wounded bear."[70] The pope, in the audience he granted for Walesa at the Vatican in January of 1981, supported Wyszynski's moderating yet supportive role of Solidarity.[71]

On January 25, a general strike began in Bielsko-Biala in which Lech Walesa perceived that a deadlock had been reached and thus requested the Church's direct involvement in the negotiations as a mediator. Walesa believed that the Church's presence would serve as a guarantee of the fulfillment of both side's obligations.[72]

With the Church's intervention, a solution was reached after ten days of the general strike. Another important instance in which the Church played a mediating role occurred during the negotiations for the establishment of Rural Solidarity. The Church had a considerable stake in this matter, given the traditional strength and close involvement of the Church in the countryside. In sermons, official communiqués, and private talks with government leaders, Wyszynski constantly emphasized the importance of a union for private farmers. Rural Solidarity was finally registered on May 12.

The Church's influence over social affairs appeared to decline after this event. Both the assassination attempt on Pope John Paul II on May 13 and the death of Cardinal Wyszynski on May 28, 1981 seemed to lessen the Church's calming influence over society. Even the pope's appeal for thirty days of mourning and national mediation after Wyszynski's death seemed to have had no perceptible effect on the country's stability.[73] The diminished influence of the Church as an institutional force seemed evident at the Solidarity National Congress in September–October 1981, when despite the symbolic trappings of religion the extremely Catholic and moderate Walesa (who had called Wyszynski "my number one adviser" and saw him as "the protector of national traditions")[74] barely managed to get reelected to his leadership post. During 1981 splits in Solidarity were attributed to religious as well as political differences, with reports circulating that radically oriented leaders felt Walesa had bowed to the Church's call for moderation and that the organization might become identified as "a Christian-Democratic union."[75]

On September 15, the Vatican issued John Paul II's third papal encyclical, "On Human Work." The Polish Bishops'

Conference of September 1981 pointed to the lessons to be taken from the document. It asserted that labor unions are indispensible to modern industrial society, but contrary to the Marxist orientation, their struggle should be one for general social justice and not a class struggle. The obvious support offered for Solidarity was tempered with the admonition that trade unions should take into account the general economic situation of the country in which they are struggling and also avoid assuming an expressly political role.[76]

The last major attempt by the Church to mediate between Solidarity and the state was at the highly touted political summit in Warsaw on November 4, 1981. In a three-way meeting between Wyszynski's successor, Primate Jozef Glemp, Prime Minister and Party First Secretary Wojciech Jaruzelski, and Walesa, views were exchanged on how to overcome the crisis. Discussion of the construction of a Front of National Accord took place; this was to serve as a permanent forum for dialogue between the major institutions of Polish society. This "social corporatism" approach—"in the sense of two or three independent organizations of society, Church and Solidarity (perhaps also Rural Solidarity), negotiating with the ruling party in the name of society as a whole within the context of a partially independent public sphere"—represented a possible way out of the political impasse that had been reached.[77]

Yet Solidarity distrusted the arrangement, suspecting that the party was seeking to coopt them into a front in which they did not share effective power, but which would give some credibility to the regime.[78] Thereafter, while the state and Solidarity continued to hold bilateral negotiations, a polarization process gained momentum: Solidarity took increasingly radical stands, while the party became unyielding and reactionary.

Social tensions intensified as both workers' and students' strikes occurred throughout the country. When the government utilized force to break up a strike by cadets of the firefighting training school in Warsaw on December 2, Solidarity called for a day of national protest on December 17. Meanwhile, the party asked the parliament for an "emergency powers act" in the event

of the threatened general strike. All of this led to the now famous tape-recorded conversations of a December 6 Solidarity
meeting in Radom in which Walesa spoke of an "inevitable
confrontation."[79]

In the interest of national peace, Archbishop Glemp made a
last attempt to defuse the tension on December 9, when he sent
letters to the parliament, Jaruzelski, Walesa, and the Independent Student Union. Although each of the letters was tailored
to each addressee, they were all of the same general theme,
calling for reduction of the potential for conflict and encourag-
ing the resumption of negotiations. The gravity of the situation
and the responsibility that the Church felt is evidenced by the
fact that this was the first time the Church had sent formal
letters to the government that were also made public. Unfortunately, this mediating effort was not enough. On December
12, Solidarity's national leadership voted to hold a national ref-
erendum in February to tap the nation's confidence in Jaruzelski: whether it favored establishing a temporary government
and holding democratic elections, whether it supported providing military guarantees to the Soviet Union in Poland, and
whether the communist party should be the institution acting
for society in implementing such guarantees.[80] On December
13, martial law was proclaimed.

THE CHURCH, MARTIAL LAW, AND THE NATION'S FUTURE

The military crackdown was effectively initiated, but constituted a profound shock to the nation. The pronunciation of a
multitude of regulations and decrees, including the suspensions
of basic civil rights and the prohibition of public gatherings
except, significantly, church gatherings, was meant to crush
Solidarity. In his speeches, General Jaruzelski appealed to national feelings of patriotism: "Poland is one. By common efforts
we must lift it out of misfortune. No one will help us out in
this. Let us extinguish in our home the hotbeds of trouble, strife
and hatred."[81]

When Jaruzelski spoke to the nation, his intention was to appear as a Polish nationalist and not as a communist. This emphasis on national values was no accident; if Jaruzelski was to obtain any popular legitimacy for the coup, he would have to appear as if he was saving the nation from civil war and external intervention. The attempt to present himself as a national savior recalled Jozef Pilsudski's military coup of 1926. Perhaps Jaruzelski believed that an increasingly exhausted and economically strained Polish population would connect him with Pilsudski, who during the Solidarity period had enjoyed somewhat of a national revival. The martial law regime even called itself the Military Council for National Salvation, but in order to achieve societal accord, at least the passive support of the Church would be necessary. The Jaruzelski leadership was not the only force looking for Church support. As in past times of national peril, the nation looked to the Church for solace and hope.

The first priority of the Church was to avoid bloodshed. In an early statement stressing national values, Archbishop Glemp emphasized that it was urgent "that peace be preserved and that passion and anger be reduced."[82] During a meeting over Christmas week, Glemp instructed parish priests to avoid political activity and public pronouncements on martial law. Some dissension within the Church's hierarchy was apparent, however. For example, on January 21, 1982, two Episcopate letters were issued. One, from Glemp, emphasized peace and freedom so as to avoid divisions in Polish society; the other letter was different in tone and considerably "tougher."[83]

The Church recognized immediately that its pre-crisis role as mediator between society and the state had become even more critical. Thus, it was careful not to cut off lines of communication with the authorities. General Jaruzelski and Archbishop Glemp met on January 9 and have subsequently communicated with each other in letters. The authorities recognized this potentially mediating role to be worthwhile and offered good-will gestures. Priests were allowed to minister to those interned under martial law measures, on Christmas Eve the curfew was extended, and regular Sunday broadcasts of masses were resumed on January 17. Glemp in that first radio broadcast offered the Church as a "bridge between both sides of a divided nation."[84]

At no point, however, has the Church signalled approval of martial law itself. Very shortly after its implementation, the Church declared, "The decision of the authorites to introduce martial law constitutes a blow applied to the hopes and expectations of society that one could solve long-term problems by means of a national understanding."[85] The Church was firm in advocating the freeing of prisoners, the revival of the labor union and its legitimate activities, and the restoration of an authentic national unity. When the state instituted a procedure requiring loyalty oaths to be signed by many citizens in order to keep their jobs, Glemp strongly criticized the action and noted that statements attained under such duress cannot be considered valid—a point subsequently reaffirmed more strongly by Pope John Paul II.[86] During the first six months of 1982, the Church's support for these stands has not wavered and has apparently even strengthened.

While carefully maintaining its position as potential arbiter of Poland's political impasse, the Church has been extremely visible in carrying out social and humanitarian functions. Church groups are carrying out measures to sustain the well-being of the internees and their families. The Church is also involved in a multitude of activities that assist those who are suffering from the economic hardships imposed by the current crisis. However, for some lay priests, the Church should do more. Most churches have been decorated in ways that stress the "martyrdom" of the nation. A small number of politically outspoken priests have even been arrested.[87] According to unsubstantiated accounts, some churches have served as meeting places and points of distribution of literature for Solidarity supporters. Yet the general impression remains that the Church as a whole is clinging to a course of moderation designed to maintain social peace, but to also promote the cessation of martial law.

The relative calm of January through April was broken by mass protests in May and June of 1982 which as of this writing, may signify a turning point for the martial law regime. On May 1, the traditional communist labor day holiday, there were two Warsaw parades, one supported by the party and the second developing spontaneously at the close of a Catholic mass. The thirty thousand people who participated in the second demonstration brandished leaflets calling for an end to martial law, a release of the internees, a one hundred percent raise in wages, and an end to unemployment. With a sense of the Polish nation versus the state, the national anthem was sung at this alternative demonstration, along with religious hymns. Chants of "Free the Nation" and "Long Live the Primate" were also offered. The nationalism of these protests was strongly visible in the May 3 demonstration. May 3 is the anniversary of the Polish constitution of 1791 and is a traditional occasion for the opposition to celebrate Polish nationhood and democratic aspirations. It was an event unrecognized by the communist party until last year, when it participated in a wreath-laying ceremony. On this May 3, 1982, ten thousand assembled in the old town of Warsaw, chanting for Solidarity. This demonstration ended in violence, however, with confrontations between the authorities and the crowd. The Church subsequently denounced the violence, arguing that such disruptions could only delay social accord. In a May 5 communiqué, it called for talks in an atmosphere of peace, talks that must, they stressed, include Solidarity.[88] At a mass in Bialystock on May 23, Archbishop Glemp felt moved to urge the congregation to remain peaceful despite the suffering of Poland. He emphasized, however, that the nation was in a period of "pain, conflict, failure, and crisis" because the prisons contained "those who had such noble intentions and their noble intentions were rejected."[89]

This is the context that perhaps explains the intense discussions between the Church and the party regarding a mid-1982 visit by Pope John Paul II. The occasion for the visit was supposed to be the six hundredth anniversary celebrations of the Black Madonna of Czestochowa, a cherished religious symbol in Poland. Rumors were circulating that prior to the visit most internees would be released and martial law be lifted. Both the Church and the authorities were anxious over the more regular outbursts of violence. The Church continues to apply moral pressure on the party, while cautioning the population that realism dictates that bloodshed must be avoided. The military regime continues to hope that the Church will cooperate with it in restoring social order. Despite these mutual concerns, as we write the outlook appears bleak. New instances of violence suggest that continued turmoil lies ahead.[90]

Our analysis has shown that the fate of the Polish nation is intimately tied to Catholicism. Religion has been both a spiritual and cultural force maintaining national identity in a country historically vulnerable to external domination. As a consequence of the lack of legitimacy of the various authorities during most of Poland's modern history—from the partitioning powers to the Nazi occupation forces to the postwar communist regime—the Church has become in popular consciousness the most credible and respected national institution. Its stature under the present political circumstances may be at an historical apex. At the very least, society, the military authorities, and Solidarity look to the Church for support and mediation.

The interaction between the Church, Solidarity, and the authorities has not been based, however, on their respective ideological or spiritual perspectives. The socialist state has with great difficulty come to accept the permanent presence of the Church as a national force in Poland—one that challenges their materialist ideology, but whose lack of overt opposition is essential to the party's (and now the military's) continued political hegemony. Since August of 1980, the authorites have even come to depend upon the Church for assuring social harmony. The Church, too, has learned over the years that its own autonomy and fulfillment of religious functions are best assured through practical accommodations with the ruling authorities— accommodations that do not compromise its spritual mission. Confrontation over the legitimacy of the communist regime in Poland has given way to a tolerance of existing political realities. The relationship between the Solidarity movement and the Church was not based on identical goals. Solidarity, by forging a tacit alliance with the Church, became more than a trade union; it developed into an authentic national movement. The Church, while not a radically democratic and pluralistic organization like Solidarity,[91] signified its comprehension of concerns for political freedom and social rights to a Polish nation ever more demanding in these areas. Certainly the Church secured gains in its own domain by supporting the broader aspirations of Solidarity.

The political impasse in which Poland finds itself presents imminent dangers to its national existence. For many, martial law means that Poland has once again become the martyred "Christ of nations." As the historical protector of Polish nationhood, the Catholic Church remains a key institution for assuring its continued survival.

NOTES

1. Adam Bromke, "Poland's Idealism and Realism in Retrospect," in Adam Bromke, ed., *Poland: The Last Decade* (Oakeville, Ontario: Mosaic Press, 1981), pp. 1–23. Also see Adam Bromke, *Poland's Politics: Idealism vs. Realism* (Cambridge: Harvard University Press, 1963).

2. Jerzy J. Wiatr, *Polska-nowy narod* (Warsaw: Wiedza Powszechna, 1971). This short study presents postwar Poland as a new socialist nation.

3. Joseph R. Fiszman, "Poland: The Pursuit of Legitimacy," in Ivan Volgyes, ed. *Political Socialization in Eastern Europe: A Comparative Framework* (New York: Praeger Publishers, 1975), pp. 137–138.

4. "For a Further Dynamic Development of Socialist Construction and for a Higher Quality in the Work and Living Conditions of the Nation," Report of the First Secretary of the Central Committee of the PZPR, Comrade Edward Gierek, to the Seventh Congress, in *For a Further Dynamic Development of Socialist Construction* (Warsaw: Interpress Publishers, 1976), p. 174.

5. For discussions of internal party developments, see Jan B. de Weydenthal, *The Communists of Poland: An Historical Outline* (Stanford: Hoover Institution Press, 1978). Also see M.K. Dziewanowski, *The Communist Party of Poland* (Cambridge: Harvard University Press, 1976).

6. Jerzy Szacki, *Polacy o sobie i innych narodach* (Warsaw: Osrodek Opinii Publicznej i Studiow Programowych, 1969), Table 39, p. 43. The survey was conducted in 1966 and included 1,907 respondents—a representative sample of the urban population.

7. See also the discussion in Jerzy Wiatr, *Polska-nowy narod*, pp. 114–126.

8. Stefan Nowak *et al.*, *Ciaglosc i zmiana tradycju kulturowej* (Warsaw: Zaklad Metodologii Badam Socjologicznych Institutu Socjologii Uniwersytetu Warszawskiego, mimeo, July 1976), Table 15–1, p. 375.

9. Ibid., Table 15–62, p. 377.

10. Jan Jerschina, *Narod w swiadomosci mlodziezy* (Krakow: The Jagiellonian University Press, 1978), pp. 142–153. The sample consisted of one thousand students completing the eighth grade in elementary schools. The methodology is discussed in pp. 57–61; it is not a representative sample, however.

11. J. Gesek, S. Szostkiewicz, and J. Wiatr, "Z badan opinii spoleczenstwa o wojsku," *Studia socjologiczno-polityczne*, no. 13 (1962), cited by George Kolankiewicz and Ray Taras, "Poland: Socialism for Everyman?" in Archie Brown and Jack Gray, eds., *Political Culture and Political Change in Communist States* (New York: Holmes and Meier, 1979).

12. See for further discussion Robert Darnton, "Poland Rewrites History," *The New York Review of Books*, Vol. XXVIII, No. 12 (July 16, 1981), pp. 6–10.

13. For an interesting critique of the nationalist explanation, see Leopold Trymand, "Notes on the Polish Question," *Policy Review*, No. 20 (Spring 1982), pp. 83–101. Trymand's discussion, however, includes examples of the strength of traditional Polish national values—e.g., love for the 1791 May Constitution, attachment to the Catholic Church, anti-Russianism.

14. Two interesting discussions of the Catholic Church are John P.C. Matthews, "Renewal in Poland," *Worldview*, Vol. 24, No. 6 (June 1981), pp. 7–10 and Denis MacShane, "Solidarity and the Church," *Commonweal*, Vol. CIX, No. 1 (Jan. 15, 1982), pp. 14–17.

15. Zenon Kawecki, "Pzemiany swiatopogladowe mlodziezy," in T.M. Jaroszewski, ed., *Przemiany swiadomosci spoleczenstwa polskiego* (Warsaw: Instytut Podstawowych Problemow Marksizmu Leninizmu, 1979), pp. 204–205. The survey was conducted in 1977 and is a representative sample of 8,909 graduating students from secondary general and vocational schools.

16. Ibid., Table 4, p. 210.

17. Ibid., Table 5, p.211.

18. Ibid., Table 3, p. 194.

19. Lawrence Weschler, *Solidarity: Poland in the Season of its Passion* (New York: Simon and Schuster, 1982), p. 20.

20. Quoted in MacShane, "Solidarity and the Church," p. 15

21. "Spoleczne zaufanie do instytucji politycznych spolecznych i administracynych," Komunikat z badan, Osrodek Bandania Opinii Publicznej i Studiow Programowych, Nr. 16/207 (May 1981), Table 1, p. 2.

22. Z. Anthony Kruszewski, "Nationalism and Politics in Poland," in George Klein and Milan J. Reban, eds., *The Politics of Ethnicity in Eastern Europe* (New York: Columbia University Press, 1981), p. 149.

23. For this argument, see Perry Anderson, *Lineages of the Absolutist State* (London: New Left Books, 1974).

24. Kruszewski, "Nationalism and Politics in Poland," p. 151.

25. Roman Szporluk, "Poland," in Raymond Grew, ed., *Crises of Political Development in Eruope and the United States* (Princeton: Princeton University Press, 1978), pp. 386–87.

26. Szporluk, "Poland," p. 407.

27. Norman Davies, *God's Playground: A History of Poland in Two Volumes—Volume II: 1795 to the Present* (Oxford: Clarendon Press, 1981), pp. 212–13.

28. Kruszewski, "Nationalism and Politics in Poland," p. 150.

29. Peter Brock, "Polish Nationalism," in Peter F. Sugar and Ivo J. Lederer, eds., *Nationalism in Eastern Europe* (Seattle: University of Washington Press, 1969), p. 330.

30. Ibid., p. 338.

31. Davies, *God's Playground*, p. 224.

32. Kruszewski, "Nationalism and Politics in Poland," p. 151.

33. M.K. Dziewanowski, *Poland in the Twentieth Century* (New York: Columbia University Press, 1977), p. 140.

34. Kruszewski, "Nationalism and Politics in Poland," p. 163.

35. Ibid., p. 151.

36. Davies, *God's Playground*, pp. 224–25.

37. See, for example, M.K. Dziewanowski, *The Communist Party of Poland* (Cambridge: Harvard University Press, 1976).

38. See Jan Nowak, "The Church in Poland," *Problems of Communism*, Vol. 31, No. 1 (Jan.—Feb. 1982), pp. 5–7.

39. Ibid., pp. 8–10.

40. The self-organization of society refers to the process by which society organizes itself outside the institutions and limits of the state, as in the "Flying University" and independent, non–state-controlled trade unions.

41. For the text, see *Zycie Warszawy*, No. 20, (Dec. 21, 1975).

42. Jacque Rupnik, "Dissent in Poland, 1968–78: The End of Revisionism and the Rebirth of Civil Society," in Rudolph Tokes, ed., *Opposition in Eastern Europe* (Baltimore and London: Johns Hopkins University Press, 1979), pp. 87–89.

43. Anton Popieszalski, "Lay Catholic Organizations in Poland," *Survey*, Vol. 24, No. 4. (Autumn 1979), pp. 243–45.

44. Anna Kaminska, "The Polish Pope and the Polish Catholic Church," *Survey*, Vol. 24, No. 4 (Autumn 1979), p 218.

45. See Rupnik, "Dissent in Poland."

46. Tadeusz Szafar, "Contemporary Political Opposition in Poland," *Survey*, Vol. 24, No. 4 (Autumn 1979), p. 53.

47. See Adam Michnik, *Kosciol, Lewica, Dialog* (Paris: Instytut Literacki, 1977).

48. Rakowski's comments are reprinted in "Bases of Cooperation and Dialogue," *International Journal of Politics,* Vol. 9, No. 1 (Spring 1979), pp. 69–89.

49. William Robinson, "Church and State in Poland: From Dialogue to Cooperation?" *Radio Free Europe Research,* Vol. 3, No. 28 (July 12, 1978).

50. J.B. de Weydenthal, "Poland's Politics in the Aftermath of John Paul II's Election," *Radio Free Europe Research,* Vol. 3, No. 47 (Nov. 29, 1978).

51. The Polish text appeared in *Tygodnik Powszechny* (Nov. 12, 1978) with parts of it translated in Ibid.

52. Hansjakob Stehle, "Church and Pope in the Polish Crisis," *The World Today,* Vol. 38, No. 4 (April 1982), p. 139.

53. This argument is presented in Stanislaw Starski, *Class Struggles in Classless Poland* (Boston: South End Press, 1982), p. 55.

54. See "Poland Situation Report," *Radio Free Europe Research,* Vol. 4, No. 52 (Dec. 20, 1979).

55. See "Poland Situation Report," *Radio Free Europe Research,* Vol. 5, No. 20, (May 9. 1980).

56. See "Poland Situation Report," *Radio Free Europe Research,* Vol. 5, No. 33 (Aug. 5, 1980).

57. For an elaborate account of the events leading up to the establishment of Solidarity, see William Robinson, ed., *August 1980: The Strikes in Poland* (Munich: Radio Free Europe Research, 1980).

58. Reported in Ewa Celt, "Polish Episcopate Defines its Stand on the Current Crisis," in Robinson, ed., *August 1980,* pp. 137–38.

59. Stehle, "Church and Pope in the Polish Crisis," p. 142.

60. Starski, *Class Struggles in Classless Poland,* p. 66.

61. Ibid., p. 82.

62. For an account of the ceremonies, see Neal Ascherson, *The Polish August: The Self-Limiting Revolution* (New York: The Viking Press, 1982), pp. 13–18.

63. J.B. de Weydenthal, "Solidarity's First National Congress: Stage One," *Radio Free Europe Research,* Vol. 6, No. 65 (Sept. 21, 1981).

64. Michael Szkolny, "Revolution in Poland," *Monthly Review,* Vol. 33, No. 2 (June 1981), p. 10.

65. See *Kierunki* (October 5, 1980).

66. The Polish text appeared in *Tygodnik Powszechny* (June 21, 1981) and parts of it were translated in Nowak, "The Church in Poland."

67. Stehle, "Church and Pope in the Polish Crisis," p. 142.

68. Ibid., p. 143.

69. See "Poland Situation Report," *Radio Free Europe Research,* Vol. 6, No. 2 (January 15–16, 1981).

70. Quoted from Jonathan Spivak, "Delicate Diplomacy—Poland's Churchmen Wield Power Carefully in State-Worker Crisis," *The Wall Street Journal* May 15, 1981.

71. Stehle, "Church and Pope in the Polish Crisis," p. 144.

72. J.B. de Weydenthal, "Polish Church Acquires an Active Political Role," *Radio Free Europe Research,* Vol. 6, No. 9 (February 6–13, 1981).

73. Stehle, "Church and Pope in the Polish Crisis," p. 145.

74. Cited in Michael Dobbs, "Lech Walesa: Symbol of the Polish August," in Michael Dobbs, K.S. Karol, and Dessa Treyisan, *Poland—Solidarity—Walesa* (New York: McGraw Hill Book Company, 1981), p. 118.

75. Spivak, "Delicate Diplomacy—Poland's Churchmen Wield Power Carefully in State-Worker Crisis," p. 23.

76. "Excerpts from the English Version of the Pope's Encyclical 'On Human Work'," *The New York Times,* September 16, 1981.

77. Andrew Arato, "Empire vs. Civil Society: Poland 1981–82," *Telos,* No. 51 (Winter 1981–82), p. 27.

78. Ibid., p. 31.

79. For an intelligent discussion of the background to this event, see Martin Malia, "Poland: The Winter War," *The New York Review of Books,* Vol. XXIX, No. 4 (March 18, 1982), pp. 21–26.

80. Cited in Weschler, *Solidarity: Poland in the Season of its Passion,* p. 200.

81. *The New York Times,* December 25, 1981.

82. Ibid., December 15, 1981.

83. See J.B. de Weydenthal, "The Church and the State of Emergency," *Radio Free Europe Research,* Vol. 7, No. 8 (February 26, 1982).

84. Ibid.

85. *The New York Times,* December 15, 1981.

86. Nina Darnton, "The Subtle Power of the Polish Church," *The New York Times Magazine,* June 6, 1982, pp. 100–102.

87. Ibid. p. 102.

88. For an account of the early May demonstrations, see David Ost, "Poles Take it to the Streets," *In These Times,* May 26–June 1, 1982, p. 7. The communiqué was reported in *The New York Times,* May 7, 1982.

89. *The New York Times,* May 24, 1982. This same article quotes a recently released Solidarity leader as stating that the Church has "unequivocally expressed itself on the side of the nation."

90. Outbreaks occurred in Wroclaw and Poznan. The Polish Catholic Church had stated that the pope would visit his homeland this summer "only if he was sure of a peaceful welcome." *The New York Times,* June 30, 1982.

91. Andrew Arato argues that the alliance between the Church and the democratic opposition was a conditional alliance based on their common opposition to the regime. Their different structures predispose each organization to seek different kinds of solutions: the Church with its hierarchic structure seeking an authoritarian solution, and Solidarity a radically democratic one. See Arato, "Civil Society Against the State: Poland 1980–81," *Telos* No. 47 (Spring 1981), pp. 40–42.

EIGHT

Modern Japanese Nationalism: State Shinto, the Religion That Was "Not a Religion"

Wilbur M. Fridell

INTRODUCTION

This paper is about State Shinto in Japan during the eight decades of that country's modernization prior to the end of the Pacific War in 1945.[1] During this critical period, Japanese authorities recognized the need for a national ideology around which to unify the people in their great leap forward. Thus, from the time in the 1860s when Japan opened her doors to the West and emerged from a long period of isolation, Shinto moved to the fore as the great energizer for the national effort, with focus on the sacred Emperor as the living object of the people's loyalty.

Shinto is rooted in the prehistoric mythic experience of the Japanese people, and is the closest thing to a Japanese indigenous religious tradition. As Japan reached forward, therefore, to embrace the new in the modern period, it consciously looked to the Shinto heritage of the distant past as the sure basis on which to strengthen the nation. Thus mobilizing tradition on behalf of modernization, Japanese leaders rallied the people and embarked on a crash program of modernization in all important dimensions of social, political, economic, intellectual, and much of cultural life. It was not as smooth a process as is sometimes suggested. There were severe tensions and contradictions. But compared with China, India, Iran, etc., it has been a kind of modern miracle.

My plan is to divide the topic into three segments: (1) a short discussion of terminology; (2) a brief review of the mythical and historical background of State Shinto; and (3) five phases of national ideological policy in the pre-World War II period, with some summary concluding remarks.

TERMINOLOGY

Sociologists of religion speak of two broad types of religion. The first is what is often called conventional religion—religion organized in specifically religious forms, such as churches, temples, synagogues, etc. We are dealing here with traditional religious patterns: Christianity, Buddhism, Islam, Zoroastrianism, and so forth.

The second type of religion is broadly social, and consists of what Joachim Wach called the "religion of natural groupings:" family, clan, and nation. Emile Durkheim noted that every group in society has a religious dimension, and that the clan has played a kind of godlike role.

Ikado Fujio, a Japanese sociologist, calls this "culture religion." At its heart are shared values set against the broadest framework of a society's worldview. If that society is a nation, culture religion is the great unifier overarching all, providing national orientation to ultimate things, however conceived. So speaks Professor Ikado.

While various terms have been advanced for this phenomenon by Wach, Ikado, etc., I prefer to call it collectivity religion. Just as collectivity religion operates in relatively small groups like clans, so it can extend even beyond the nation-state to assume international and transcultural dimensions. Thus, Marxism is increasingly being seen as one of its forms.

In between clans and Marxism are other representative types of collectivity religion at the level of the nation-state. One such is State Shinto as it functioned in Japan up to the end of the Pacific War in 1945.

But, one may ask, can this kind of socially grounded religion really be regarded as religious? Is it not at best a kind of quasi-religion? I wish there were time to consider this question, but let me simply stand on the evidence that scholars of religion are increasingly recognizing sacred national ideologies as constituting a type of religion, broadly conceived. It is this to which I point when I speak of State Shinto as an instance of "collectivity religion."

Sacred national ideologies fit Paul Tillich's description of religion as that which relates to "ultimate concerns." Or, take a definition of religion given by my colleague at Santa Barbara, Raimundo Panikkar: namely, religion is a "way of salvation"—salvation for an organized society, as well as for individuals in it. Specifically pointing to the type of thing we are talking about in collectivity religion, Panikkar has put it this way: "Do religions [of the conventional type] have a monopoly on 'religion?' "

All of this is by way of setting out basic categories for the introduction of my topic of State (or National) Shinto, a collectivity religion which played a major role in the modern pre-1945 Japanese experience.

MYTHICAL AND HISTORICAL BACKGROUND

Mythical tradition and government-religion relations. In order to understand the traditional pattern of government-religion relationships in Japan, one that carried right up to the modern period, we must go back to the Japanese national myth, officially taught as historic fact in the decades immediately prior to Japan's military defeat in 1945.

The Japanese cosmogonic myth begins with sacred *kami* (spirits) in the High Plain of Heaven (Takamagahara). Two great creative *kami,* Izanagi (male) and Izanami (female), were

parents of the Japanese race. These two came down from
Heaven to a rainbow bridge which arched over an oily mass
below. Izanagi, the male, reached down his spear, stirred and
withdrew it, and drops of liquid fell back to form islands below. The two *kami* then descended to the islands, and by a
process of natural generation produced the Sacred Land of Japan—all of nature: rocks, trees, waterfalls, etc.—and also a
series of other sacred *kami* spirits.

The age of the original *kami* and their descendants flowed
without break into the age of humans, including the chief humans, the line of Sacred Emperors. The imperial line was com-
missioned by the great sun *kami* Amaterasu to reign over the
land in unbroken succession forever.

Not only was the land of Japan sacred, and the line of emperors, but also the People—at least, potentially so. According
to the myth, the whole nation of people descended from the
central imperial line, like the branches of a tree, and thereby
shared in the sanctity of that line.

Given this mythic past, it is understandable that the Japanese prehistoric relationship between government and religion
should have been like that of other such primitive societies:
virtually indistinguishable. This basic assumption about the
harmony that should prevail between these two elementary dimensions of life was early formulated in the expression, *saisei
itchi,* which means the "unity of [Shinto] rites and government." This unity of religion and government is reflected in the
ancient Japanese word for government, *matsurigoto,* which literally means "festival affairs," or more broadly, "worship."

Government and religion, coming into the modern period.
We turn our attention now to government and religion as Japan came into the modern period. Thus far, the "modern period" has spanned a little over one hundred years, beginning
with the opening of Japan to the West in the middle of the
nineteenth century. This is a fascinating, highly complex history. Here we can only highlight the several major policies and
programs relating to government-religion relations, within the
context of rapid modernization.

First, the situation in which the Japanese found themselves in the mid-1800s. They had been virtually isolated from the out-side world for two and a half centuries. Western powers now came knocking on Japan's door, demanding that it open to trade. In 1853 Commodore Matthew Perry of the United States Navy anchored American warships in Tokyo Bay, and insisted in the name of his government on negotiations with the Japanese authorities. Other Western powers, notably the Russians, moved in the background, preparing advances toward Japan.

Japan was sadly unprepared to make any kind of vigorous response to this situation. For two and a half centuries the Tokugawa family had ruled the country in a feudal dictatorship, but by the time Perry arrived, their rule was a façade that scarcely hid incompetence and extreme weakness at the heart of what could almost be called a national "non-government."

With the Tokugawas incapable of rallying any kind of effective, unified national response to the Western threat, imperial loyalists stepped into the power vacuum with the cry, "Restore the Emperor!" The Emperor was the latent symbol of national unity. Emperors had pretty much lost their prominence for many centuries, having sat on the throne in Kyoto, above the business of government, with virtually no influence on affairs, Now, in the national emergency, imperial loyalists appealed to the ancient tradition of the sacred imperial family as the focal point for pulling the nation together.

Thomas O'Dea, until his sad death our colleague in the Religious Studies Department at Santa Barbara, used to speak about this whole phase of Japanese history as an example of the well-known "challenge-response syndrome." The challenge was the threat of encroachment on a weak Japan by Western powers, who were even then slicing up China into "spheres of influence" and humiliating this proud continental giant with its impressive cultural heritage. The Japanese were well aware of what was happening to China, and were determined that it would not happen to them. Their response to this crisis, therefore, was to restore the Emperor, sanctified by mythic origin, to his traditional position in national life: namely, as the highest sanction for government, and the symbol of national unity. The Emperor must be the focus of loyalty, to rouse the nation to decisive action.

Fortunately, during the latter part of the Tokugawa period, there had developed in Japan a school of Shinto thought, "National Learning" (*Kokugaku*), which produced important scholarly work with ancient Shinto texts, including one source of the national mythology, the *Kojiki* (Records of Ancient Matters). With the anxiety produced by the Western threat, this school of Shinto thought, until then apolitical, was rapidly brought forward by supporters of the imperial cause as the ideological justification for the restoration of the Emperor to national prominence. In this politicized form National Learning has been called, in retrospect, "Restoration Shinto."

The young emperor thus restored came to be known as Meiji (his reign name), and the date of his coming to the throne, 1868, marks the beginning of the Meiji period, when Japan launched upon its great national campaign to modernize along Western lines. The new emperor was only a young lad in his teens when he assumed his imperial position, but he soon became a substantial, much-revered personage, with considerable influence on his ministers, and through them on government. Emperor Meiji was what the Japanese call *tennō rashii,* or "emperor-like." He served Japan well until his death in 1912, a forty-four year period which was highly crucial in the experience of the nation.

FIVE PHASES OF NATIONAL IDEOLOGICAL POLICY

I don't wish to spend too much time on the historical account, but we need to review five major phases of national ideological policy and program in order to get the situation before us, and as a basis for certain concluding observations.

Shinto as the official patriotic religion (1868–mid-1870s) The first ideological phase was an attempt by the new Meiji government to establish Shinto as *the* official patriotic religion of Japan, "Shinto" being the same Restoration Shinto that had helped to restore the Emperor as the symbol of national loyalties.

Under the intense pressures of the time, Restoration Shinto was quickly institutionalized in a rather extreme, even emotional manner. For three or four years leaders of the new government actively attempted to nationalize all Shinto shrines, and aggressively propagated a somewhat eclectic collage of maxims and admonitions called the "Great Teaching," which was heavily Shintoist in nature. Emphasis was on loyalty to the new regime, in the name of the Emperor.

This first Shinto venture soon failed—it was too drastically overt, and it threatened too many interests. Thus, the Japanese Buddhists, who had seemed almost moribund, reacted strongly against the Shintoistic Great Teaching at the grassroots level. Also, certain Japanese liberals objected to what struck them as a throwback to premodern patterns.

What really killed this early propagation of Shinto as the official patriotic religion, however, were the clear and forceful protests of Western powers. These countries had recently inflicted on the Japanese certain unfair trade treaties, which the Japanese hated and resented; and they made it clear that these treaties would not be revoked unless the Meiji government established a policy of religious freedom. The Westerners said they were concerned that an official Shinto religion would make it difficult for Christian missionaries to do their work. An even more important reason had to do with the pocketbook: they feared that a Shinto state religion would generate anti-Western sentiments, thereby blocking trade relations with Japan.

Painfully aware of their weakness vis-à-vis the Western powers, Japanese leaders accommodated to the foreigners' demands and declared religious freedom. In so doing, they abandoned for the time being official efforts to establish a national Shinto cult with the focus on the Emperor.

"Western intoxication" (*c. mid-1870s–mid-1880s*). There followed a little over a decade, a brief time which has been called the period of "Western intoxication." Japanese authorities

launched a crash program of modernization along Western lines, in order to strengthen the country in every possible way: Western industry, a Western-type army and navy, a Western school system, political institutions, etc. were all rapidly established.

Along with Westernization in these basic dimensions of national life, there were superficial areas as well in which things Western took hold. Caught up in the faddish Western craze, people in high places aped foreign ways, such as dress—even social dancing, a scandalous departure for a traditional Japanese. Such developments shocked many Japanese, and a sharp conservative reaction was quickly mounted. Although this reaction focused on the highly visible social excesses of the Western craze, it was motivated by a deep feeling among many Japanese that their country was borrowing indiscriminately from the West in fundamental ways (such as political and educational institutions), thereby introducing changes that threatened the continuity of traditional value patterns and the well-established sense of Japanese national identity.

Conservative reaction (especially from the mid-1880s). The reaction to the period of "Western intoxication" gathered strength in the 1880s, or the second decade of the new regime. The general sentiment was neatly encapsulated in the slogan, "Eastern ethics, Western science."[2] In other words, we'll take your Western science and technology to strengthen the nation; but we'll not sacrifice our Eastern (Japanese) ethics, our values. This dimension of national life, the inner citadel of Japaneseness, must be protected at all costs.

With the new mood of conservatism, government leaders produced the Meiji Constitution of 1889. Patterned after the Prussian constitution under Bismark, it was by no means a progressive or liberal document: that is, it served to protect certain traditional Japanese values and loyalties. At the same time, it clearly represented an effort to move into the modern world.

Within the Japanese context, one of the modern features of the Meiji Constitution was its provision for freedom of religious belief. Article 28 was framed as follows: "Japanese subjects shall, within limits not prejudicial to peace and order, and not antagonistic to their duties as subjects, enjoy freedom of religious belief."[3] As can be seen, modern Japanese religious freedom was seriously hedged about by certain crucial limitations.

Still, this constitutional declaration was sufficiently explicit to make it impossible thereafter for the government ever to favor one religion above others as an official state religion. From this time on, Japanese authorities would be seriously handicapped in any effort to promote an official State Shinto if it was represented to be religious in nature. To make Shinto religious observances incumbent on all Japanese subjects would run counter to the freedom of religion provision in the constitution. This constitutional provision for religious freedom, and the limitations it placed on efforts to promote an official State Shinto religion, largely determined the thrust of subsequent phases of policy in regard to government-Shinto relations right up to the end of the Pacific War in 1945.

Ethics instruction in the schools (1903–1945). Japanese authorities had been stung in the matter of an official Shinto religion in the early Meiji years; and conditions were not yet ripe for the promotion of a government-backed Shinto "non-religious" cult. That would come later. Therefore, the leaders temporarily shelved all efforts to establish State Shinto and tried another, less controversial, tactic to accomplish their ideological aims: namely, ethical instruction in the public schools.

This program was implemented through a whole series of officially produced ethics textbooks and teachers' manuals, which were used in the public schools from 1903 until the end of the Pacific War in 1945. The instruction was carefully identified as being ethical, not religious, so as to avoid conflict with the freedom of religion provision of the Meiji Constitution. It was, in fact, called *kokumin dōtoku,* the "national ethic," and was held up as the ideal to which every patriotic Japanese should commit himself, regardless of personal or household religious affiliation.

In numerous places, the government texts reflected a German theory of state absolutism (*kokka yūkitai,* or "state organism"). However, the two most important dimensions in the ethics lessons were rooted in Japanese tradition: a Confucian element, and a Shinto element.

The Confucian element centered in filial piety and loyal devotion to parents, which was then transferred upward to the Emperor, the father of the nation within the great "national family" (*kazoku kokka*). The more prominent Shinto element emphasized the retelling of the national myth, presented as historic fact. The focus here was on the sacred charge given by the highest Shinto *kami,* the "Sun Goddess" Amaterasu, to the imperial line of emperors, commissioning them to reign in unbroken succession forever.

There is a sense in which Meiji ideologues were transmuting for the modern Japanese situation the Bushidō samurai ethic of loyalty that had been formulated in the late Tokugawa period. Only now, we see these basic changes taking place: (a) whereas samurai loyalty had focused most intensely on one's immediate feudal lord, Meiji loyalty was now clearly shifted to the Emperor; and (b) what had been an ethic for the samurai elite was now propagated as the expected norm for every loyal Japanese subject. In effect, emperor-loyalty became the super-creed for all the Japanese people.

Shinto as the non-religious national patriotic cult (especially from mid-1920s–1945). We come now to the final phase in our historical overview: namely, the second effort to exalt State Shinto—this time not as a religion, as had been unsuceessfully tried in early Meiji, but rather as a "nonreligious" patriotic cult. This time the effort was a success.

The history of this phase is a complex one, involving not only government relations with Shinto, but also with the Buddhists, the Christians, and various popular "new religions." Here I shall simplify things drastically, focusing our attention on Shinto.

From as early as 1899, the government had attempted to pass bills in the national Diet to tighten oversight of the religions. "The religions" meant everything except State Shinto, which already at this time was implicitly treated as a nonreligious national ethic. The 1899 bill lost in the Diet, and for some years thereafter the attention of the nation's leaders was deflected from the government-religion problem.

Finally, in 1926, in response to insistent demands from conservatives, the authorities appointed a Religious System Inquiry Commission (*Shūkyō Seido Chōsakai*) to consider how the government should regulate the religious bodies of the country. In 1929 they created a corresponding Shrine System Inquiry Commission (*Jinja Seidō Chōsakai*) to study the whole question of State Shinto.[4] In this second commission, particular attention was devoted to the nature of State Shinto and how it related (a) to Japanese national life; and (b) to the conventional religious traditions: Buddhism, Christianity, sect (denominational) Shinto groups, and the "new religions."

In tackling the thorny problem of the nature of State Shinto, the Shrine System Inquiry Commission addressed itself to this basic question: was the national cult a religion, or a national ethic? The not-so-hidden agenda of the government representatives on the commission, of course, was to come up with the conclusion that it was a national ethic, *not* a religion.

Beginning with the formation of the Shrine System Inquiry Commission in 1929, interminable studies and discussions were held by that body over the years, right into the 1930s, without conclusive results. As nationalistic tensions mounted in connection with Japan's military ventures on the Asiatic mainland from 1937, the authorities increasingly looked to State Shinto as the main force for intensifying patriotic loyalties.

In the end, national events overrode the somewhat theoretical deliberations of the Shrine System Inquiry Commission as to the nature of State Shinto. Especially with the beginning of the Pacific War in 1941, the state cult became ever more entrenched in national life. The conventional religious groups

(Buddhism, Christianity, sect Shinto groups, and the "new religions") were swept into commitment to political and military goals that were vigorously supported by the Shinto cult and its nationalistic ideology. The authority of State Shinto over the people was left legally undefined, so that in actual fact it was unlimited. The effect was to give it free reign as an instrument for the generation and mobilization of patriotic devotion.

SUMMARY OF THE BASIC STATE SHINTO ISSUE

The charge to the Shrine System Inquiry Commission in 1929 had been to clarify the nature of State Shinto, particularly to determine whether it was a religion or a national ethic.

As we have made clear by now, if State Shinto was to be treated as a religion, it came under the provision of the Meiji Constitution, which guaranteed freedom of religious belief. This would make Shinto a matter of personal choice, for, if it was a "religion among religions," a Japanese subject would be free to align himself with it or not, according to inclination.

This was not good enough for the authorities. When it came to participation in the national Shinto patriotic cult, they did not wish to permit any choice. For this reason, State Shinto was officially understood to be a nonreligious national ethic, to which the religious freedom provision of the Meiji Constitution did not apply.

Thus, the Japanese were not to relate to the State Shinto cult on a voluntary basis. Rather, observance of its rituals was incumbent on every loyal subject, regardless of his private religious associations. In effect, this made State Shinto a kind of superfaith of national loyalty, with its rites given the importance which attached to official governmental sponsorship.

My good friend Charles Iglehart, long a respected Methodist educational missionary-scholar in Tokyo, and the man with whom I once climbed Mt. Fuji, wrote a history of Protestant Christianity in Japan, from which I wish to quote. In speaking of the national ethic that was propagated at the heart of State Shinto, he wrote,

This ethical system was construed as being not religious. It must not, however, be thought that this was . . . viewed as being beneath religion, or of minor importance. On the contrary, the official view of the makers of Japan's policy was that anyone might hold such religious views as he pleased, provided they never touched the summit of Japan's life at the Imperial center. This was so far above the vagaries of a private religious faith that they could not be classed together.[5]

Was this elevation of the "Imperial center" to a transcendent position above personal faith a distortion of true religion? From the Judeo-Christian point of view, we would have to say yes, that to exalt a national ideology above God was clearly a blasphemous perversion of religious reality.

It is manifestly unfair, however, to evaluate a Japanese religious pattern on the basis of such Western assumptions. The more correct question would be, was State Shinto a distortion of religion in the *Japanese* context?

Basically, no. State Shinto was but a modern expression of that prehistoric Japanese formulation, *saisei itchi,* or the "unity of [Shinto] rites and government." According to this pattern, Japanese government has always used religious rites for the support of political rule. Consider: there has been no transcendent religious norm for judgment over society: political symbols and institutions have always been at the very top of the Japanese value system; and, in the modern period, the Emperor was explicitly described in the Meiji Constitution as "sacred and inviolable."[6]

Given this consistent pattern throughout Japanese history, modern State Shinto was not so much a distortion of Japanese religion as it was an authentic expression of how the Japanese have always tended to be religious—in cooperation with, and in support of, government. This has not been seen as a corruption of religion. Rather, the Japanese have instinctively felt it was a good thing that the two most basic dimensions of society, government and corporate religion, were harmoniously compatible, rather than fighting each other, as has been the most characteristic pattern in the West.

The one point at which the authentic State Shinto heritage

can be said to have undergone a certain amount of distortion was in the ultra-nationalistic decades prior to and during the World War II, when the authorities so manipulated a genuine tradition that it bordered on artificiality. This period saw the systematic propagation of the state ideology and national mythology, with no contrary positions permitted, all within a police-state context.

On the one hand, this was a measure of the crisis the authorities knew they were facing; on the other hand, it may have been an instance of the Japanese tendency to push to extremes. But note that, even in their extremity (indeed, all the more because of it), these people moved with remarkable unity. Faced with all-out war, the Japanese characteristically pulled together as a national group, and in the process generated tremendous power for concerted action.

NOTES

1. When I use the term "State Shinto," I am departing from the practice of the Japanese themselves during the prewar period under discussion. That is, the Japanese expression *Kokka Shintō* (State Shinto) seems not to have been used by the Japanese in their writings during the time the national cult was actually in operation. It is true that Daniel Holtom, as well as some other foreign writers, used the term "State Shinto" in prewar English-language accounts. So also did Katō Genchi, prominent Shinto expert, and others, when they wrote in English for foreign readers.

The way the Japanese usually referred to the national shrine system in prewar Japan was simply to speak of "the shrines." Or, more formally and definitively, they used the adjectival expression, *Kokkateki Shintō* (National Shinto). *Kokka Shintō* in the Japanese language, therefore, was a term created *ex post facto* following the Pacific War to designate an identifiable series of Shinto events and institutions in the prewar past.

The Shinto elements caught up in the expression *Kokka* (State) *Shintō* were not neatly delineated, but were rather a rich conglomeration of nationalistic values and socio-ideological patterns that broadly shaded off into other phases of Shinto, as well as Japanese life in general. One could almost say that State Shinto was more a focus then a clearly prescribed area.

It will be noted that, in moving from the earlier adjectival form "National (*Kokkateki*) Shinto" to the nominative form "State (*Kokka*) Shinto," we have passed from a soft adjectival to a hard nominative expression, a transition that reflects a reification process over time in both thought and language.

What thus began as a flowing succession of dynamic happenings at the time of their occurrence acquired a static label as a means of identifying a certain series of related events in retrospect. This is probably standard for any historical sequence as it is viewed, first at the time of its occurrence, and later after it has been crystallized in historical perspective. In other words, all historical events are dynamically moving episodes when they occur, and only after the fact are they reified into conceptual notions: "State Shinto," "French Revolution," "Protestant Reformation," "Great Leap Forward," etc.

This reification is really inescapable, for we need convenient labels if we are to talk about historical epochs at all. But we must constantly be alert to the danger that, in using such hardened expressions, we will lose something of the dynamic quality of events as they happened in real life.

As a postscript to this note, I would like to observe an interesting similarity between the writing of history and the practice of that highly experience-oriented religious tradition of Zen. In Zen they constantly emphasize the need to grasp life directly, without filtering it through mental constructs, for in the filtering we experience not life itself, but rather concepts *about* life, once removed from the real thing. We are enriched to the extent that we can read historical records and follow historical events in this same direct, living way.

2. Coined by Sakuma Shōzan (1811–64), late-Tokugawa samurai intellectual and champion of Western technology.

3. Hugh Borton, *Japan's Modern Century* (New York: Ronald Press, 1955), p. 494.

4. Information about the Shrine System Inquiry Commission is taken from the official minutes, the *Jinja Seido Chōsakai Gijiroku,* which includes the records of a long series of *sōkai* (general meetings) and *tokubetsu iinkai* (special committee meetings), running from 1929 to 1940.

5. Charles W. Iglehart, *A Century of Protestant Christianity in Japan,* (Rutland, Vt.: Charles E. Tuttle Co., 1960), pp. 109–10.

6. Hugh Borton, op. cit., p. 491.

NINE

The Case of Pakistan

Barbara Metcalf

In any consideration of nationalism, and, in particular, any consideration of the relation between religion and nationalism, the case of Pakistan is one of great fascination. Here the symbols of nationalism do not simply have features analogous to the symbols of religious mythology but are themselves meant to be part of a religious structure of meaning. Moreover, Pakistan stretches the classical definition of nationalism set out by Professor Smart to the extreme of its limits.[1] Third World countries in general, shaped by the arbitrary boundaries of colonial rule, fit this definition uneasily at best, their origins often at conflict with ethnic realities. Pakistan at its birth defied virtually every criterion of nationhood. Its territory, far from contiguous, was separated into two segments divided by a thousand miles of alien territory. Its international border segmented two core regions of the subcontinent, Punjab in the West and Bengal in the East, each united by custom and language and ethnic pride. The case of Bengal was particularly striking, for it had long been known as an area marked by regional consciousness and common language, a region whose Hindu and Muslim population both seemed to have the potential hallmarks of a modern nation. As for a cherished history shared throughout the area, much of the population had been unaffected by the historical interpretation and present policy that the leaders of the Pakistan movement, themselves from elsewhere in the subcontinent, had finally seen triumph. As for language, it was the mother tongue of these leaders, Urdu, that was initially set up with English to be the official language of the new state. Urdu was the first tongue of a mere four percent of the population; English was the second language of only a handful.

The short history of Pakistan is also absorbing to the Western scholar for the haunting resemblances it bears to that of the other postwar state based on religious nationalism, that of Israel. The size of the two countries is certainly not analogous, nor is the fact that, from a Third World perspective, Pakistan represents a resurgence against colonialism, while Israel is held to be one of the last gasps of European domination of a Third World area. Yet both shared at their inception a vision of themselves as a refuge and a homeland for the persecuted, while tragically and ironically finding themselves subsequently the oppressor of Arabs and Bengalis, respectively. Both were opposed by substantial numbers of their religious leadership who held aloof from the secular goals of the political leadership and even from the concept of a nation.[2] Both countries have groped for self-justification, shifting in their ideological formulations between what in the South Asian case is called communal interests on the one side—the preservation of the lives, interests, and culture of a community—and religious on the other—the creation of a utopian society on religious principles. Both, indeed, have cherished the vision, now tarnished for both, as countries militarily impregnable on the outside and justly and humanely ordered within.[3] Both finally bear, along with Ireland, the heritage of British control that by its idiom of rule and its deliberate policy, exacerbated in all three cases the divisions that have given these areas their shape.

The creation of Pakistan, the movements in its favor, the pressures that in the end seemed to necessitate it, all this together forms a complex story. The role of the British, who had

ruled the areas that came to make up the new country as part
of the Indian Empire for between a hundred to one hundred
and fifty years, was of course central, both because their policies in education, justice, and politics encouraged religious
identity and because the social and economic changes that came
in the train of imperial rule fostered new forms of horizontal
loyalty. In 1947, the British, weary of war and of an increasingly aggressive nationalist movement, justified their transfer
of power to two sovereign nations on the grounds that the Hindus and the Muslims were in fact two separate nations defined
in religious terms. The focus of this brief essay is not to examine the legitimacy of that claim or the process that made it
necessary, but rather the situation afterward when Pakistan
found itself in existence.[4] For that, history is only relevant for
the construction it is given in the present.

Pakistan has had not only to come to terms with its history
but with two of the great tragedies of the twentieth century.
The first, 1947, when the country was born in chaos and
bloodshed, with a terrified migration of Hindus and Sikhs toward India and Muslims toward Pakistan. Perhaps ten million
people moved; an estimated one million died. Barely twenty-
five years later, faced with demands for autonomy from Bengal, the central, West Pakistani-dominated government, joined
battle with the East. Ten million refugees fled to India, Bengalis were brutally massacred, the Indian army moved in, and
Pakistan was humiliated by the capture of 100,000 of its soldiers. Pakistan was reduced to its Western provinces, its claim
to be a Muslim homeland undercut by its reduction to the third
largest Muslim population of the subcontinent, following those
of the new nation of Bangladesh and that of India itself.

Against such an origin and such a history, it is not surprising
that Pakistanis have been absorbed in self-justification and that
the country has produced a rich variety of nationalist interpretations. The feature celebrated throughout—to use Professor
Smart's term—has been Islam. To say this, however, is only to
begin, for the socio-political and even spiritual implications of
Islamic interpretations have varied substantially. Virtually every

political figure has made his proposals in an Islamic framework. Secondly, every figure has implicitly or explicitly set his interpretations in an international context. In the first two decades, which in terms of nationalist symbols forms the first period, that context was opposition to and distinction from India. In the decade of the '70s after Bangladesh, the second period, the context has been identification with the countries of the Middle East. The passionate, self-conscious identification of Pakistanis with Islam is notable even to other Muslims.

Is it possible to distinguish patterns in the various Islamic ideologies that have been expounded? Much as opponents may do it, one can certainly not distinguish between some authentic statement of Islam on the one hand and the opportunistic use of Islam on the other. One distinction, alluded to as significant in Israel as well, is that between the more communal emphasis on the one hand and the more radically religious on the other. The first has primarily stressed the interests of the Muslim community and the protection of its culture. It has passionately embraced the glories of the high period of Muslim culture and determined to make Muslims powerful again. It has even been called secular. It has often looked to the West, not only for technology but for the radical disjuncture of domains, so that such areas as economics are guided by principles apart from religion. In this sense it is modern; in the context of the subcontinent, it is associated with the "Aligarh perspective." Listen to a young Pakistani student speaking at the University of Southern California in April 1948:

. . . I only want to tell you of the Islam that was the burning light of yesterday, the ember that it is today, and the celestial flame of tomorrow, for that is how I envisage the future of Islam. I must also tell you that religiously speaking, I am not a devout Muslim. I do not say my prayers regularly, I do not keep all the fasts, I have not yet been on a pilgrimage to Mecca. Therefore religiously speaking, I am a poor Muslim. However, my interest is soaked in the political, economic, and cultural heritage of Islam.

This was Zulfikar Ali Bhutto, then a student at Berkeley, rejoicing in the creation of Pakistan and looking ahead to a confederation of Muslim peoples.[5] He defined religion in terms of personal piety and the power and protection of Muslim peoples, not as a guide to social and political life. Generally speaking, this "communal" position has been socially conservative and has been identified with the preservation of vested interests of landowners, businessmen, the army, and politicians. It has dominated Islamic ideology throughout most of the history of Pakistan.

The more radically religious interpretation of Islam looks less to the glorious peaks of Muslim civilization for its inspiration than to the pristine revelation of the Prophet itself. It sees in it social revolution, the overthrow of the oppressive exploitative powers, the end of the contempt and pride of the rich in favor of egalitarian and human social principles. This ideology was a secondary stream in the Pakistan movement, associated with the urban Punjabi movements of the '30s, notably the Ahrar, and with the grassroots Muslim League support in Bengal organized by Abu'l-Hashim.[6] The radical interpretation was also present in the beloved poetry of Iqbal, a side of him recited but rarely heard. It emerged again in the ideology of the PPP, the Pakistan People's Party, led by no one less than that same Bhutto, whose party, in the wake of skewed economic development and disruptive social change, in the late '60s embraced a platform of what was called "Islamic socialism." It is significant that even at its inception Pakistan was not merely a sanctuary for Muslim landed, merchant, and professional groups in search of their own interests but also was a focus for radical social aspirations, a vision that has had the potential of periodic reassertion.[7]

Keeping in mind that all is set in an Islamic framework, one can distinguish three strands in Pakistani nationalism in the first period. The first represented espousal of the European model of the elements that make up a state, known of course through British example and education. The second, whose form derived from the nature of great power relations and general post-war concerns in the new states, emphasized the symbols and realities of modern technological development, coupled closely in this case with a high valuation of law and order.

The third, itself consisting of complex parts, concerned the attempt to shape a cultural consensus through a commonly understood history, a current destiny, and a cultural heritage, summed up above all by the place of the respective languages of diverse populations. Here, as in the second period discussed below, one is struck by the extent to which these symbols do not evolve autonomously, but in the context of a highly integrated world economy and of political rivalries and involvements of the more developed nations.

In the post-colonial states in general, the leaders of the newly liberated states had wholly assimilated the requisites of a state on the European model. A capital, a flag, an anthem, a constitution, parties and elective bodies, army, and bureaucracy were all to be acquired. Jinnah, the nation's founder, indeed took pride in being more cosmopolitan, more constitutionalist, than Gandhi.[8] Pakistan comprised the corners of a previously united polity and initially operated out of provincial offices, but rapidly set about to create the hallmarks of an independent state. Its new capital, set in the beautiful, rolling Margalla foothills of the Himalayas, was to be Islamabad, "the abode of Islam," its simple and elegant white buildings the work of a Philadelphia architectural firm—a mix of Muslim identity and technical expertise that was perhaps the heart of the ideal of the early leaders. The pride in the institutions of the country was the greater since they seemed to appear from nothing.

The European model of how to create a country is clear in a book that most Pakistanis would have considered eccentric throughout, *Pakistan: The Fatherland of the Pak Nation,* by Choudhary Rahmat Ali.[9] First printed in 1935, it was reprinted in several editions. Rahmat Ali is best known for his coining of the acronym that was to be name of the new country—symbol of a nation par excellence—while a young student in London in the early 1930s.[10] He subsequently committed himself to propaganda in favor of the creation of a number of Muslim homelands throughout the subcontinent with the vision of ultimately winning the whole subcontinent to Islam. How does one control an area? In part, as Edward Said has recently argued for European colonialists, by knowledge, and by presumed mastery of the culture and terrain of an area.[11] Rahmat Ali set out to do the same by cataloguing every detail of the area he hoped to be Muslim: frontiers, coastline, and islands; physical features and climate; flora, fauna, and forests; agriculture and minerals; industry, commerce, and communications. He surveyed the human geography as well—"Provinces, States, Enclaves, and Notable Places" with attention to history and archaeology. He discussed the people, as had the colonial bureaucrats before him, on the basis of racial and ethnic stock. He described and tried to shape the symbols of the nation: faith, flag, calendar, festivals, language (Urdu), laws, "code of honour" and "courtesy titles." He summarized a "National Story" and (in the third edition) what he saw as betrayal at the time of partition.

That Pakistan was to have the shape of a nation-state in the far reduced area that was to be its, was, in a sense, taken for granted. The ideals of the new state were somewhat less so. If, however, a central vision of the leadership were to be elicited from the early period of the country's history, particularly from the late '50s to the late '60s, it would be the celebration of technological and economic development. It was this, rather than any cultural or immediately human concerns, that dominated the actions and goals of the leadership. A corollary to this, in part the legacy of the imperial state that had nurtured them, was an overriding concern with law and order and an impatience with political activities. To be sure, the base for democratic political activities was very weak: a heterogeneous area, much of it never integrated into even the limited political institutions created by the Raj, and no coherent and long-lived political organization like the Indian National Congress to be a force for stability. The very powerful bureaucracy and the army together grew impatient with the faction-ridden, landlord-dominated political institutions unsympathetic to central authority and economic change. On October 7, 1958, the army and the president assumed military rule. The subsequent mixture of an emphasis on stability and modernization was helped by the international political alignments of the period, above all by the congeniality found between American political leaders and Pakistani bureaucrats and generals. The Americans, dubious of India's nonalignment and mystified by her culture, found, as had the British before them, the sturdy Muslims of the Northwest far more to their liking.

Helped not only by American foreign policy but by American scholars, Ayub Khan, the Chief Martial Law Administrator and President, joined by generals and elite civil servants, embraced a theory of development that urged rapid growth with no concern whatsoever for distribution either among the regions or the classes. Rapid growth overall was to make the entire pie larger so that all would benefit. This was classic modern Western economic theory, in which economics was wholly divorced from moral considerations and seen instead as subject to its own laws. Mysteriously, the whole enterprise would conduce to the good. The oft-quoted title of a work by one of the American economists summed up the short-term implications: "The Social Utility of Greed."[12] The result of course was growth, but skewed so much that one could speak of the "twenty-two families" that controlled virtually all of industry, insurance, and banking. As the civil war was to make clear, there was not only inequality but inequality increasing at an accelerated rate.[13] Ayub Khan, as military dictator from 1958–68, explicitly made economic growth the basis for national unity. He was not unaware of regional disparities and sought to redress them, but his efforts were too few and his political base too exclusive. The very symbolic weight put on development made its failures the greater. An East Pakistani intellectual made the point: "the elevation of economic goals to the level of symbolic and transcendental ends . . . *created* conflicts concerning solidarity and identity."[14]

Although opponents at the time and historians later have criticized Ayub for using Islam as a veneer to protect vested interests and justify authoritarian rule, such a conclusion is only circumstantial. Personally pious and known to rely on the *pir* (spiritual leadership) of Golra Sharif,[15] Ayub justified his system as serving the interests of Muslims and of Islam. His Islam was thus modernist in the sense of not providing a blueprint or guide to policies or actions but by being the ultimate interest served by the policies followed. This had an appeal. But the contradictions of this style of Islamic emphasis, and the scepticism it produced in many, were felt by Ayub himself. He spoke of the urgent need to find a concept to "weld the people into unity," "an answer which is comprehensive, tangible, arouses spontaneous and consistent enthusiasm, and is workable in the light of the requirements of modern life." "I have not been able to find an effective answer so far."[16] Nor would he in the whole of his rule.

The nationalist rhetoric of the regime focused on what we have called Islam in its communal sense: the place of Pakistan as a homeland and a refuge and as a guarantor of the rights of some fifty million Muslims in India. It was fueled by the continuing sense of being mistreated and misunderstood, above all over the issue of Kashmir. The present plight was made the more poignant by the creation of a Pakistani historiography that read back into the past the self-conscious religious identity of the present: found heroes in the military conquerors and proponents of legalist, uneclectic Islam; and generally painted a picture of a glory that was to be reclaimed. The anger channeled against India and the pride in a Muslim state were expressed in the 1965 war, a defeat both to the hopes of seizing Kashmir and to the belief in military might.

The religious style espoused by the state lacked coherence and popular support. The treatment of Islam by the elite had two significant elements. One was its modernist orientation; the other, more implicit, was its contempt for regional expressions of Islam, a corollary of its economic and governmental policies. The influence of the religious leadership in these formulations and on the government in general was always peripheral. Its strength was felt in the Punjab disturbances of 1953, an outburst of the always simmering antagonism felt toward the highly cohesive and upwardly mobile sect of the Ahmadiyyah. But the involvement of the ʿulama on that occasion and the subsequent judgment of the commission of inquiry that the religious leadership was ignorant even of its own texts, increased the impatience of the elite with the "traditionalists." Nonetheless the pressure of the *ᶜulama* was sufficient to bring about a statement in the Constitution of 1956 that no laws would be enacted repugnant to Islam as laid down in the Qur'an and *sunnah* and that existing laws would be revised in conformity with Islam. A commission was to be appointed to carry out these provisions. As a constitutional authority dryly noted, "Nothing effective appears to have been accomplished in the exercise of these functions."[17] After the military coup, the new constitution of 1962 continued the repugnancy clause, but deleted the reference to *sunnah,* which was viewed as an effort to introduce modernist reforms and subsequently amended. More significant was the provision that the effective implementation of this principle was assigned to an Advisory Council on Islamic Ideology whose members, appointed by the President, not only were to be scholars of Islam but experts on the "economic, legal and administrative problems of Pakistan."[18] This ensured a modernist interpretation of Islam.

For those of the elite committed to a Western-style state and technological advancement, religion was to be modern too. True Islam was understood primarily as personal piety; when it intruded on socioeconomic issues, it did so in conformity with Western standards of practice and interpretation. One of the most distinguished advisors to the government, Professor Fazlur Rahman, in retrospect, suggests Ayub Khan's instrumental motive for even addressing the Islamic aspects of his policies: that without attention to Islam "it might become difficult for East Pakistan and West Pakistan to stay together, for apart from their attachment to Islam, linguistically and culturally the two wings had little in common. As time went on Ayub Khan became more and more convinced of the importance of Islam as the basis of the Pakistani nationhood."[19] In the end the style of Islam espoused was to be more disruptive than unitive.

The interpretations offered by the advisors to the government represented a jurisprudential position that had its roots in nineteenth-century reform, one that was confirmed by the scholarship of some Western orientalists. It denied the validity of the recorded sayings of the Prophet, a major source for the historic interpretations of the Law, and even questioned the eternity of the legal injunctions of the Qur'an. Perhaps the issue best known of those they considered was that relating to family law, for in acts passed in 1961 Pakistan moved decisively outside what were considered the legal injunctions of Islam on issues related to polygamy, divorce, and the inheritance of orphaned grandchildren. A related, equally inflammatory attempt to argue the sanction of Islam for family planning was meant to bolster the foreign aid projects of USAID and UNICEF (whose offices, moreover, were to be a focus for political support for the regime).

As well as these attempts to define the content of Islam, certain acts of the government specifically threatened the financial base of the religious leadership. Notable were central government efforts to control pious endowments and the canonical tithe, a sum of money estimated at one point to be potentially twice the income of central government revenues. The center moreover took over such duties as the sighting of the ʿId moon, trading romance and tradition for the scientific accuracy of the Meteorological Department.

Fazlur Rahman himself, again looking back, speculated that the attempt to interpret Islam "in rational and scientific terms to meet the requirements of a modern progressive society," had three possible effects: the desired one of increasing the interest of the educated in serious attention to Islamic issues, or the effect of driving the educated to secularism and strengthening the "traditionalists."[20] It was to be the latter two that happened. A later scholar has judged that the advisors lost all credibility because of their failure to address the principles of the whole system of Islam in favor of piecemeal change based on jurisprudential radicalism, an approach which made them seem only opportunist, the tool of the ruling elite.[21]

The second element in the particular kind of Islam fostered by the regime was its rejection of regional forms of Islam. Both

Khalid bin Sayeed and Nasim Jawed have argued in analyses of the separation of Bangladesh that the modernist Islam of the regime was much closer to the scripturalist and legalist Islam current in some circles in the West than to the Islam of Bengal.[22] Bengal, with a population almost one-fourth Hindu, and with a tradition of openness to Bengali literature and folkways, was deemed religiously suspect. This view of Bengali Islam was shared, in fact, not only by the elite but by the organization that most consistently opposed the Islam of the ruling class, the Jama'at-i Islami led by Maulana Abu'l Ala Maududi, a proponent of pervasive Islamicization on the basis of the historically evolved schools of law.

Besides Islam, the elite attempted to make certain other symbols a focus of national loyalty. Their consistent policy was to downplay the importance of the regional cultures in favor of central symbols, a policy which in retrospect could only bring opposition in such an ethnically and culturally diverse population. Pride of place was given to the elite culture of the North, a culture expressed above all in Urdu and embodied in poetry, art, music, and dance. This not only clashed with the regional languages, which had their own traditions, but also, one might note, at least in part with the puritanic values of the "traditionalists."

Urdu, from the late nineteenth century on, had become the symbol par excellence of Muslim communal interests in North India and fears for its place as a government language and language of education were one of the motivating forces for opposition to Congress politics. Used as an official provincial language by the British, it had undergone a literary flowering in new genres of both prose and poetry. It had, moreover, become a major vehicle for disseminating Islamic religious values, especially the tenets of a more informed Islam, as part of the reform movements of the modern period. Knowledge of Urdu defined one as a person worthy of respect, and cultivation of that form of the common language, written in Perso-Arabic script and including large numbers of Persian and Arabic loan words, increasingly defined one as a Muslim, one apart from those who used Hindi written in Devanagari. The importance of language as a symbol of group identity perhaps transcends all others.

To adopt Urdu as the national language seemed only logical. It was the mother tongue of the *muhajir* who had fled from North India and settled in cities, especially the cities in Sind, which underwent a demographic revolution as their majorities became Urdu-speaking.[23] It had as well the most developed tradition of use as a language of government and education. Not only the first language of the migrants, it was the second language of elite groups throughout the new country, among them the upper class, or *ashraf*, of Bengal. Many had attended elite institutions, in what is now India, places like Aligarh University and the theological academy at Deoband, and had mastered standard Urdu. Ayub Khan himself, from the North West Frontier, described his own experience as a student at Aligarh, sensitive about his rough speech but soon master of a more refined diction. Such hard-won accomplishment seemed the more valued.

Decisive in the relative success of Urdu as the national language was its position in Punjab, which was not only the dominant province in the West, comprising about two-thirds of the population, but, as study after study has shown, the region that controlled both the civil service and the army. Urdu had long been the language of education for all communities in the Punjab. Punjab had, moreover, its own tradition of Urdu literature, capped by the triumphs of Iqbal. Urdu was closer to Punajbi than to any other regional language, both in grammar and in a heavily overlapping vocabulary. It was already effectively the second language of most of the province.[24]

Not surprisingly, language proved to be a major source of tension both between the two wings and within the West. Before the first decade was over, Bengali language riots had at least on paper, assured equal status for Bengali as a national language. Bengali was one of the most developed languages of the subcontinent, with a distinguished literary tradition of its own. That the giants of that tradition were entirely Hindu—

and valued nonetheless by Muslim Bengalis—did not make this concession, as it was seen, the more palatable. Despite the accommodation, a legacy of bitterness remained.

The same problem of linguistic self-assertion was evident in the West. In Sind, for example, which had never had the tradition of Urdu as a second language, the new place of Urdu was particularly charged, because it was associated with the now economically dominant new settlers, whose role aroused predictable antagonism. Movements for Sindi provincial autonomy, focussed on the place of language, grew as the '60s progressed. In the Frontier and Baluchistan the opposition to the domination of the center was potentially more far-reaching than mere demands for language reform, since both had a tradition of looking to their ethnic fellows across the Afghan border and of threatening wholesale separatism. Even in Punjab there were cultural movements in Lahore and elsewhere as early as the '50s. Held in check by martial law, they again became prominent in the '70s. In all the provinces proponents of the local language fostered its use by politicians, patronage to literary circles, increased publication and demands for television broadcasting.

From 1967 civil unrest in Pakistan grew. Every symbol of the regime was called into question. The economic changes of the development policy led to a sense of gross socioeconomic injustice on the part of industrial workers and others who felt excluded from adequate returns. Those who had profited, including urban professionals and rural smallholders caught up in the green revolution, felt excluded from the political process. Antagonism to India continued virulent, but Pakistani aims appeared thwarted by military failure in the 1965 war and diplomatic failure at Tashkent. The religious policy of the regime was wholly discredited. Indeed, all discontent was focussed, as so often happens, on religious symbols; it was the religious leadership who became the focus for protest in urban areas. The Islamic policies in general and the writings and decisions of Fazlur Rahman in particular were major targets. In Bengal the continued insults to cultural self-esteem and the ever-worsening economic disparities led to increased demands for autonomy.

The elections of 1970 saw the decisive victory of Bhutto's Pakistan People's Party in the West and Shaikh Mujibu'r-Rahman's Awami League in the East. The failure to grant Mujib the premiership he had won and to accommodate the six demands for provincial autonomy he requested resulted in the tragic civil war and the end of Pakistan as it had existed. The subsequent decade was one of substantial change in Pakistan, and, not surprisingly, of a dramatic reordering of national symbols.

The PPP, which controlled the government until 1977, was led by a cosmopolitan, personally secular figure, and focussed on anti-Indian sentiments and a radical socialist rhetoric. Against India, Bhutto swore a war of a thousand years. Against the propertied and wealthy, he promised a redistribution of economic goods for the common man. Significantly, the party aligned itself with a group led by Hanif Ramay, who called themselves Islamic Socialists; the rhetoric of the party was wholly Islamic. The symbol the party chose summed up the elements of its platform. It was the carved sword or scimitar of ʿAli, the heroic grandson of the Prophet, and hence pointed simultaneously to the party's leader, who was felicitously named Zu'l-faqar. This means literally "the cleaver of the vertebrae," the name of the sword of a slain unbeliever that passed to Muhammad and thence to ʿAli. It was thus held to be the sword of victory over one's foe and, in the hands of ʿAli, the sword of social justice.[25]

Bhutto rejected the foreign policy of his predecessors, turning dramatically away from Pakistan's long alignment with the United States and calling for bilateral rather than bloc agreements. He established close relations with China and at the same time, aided by the new-felt power of the oil producers in the early '70s, sought to ally himself with the Muslim states of the Middle East. The web of substantial relationships with Middle Eastern countries grew, with Pakistan seeing itself as a potential source of sophisticated technical training for overseas

students and, at the same time, as a seemingly bottomless res-
ervoir of unskilled manpower for the wealthy oil states. Never
losing its self-image as a military fortress, it called itself the
qila^c or fortress, the Eastern outpost of Islam. The highpoint
of Bhutto's turning toward the Middle East came in the Islamic Summit Conference held in Lahore in 1974, when the
attention of the population was riveted on the presence of such
figures as King Faisal, Colonel Qaddafi, and Idi Amin. A review of Pakistan's relations with the Islamic States, published
in 1977, insisted that these links were the true orientation of
Pakistan, the legacy of Indian Muslim involvement in the Khi-
lafat movement. Pakistan had been only temporarily diverted
by the short-sighted policies of a misguided military regime,
which led to such embarrassments as the Pakistani position on
Suez:

After the confusions of the past . . . after the hypocritical separation of the
Islamic loyalty from the Islamic imperatives of justice between people and
regions which was responsible for the disaster of 1971, Pakistan has now
rediscovered its Islamic identity and set its feet firmly on the path ordained
for it by its everlasting faith. The path is that of promoting the brotherhood
of all Muslim peoples and helping to banish divisive prejudices. It is that of
participating with the fellowship of other Muslim countries, in humanity's
struggle toward an equitable world order. During the last five years, Pakistan
has provided proof that it will suffer no deviation from that path.[26]

Bhutto had in fact turned his back on the subcontinent. No
longer was it to be the emotional other against which the country defined itself. At the end of his career, a broken man awaiting execution at the hands of the man who overthrew him,
ironically perhaps yet wisely, he saw the greatest accomplishment of his whole career as nothing other than the agreement
of June 1976—the restoration of diplomatic relations with India.[27]

In keeping with this, the image of Pakistan as homeland and
protector of Muslims was no more. Pakistan was now to be a
Middle Eastern state, its attention toward its West and not its
East. One important expression of this new orientation was the
attempt to emphasize the regional continuity of Pakistan. As

expressed by the distinguished archaeologist Professor A.H. Dani, it took the form of identifying a continuing Indus civilization from a Gangetic pattern. The former was the "life-blood of Pakistan," the latter, "the fountainhead of Hinduism."

Punjabi and Sindhi are part of the Indus system as also are Pashtu and Baluchi [i.e. the four provincial languages]. Hence all the symbols—whether language, music, dance, decorations, arts and crafts, clothes or dress, pottery and food habits, behavior patterns, etc.—associated with them belong to Pakistan. . . . Islam has imbibed the ethno-cultural elements of this land.[28]

Gone were the emphasis on a separate political identity of Muslims throughout Indian history, the attempts of the majority to deny Muslims their culture, and the need for a separate homeland; in its place was the acceptance of a territorially defined nationality. Dani's interpretation is the more significant as an attempt to argue a fundamental union and coherence to what remained of Pakistan, itself internally divided by ethnic loyalties. Regional tensions in fact increased as Bhutto continued the policy of extreme centralization.

For both economic and political reasons Bhutto sought to eliminate all intermediaries between the central government and the people—provincial authorities, tribal chiefs, landlords, powerful industrialists, *sufi pirs*. The so-called twenty-two families were to be broken up. Government moved to take over the cotton, insurance, banking, and rice industries. Land reforms were passed in 1972 and 1976 to make real the election slogan, "land to the tillers." The powerful shrines—in a coupling of scripturalist reform and political interest—were to be controlled by government officials and the potentially charismatic scions of the saintly families were to be mere caretakers.[29] The ideals of the party soon gave way to deals with bureaucrats, landlords, and the old industrial elite. The result was the same: economic grievances, now fueled by inflation, public protests, and virtual civil war in the provinces, this time in Baluchistan.

The military coup of Zia'u'l-Haqq on July 5, 1977 was seen as an attempt to restore law and order and, increasingly, as the vanguard of an even more self-consciously Muslim state. Supported by the Jama^{c}at, Zia moved simultaneously to bolster his own position and to implement certain Islamic measures: criminal penalties, special court benches to review very limited segments of law, and government collection of the tithe.[30] As before, Islam is now the ideology of vested economic and political interests. It continues to impose a narrow definition of Islam, this time fundamentalist. Pressure in this direction was evident even before the coup in the anti-Ahmadiyyah riots of 1974, which were followed by an unprecedented act in Muslim history: a government declared a sect to be un-Muslim. Its narrowness is evident today. Newspapers report civil protests by what appears to be a growing Shi^{c}ah population against measures they deem acceptable only to Sunni Islam.[31] The Islamic symbols of the regime, while clearly salient to those associated with and sympathetic to the Jama^{c}at, will have little appeal to the sectarian minorities or to those, whether motivated by Islam or by secular ideologies, who are committed to a humane reordering of society. Other symbols of national identity appear to be anti-Americanism, evident in the seizure of the embassy in Islamabad in November 1979, and a decreased role for English as a medium of elite education, coupled with a concern for economic and military power of their own epitomized in the development of a controversial nuclear reactor.

One is tempted to argue that the short history of Pakistan has seen an increasing convergence of "religious myth and nationalism," but such a conclusion is probably unwarranted. There has not been a "rebirth" of Islam in Pakistan. A passionate attachment to a Muslim identity has been the constant in Pakistan's self-image and in the rhetoric of its politicians. The content given that identity has shifted, particularly in its "charged story," moving from one that emphasized its subcontinental role as a homeland for the persecuted to one that stresses its geographic place with other Muslim states. At the same time, the interpretation of Islam fostered by the state has changed from one that sought to be "rational and scientific" to one that stresses adherence to what can, cynically but legitimately, be called the cosmetic and highly visible symbols of

Islam—e.g., certain public punishments and the prohibition of alcohol. Only fleetingly have there been spokesmen for radical Islam who have challenged vested interests and the status quo. The changes in the symbols of national unity are related above all to shifting international currents. In the first phase, the rivalry of the Americans and the Soviets in the subcontinent led Pakistan to throw in its lot with the Americans, politically, economically, and even ideologically. In the second phase, after Bangladesh, the hegemony of India in the subcontinent led Pakistan to turn away from it as a focus of political activity, and to forge ties to the newly assertive countries of the Middle East. Nationalist symbols have not evolved autonomously. Throughout this, the most central of these symbols for most Pakistanis has been Muslim identity, whether defined primarily as a push away from India or a pull toward the countries of the Middle East. That that symbol is sufficient to sustain Pakistan as it is currently structured is a matter of considerable doubt. Judging from the past, one might argue that de-emphasis on a highly centralized state and its symbols would in fact contribute to the state's coherence. One might further venture that the territorial emphasis (rather than an emphasis on a Muslim homeland) is a promising one, particularly if it leads to an appreciation of Pakistani ties to and common interests with India.

Pakistan, a new nation, has borne the heavy burden of a troubled origin, an intractable ethnic and geographic diversity, and a vulnerable international position, both politically and economically. Its nationalist symbols have often proven incapable of sustaining the loyalty of its people. Its very survival, however, and that it does now have a past and some ideological ferment, do mean that Pakistanis continue to hope that their potential—for it was that and not any existing condition that justified their nation's creation—may yet be realized.

NOTES

1. Ninian Smart, "Religion, Myth, and Nationalism," in this volume.
2. See Yohanan Friedmann, "The Attitude of the Jam‘iyyat-i ‘Ulama’-i

Hind to the Indian National Movement and the Establishment of Pakistan," in Gabriel Baer, ed., *The ʿUlamaʾ in Modern History* (Jerusalem, 1971), pp. 157–183.

3. Leonard Binder, "Prospects for Pakistan" (University of Chicago, Muslim Studies Sub-committee Occasional Paper Series, 1972), p. 14.

4. For an excellent account of this history see P. Hardy, *The Muslims of British India* (Cambridge, 1972).

5. Reprinted in *Pakistan Economist,* February 16–22, 1974, pp. 1–7.

6. K.B. Sayeed, "The Breakdown of Pakistan's Political System" (paper delivered at the University of Toronto, May, 1972), p. 3.

7. P. Jones, "Islam and Politics under Ayub and Bhutto: A Comparative Assessment" (paper delivered at the Seventh Wisconsin Conference on South Asia, n.d.) pp. 5–6.

8. Lawrence Ziring, "The Phases of Pakistan's Political History," in C.M. Naim, ed., *Iqbal, Jinnah and Pakistan: The Vision and the Reality* (Syracuse, 1979), p. 147.

9. Choudhary Rahmat Ali, *Pakistan: The Fatherland of the Pak Nation* (Cambridge, 1947, 3rd ed.).

10. The initial letters of Punjab, Afghanistan, Kashmir, and Sind, joined to the prefix *stan,* place of. The name also has meaning in that the word *pak* means pure.

11. Edward Said, *Orientalism* (New York, 1978).

12. Gustav F. Papanek, *Pakistan's Development: Social Goals and Private Incentives* (Cambridge, 1967), p. 242.

13. Sayeed, "The Breakdown of Pakistan's Political System," p. 29.

14. Sharif al Mujahid, "The Ideology is Still Supreme," *The Pakistan Times,* March 23, 1974. Emphasis added.

15. Jones, "Islam and Politics under Ayub and Bhutto," p. 9.

16. Quoted in Ralph Russell, "Islam: Culture and Society in Pakistan Today" (unpublished manuscript,) 1967.

17. A. Gledhill, "Dustur," *Encyclopedia of Islam, 2nd edition,* p. 670.

18. Gledhill, "Dustur," p. 672.

19. Fazlur Rahman, "Some Islamic Issues in the Ayyub Khan Era" (University of Chicago, Muslim Studies Sub-committee Occasional Paper Series, 1972), p. 2.

20. Fazlur Rahman, "Some Islamic Issues," pp. 3, 19–20.

21. M. Khalid Masud, "Failure of Islamic Reformism in Pakistan" (unpublished manuscript, 1979).

22. Khalid bin Sayeed, "The Breakdown of Pakistan's Political System;" Nasim A. Jawed, "Nationalism and Islamic Consciousness in Pakistan and Bangladesh" (University of Chicago, Muslim Studies Sub-committee Occasional Paper Series, 1972).

23. The immigrants who were not originally Urdu-speaking and who came to Sind tended to learn Urdu rather than Sindi.

24. See Hafeez Malik, "Problems of Regionalism in Pakistan," in W.H. Wriggins, ed., *Pakistan in Transition* (Islamabad, 1975), pp. 60–132.

25. P. Jones, "Islam and Politics," includes a reproduction of an election poster of the PPP. Bhutto is dressed in a Western suit with a "Jinnah cap" on his head, mounted on a caparisoned, leaping horse, the flag of Pakistan in his hand and a sword and shield by his side. Across the top, under "Zu'l-faqar-i Haidari" is a picture of the sword, the width of the poster, emblazoned with the Qur'anic phrase, "With the help of Allah, victory is near." The dense epigraphy includes the attestation of faith; a quotation from a Bhutto speech promising he will sacrifice his life for the people; Bhutto's titles, "The Pride of Asia," "The Leader of the People;" a prayer to the great Sindi mystic Shahbaz Qalandar that Bhutto live a thousand years; a Punjabi denunciation of imperialism and the Indian foreign minister; and a couplet from Iqbal, "China and Arabia is ours, Hindustan is ours; Every Muslim is our fellow countryman, the whole world is ours."

26. Government of Pakistan, Ministry of Foreign Affairs, *Pakistan's Relations with the Islamic States: A Review,* 21 February 1977, p. 34.

27. Zulfikar Ali Bhutto, *"If I am Assassinated . . ."* (New Delhi, 1979), p. 223.

28. A.H. Dani, letter to the editor, *The Pakistan Times,* June, 1974.

29. Katherine Ewing, "The Pir or Sufi Saint in Pakistani Islam" (Doctoral dissertation, Department of Anthropology, University of Chicago, 1980).

30. Mohammad Zia-ul-Haq, "Introduction of Islamic Laws," address to the Nation, February 10, 1979, published by Government of Pakistan, Ministry of Information and Broadcasting, 1979.

31. An estimate of 25–30 percent appears in Salamat Ali, "Is Time Running out for Zia's Regime?" *Far Eastern Economic Review,* March 30, 1979, p. 17. The Shi'ah protests were reported in *The San Francisco Chronicle,* July 7, 1980.

TEN

Mysticism and Politics in Modern Israel: The Messianic Ideology of Abraham Isaac Ha-Cohen Kook

David J. Biale

Ever since He gave sanction to the Prophet Samuel to establish a monarchy for the Israelites, the Almighty has made it his business to interfere in the political life of his people. This divine nosiness—welcome or not—is believed by the Jews to lie at the heart of both their political triumphs and their unfortunately all-too-numerous disasters. Hence, it is only fitting that a volume on religion and nationalism should include at least one paper on a religious aspect of Jewish nationalism. If the Jews did not invent the intimate affair between religion and nationalism, they have at least kept it persistently alive for as long as anyone else.

This connection between religion and nationalism can be discerned even in those periods when the Jews had no state. The messianic desire to return political sovereignty to the Jews is the authentic pre-modern form of Jewish nationalism. Interestingly enough, one of the strongest impulses behind the great messianic movement of the seventeenth century, Sabbatianism, was not a pragmatic political ideology, but ostensibly other-

worldly mysticism: the Lurianic Kabbalah. This mystical theory—quite different from the passivity we typically associate
with mysticism—argued that man's actions directly effect and
are secular representations of cosmic history. Already by the
seventeenth century, therefore, the connection between mystical religion and this worldly political nationalism was firmly
established.

One might expect that the realization of the messianic dream
in the modern creation of the state of Israel would similarly
wed such ostensibly strange bedfellows. But the surprising fact
about modern Zionism is its thoroughly secular character. Here
is a militantly secular movement spurred on by a revolt against
Jewish religion. Those religious supporters of Zionism—and
they remained a minority of the religious world until after World
War II—assiduously excluded messianic ideas from their Jewish
nationalism. They saw Zionism as, at best, "the faint beginnings of the messianic era" and they conceived of their own
role as defending the interests of a religious minority in a secular movement. Hence, they fought to establish religious schools
and to safeguard the Sabbath. None of these activities—which
were secular in form if religious in content—can be construed
as a real attempt to unite religion with nationalism, or, more
radically, to suggest that Zionism might be the flowering of the
messianic times. If anything, it was the secular Zionists in both
the socialist and right-wing nationalist camps who coopted a
secular brand of messianism into their Zionist ideologies. One
of the greatest problems of the orthodox religious Zionists of
the last generation was to justify their collaboration with these
secular Zionists, whose heresies seemed to pollute any redemptive potential in the return to Zion.

Since the Six Day War of 1967, however, this religious si-
lence has been broken by the rise of a militantly religious group
who combine a nationalistic politics with a coherent messianic
theory. This is the Gush Emunim—or bloc of the faithful—
who have repeatedly set up illegal settlements in the occupied
territories and who, if not a decisive force in Israeli politics,
have become at least a very significant nuisance factor, capable

of complicating the peace negotiations and of provoking heightened Arab hostility toward the Israeli occupation.

In the years following the Six Day War, a new generation of orthodox Jews who "did not know Joseph" grew to maturity. Estranged from the Diaspora origins of their parents, they did not understand the older generation's pragmatic approach to politics. Moreover, they were justifiably disgusted with the corruption of the religious parties, which is second to none in the Israeli political jungle. The Six Day War and the challenge of the new territories represented to them an opportunity to demonstrate their political commitment independent of their parents. Too long scorned by the secular as emaciated "Yeshiva bochers," they could now prove that they were doing as much to fulfill the patriotic tasks of Zionism as their secular counterparts. (Witness, for example, the proud insistence by the orthodox that they absorbed the highest casualties of any group during the Yom Kippur War—surely a macabre way of proving one's involvement in society.) Finally, the young orthodox saw the new, post-war situation as an opportunity to put the corrupt past behind and forge a new, purified national consensus. It is no coincidence that a moral fervor pervades the Gush Emunim: they see themselves as a movement of national moral regeneration.

The vitalizing effect of the Six Day War upon orthodox youth born and raised in the Jewish state was surely connected with the results of the war: for the first time since the state was created, the Biblical land of Israel, and particularly the areas of Judah and Samaria, were in Jewish hands. The Yom Kippur War, since it accentuated pressures on Israel to relinquish the territories, heightened the feeling that the opportunity to settle and annex the land must be seized immediately. It is ironic indeed that the ideal of settlement of the land, so long the province of the socialist Zionists, has been appropriated under new slogans by the nationalist and religious right.

In the case of Gush Emunim, the motivating force behind this annexationist drive is Messianism. In the Ayatollah-like pronouncements of Rabbi Zvi Yehudah Kook, the acknowl-

edged spiritual leader of Gush Emunim (as the head of the
Merkaz ha-Rav yeshiva where most Gush leaders were trained),
we read that Messianic days are upon us. Settlement of all the
historic land of Israel is the right and role of all Jews in the
impending Messianic drama. Because political conditions are
ripe, yet may soon deteriorate, settlement and annexation are
of the utmost urgency. Zvi Yehudah Kook combines shrewd
political realism with urgent Messianism.[1]

As important as Zvi Yehudah Kook's ideas are in the context
of the current political situation, they are surely derivative and
unoriginal. My interest here is to explore the source of these
messianic notions and so to understand the ideological or, shall
we say, theological connection between religion and nationalism in the modern-day Israel. This search leads us from Zvi
Yehudah to a much more original and influential thinker—his
father Abraham Isaac ha-Cohen Kook (1865–1935), one of the
most individualistic of the early Zionist ideologists.[2] As chief
rabbi of Palestine in the 1920s and 1930s, the Rav Kook had a
significant impact on the Zionist settlement during its formative years. Although not strictly associated with the religious
Zionist parties (he was actually one of the organizers of the
non-Zionist Aggudat Yisrael) he influenced the development of
orthodox Zionism. But he also made a great impression on the
non-religious as well. In recent years, quite a legend has grown
up around the Rav Kook. He has been appropriated by some
secular and religious Jews as a paradigmatic "tolerant orthodox
rabbi" who sought to heal the wounds of a divided nation.[3]
Rav Kook argued that secular Zionists do God's dirty work
without knowing it by settling the land; although they do not
perform the *mitzvot,* they do fulfill the one commandment of
settling the land, which, according to the Midrash, is equal to
all the others. This overarching nationalism allowed Rav Kook
to accept all Jews as partners in the national enterprise. Moreover, his Messianic theory contained a universalist component
more amenable to liberal Jews than the palpable chauvinism
of other orthodox thinkers. Finally, as a personality, Rav Kook
was remarkable for his tolerance and moral sensibility.

The legend of the liberal Rav Kook has recently even played a role in the polemics against Gush Emunim. In an article in *Shdemot* (the kibbutz movement quarterly) in winter 1975, Avraham Shapira tries to contrast the Messianic statements of Zvi Yehuda Kook with those of his more illustrious father. Shapira charges that the moral nationalism of Rav Kook has degenerated into an antinomian "Sabbatianism" in the hands of his son.[4]

While by no means denying the positive impact of Rav Kook's personality, I believe that the connection between him and his son is more than genetic. Zvi Yehuda's political ideology can already be found in the writings of the Rav Kook, although without the political urgency and concreteness of the contemporary situation. I do not claim that the Rav Kook would necessarily have spoken as his son if he were alive today (clearly an unhistorical proposition) since his situation before the creation of the state of Israel generated a more abstract approach to political problems. Yet, as one of the few significant orthodox thinkers close to modern Zionism who adopted Messianic language, it should be no surprise that the Rav Kook serves as a source for the new Messianism. In fact, the Gush Emunim people quote him at least as much as do their opponents. I propose to examine briefly some of the Messianic elements in the Rav Kook's writings that could be appropriated by these Messianic radicals today.

I have already mentioned that the Rav Kook's tolerance and universalism are what prove so attractive to the non-orthodox in search of an orthodox model. Perhaps the most ingenious aspect of the Rav Kook's thought is his solution to the classic problem of the religious Jew confronting the Zionist movement: how can this movement be Messianic if its most active elements are secular? The Rav Kook argued against his anti-Zionist orthodox colleagues that there is not only room for the secular in Messianism, but they are, in fact, necessary. Using the medieval categories of form and matter, he writes that "the holy can only be built on the basis of the profane. The profane is the matter of the holy and the holy gives it form."[5] Both play necessary and balanced roles in the world. In the days of the Messiah, however, the profane paradoxically seems to increase. Rav Kook takes this idea from the Talmudic saying that "in the footsteps of the Messiah insolence (*hutzpah*) will increase." In the modern context, insolence clearly means secularism for the Rav Kook. In a striking passage in *Hazon ha-Geula* (*Vision of Redemption*) he compares the role of the secular to that of yeast in wine-making:

Just as it is impossible for wine to be made without yeast, so it is impossible for the world to exist without the wicked. Just as the yeast makes the wine and preserves it, so the crude inclinations of the wicked make possible the existence of all life. When the yeast disappears and the wine stands without it, it spoils and turns sour. The Exile has diluted the power of life of the nation and our yeast has decreased considerably until there is danger that the nation will cease to exist for lack of coarseness, which is rooted in animality, land and materiality. The Exile is a fragmented, diluted existence. . . .

But the demand for survival and the return of Israel to its land for survival is a necessary event; it creates its own yeast, namely the bearers of evil and insolence of the footsteps of the Messiah. And the end of the process will be the precipitation of the yeast to the bottom of the barrel. But while it is still productive and is necessary to go together with the wine, it makes the wine hideous and one's heart revolts at the sight of the fermentation. Only the thought of the future gives one peace and quiet.[6]

It is interesting the degree to which the Rav Kook accepted the secular Zionist analysis of the need for Jewish territoriality. The very problem with the Exile is that it is too spiritual, too holy. While the Rav Kook scarcely uses economic language in his analysis, his belief that Jewish life is physically impossible in Exile is not far from the views of Ber Borochov and other socialist Zionists.[7] Only a material, profane substrate can create the necessary conditions for the "footsteps of the Messiah." Similarly, for Borochov, only Jewish territoriality makes a socialist revolution possible for the Jews as for all other nations. For both, Zionism is an historical inevitability. Although both give man a central and active role in their respective versions of redemption, man's actions are still determined from the outset. The Marxist tension between free will and determinism that is so evident in Borochov's thought can be found equally, if unexpectedly, in Rav Kook's Messianism. Parenthetically, it should be noted against common belief that Jewish Messianism was not always a passive doctrine. A long tradition, best articulated by Moses Maimonides and echoed by religious Zionists in the nineteenth century before Rav Kook, claims that Messianic times will be brought about by Jewish political action and will not necessarily involve miracles. Rav Kook has combined this "realistic" political Messianism with his own brand of utopian, Kabbalistic Messianism.

Rav Kook is prepared to accept the secular as a temporary expedient without which the return to the land would be impossible. From an historical point of view, this theory explains why the days of the Messiah can only come after an age of secularism and assimilation. But, far from genuine toleration of secular Judaism, the Rav Kook's view is Hegelian: God cunningly uses the wicked to further his own plan until they have fulfilled their purpose. At that point, like the yeast in the wine barrel, they will precipitate out of history. Rav Kook believed that national renewal will necessarily eradicate secularism; secular Zionists are fated to return to the orthodox fold once they realize that they are actually fulfilling God's commandment in settling the land. This idea is the ideological basis for the remarkable openness of the Gush Emunim towards the secular community.

The notion of God's cunning use of the wicked goes back in the Jewish tradition to Maimonides, who saw Christianity and Islam as unwitting "road-pavers" for the King Messiah. The Sabbatians at the end of the seventeenth century were the first to apply the idea to heretical Jews: the final stages of redemption will be accomplished by the paradoxical performance of commandments through the violation of them. This doctrine of the "holiness of sin" was originally developed to explain why the Messiah, Sabbatai Zvi, had to apostasize to Islam.

It is striking how close the Rav Kook's ideas come to certain Sabbatian theories. Behind the above metaphor of the yeast we find a curious and radical Kabbalistic doctrine. While the Kabbala traditionally argued that the *klipot* (shells of evil materiality) are only maintained by the divine sparks trapped within them, the Rav Kook claims quite the opposite: the divine only exists in history by virtue of the profane and, indeed, can only be redeemed after the profane has strengthened itself. This doctrine closely resembles the Sabbatian argument that the Messiah's soul is part of the *klipot* themselves and he must apostasize in order to redeem it.

Our suspicion is further strengthened by another metaphor the Rav Kook uses for the renewal of Israel, namely that of the seed which must rot in the ground before it can sprout and flourish: "and this rotting of the seed is analogous to what the divine light does in planting anew the vineyard in Israel in which the old values are forced to be renewed by the insolence which comes in the footsteps of the Messiah."[8] This image was one of the more popular among the eighteenth-century Sabbatians to explain the dialectical process of redemption. It is unlikely indeed that the Rav Kook would have been ignorant of this fact, especially since the metaphor is quoted in an anti-Sabbatian tract probably well known to a scholar of his stature.[9] I do not mean to portray the Rav Kook as a latter-day Sabbatian, but rather to suggest that in order to justify the role of the secular within a religious framework, he came, perhaps even consciously, to similar doctrines.

Far from advocating like the radical Sabbatians that orthodox Jews break the law in order to bring redemption, he took an uncompromising position against backsliding within the orthodox world itself. For instance, in one of his responsa, he denounced orthodox Jews who followed the Reform movement in abolishing the *meḥiza* (the partition in synagogues between men and women), castigating them as "withered limbs of the nation."[10] If called upon, he could match unbridled language with the best of the orthodox rabbinate. The Rav Kook was particularly concerned with preserving orthodoxy in synagogues since in this time, the days of the Messiah, the synagogue should approximate as closely as possible the Temple which will soon be rebuilt. As if to underscore this belief, he sponsored study of the laws of sacrifice in his yeshiva.

The Rav Kook was then willing to allow heresies among the secular as part of God's plan of redemption, but he insisted that an orthodox elite retain leadership in order to prevent materiality from entirely overpowering spirituality. There is a division of labor and a hierarchy in the Jewish world. The secular perform the function of settling the land and are superior to the orthodox with respect to the "animal soul" (*nefesh*). The orthodox provide spiritual leadership and are superior to the secular with respect to the "spiritual soul" (*ruach*).

What of the non-Jewish world and its relation to the Messianic enterprise? Rav Kook's defenders have emphasized his universalism against the narrow particularism of contemporary Messianists. Again, we find that his universalism is of a very special sort. In one of his essays, he asks whether Israel is the same as the rest of the nations except for an added increment of holiness, or if it is a different kind of people altogether. Originally, he argues, God wished merely to give Israel an added measure of holiness. But, man had so degenerated that God had to purge the Jews of their profane humanity during the exile in Egypt and create a new creature, "Israelite from head to toe."[11] In another passage, he claims that it is not through being chosen by God that Israel gained its divine nature, but through "its racial character, physical and spiritual, which it did not take from chosenness nor can any corruption of chosenness eradicate it."[12] One wonders how some Jews could become secular heretics if Israel's holiness is inherited. The answer may be that since the secular fulfill a necessary role in modern Jewish history, their heresy is only apparent; once their Messianic task is finished, they will revert to their true "holy" nature.

Such a "racial" concept of the Jewish people is not a mainstream tradition in Jewish history. Judaism, after all, is a religion which welcomes converts and was even, for a period of time during the Roman Empire, actively proselytizing. But

ideas such as Rav Kook's have emerged from time to time,
particularly in Kabbalistic doctrines. In the Middle Ages, it
was Judah ha-Levi who gave them full articulation in his *Ku-
zari:* Jews inherit a certain prophetic soul that cannot be ob-
tained by non-Jews even if they convert to Judaism.

Like Judah ha-Levi, Rav Kook also believes that the land of
Israel possesses a special, intrinsic holiness parallel to the holiness of the Jewish people. Because of the uniqueness of the
land of Israel, Israel's nationalism is necessarily superior to all
other nationalisms. There are, to be sure, righteous and wise
individuals among the nations, but as a collectivity, only Israel
possesses a divine soul. However—and here is where Rav Kook
advocates universalism—through Israel's nationalism, all other
nationalisms will derive holiness:

> The nations are beginning to recognize that the basis of salvation will only
> be the holy value which carries the standard of God. The desire of Israel to
> be the living spirit of national renewal will give life to every national move-
> ment. And they will be redeemed forever through the redemption of the holy
> nation. [13]

Rav Kook and his followers believe that only when the Arabs
recognize the divine right of the Jews to their land will they
understand why Jewish nationalism also benefits their own nationalism. This belief is the theological counterpart to the secular Zionist conviction that the Arabs will learn modern politics and economic methods from the Zionists and will then
recognize Zionism out of gratitude.

We have seen that Rav Kook's tolerance and universalism
were direct products of his radical Messianism. Both secular
Jews and the non-Jewish nations play a positive and tolerated
role in God's plan for redemption of the world. But the Rav
Kook's belief in the superiority of the orthodox and the biological holiness of the Jewish people are far indeed from the liberal politics of many of his proponents. Without the eschatological dimension, the liberal Rav Kook is perhaps more
convincing. But given his goal of an orthodox holy Israel leading the nations in the end of days, his tolerance and universalism assume different meanings.

The Messianists from Gush Emunim have rightly found a spiritual grandfather (if Zvi Yehudah Kook is their spiritual father) in the Rav Kook. Their moralistic emphasis on the unity of the Jewish nation, regardless of religious conviction, is the modern version of his tolerance of the secular. The insistence on settlement of the land as the primary commandment (hence their campaign of illegal settlements which has become their trademark) is borrowed directly from his doctrine of the holiness of the land and the importance of settling it as the precondition for the coming of the Messiah. Finally, Gush Emunim's blithe neglect of the Arabs in the occupied territories is not the result of moral callousness (as is no doubt the case with the right-wing secular nationalists) but of the peculiar optimistic universalism of the Rav Kook. There is no doubt that the leaders of Gush Emunim believe that if Jews settle throughout the land of Israel, the groundwork will be laid for the Messianic peace with Israel's Arab neighbors.[14]

It is curious indeed that a religious thinker like the Rav Kook could become a model for two irreconcilably opposing positions. Both liberals and nationalist messianists use his thought as a source for ideologies to unite the Jewish nation. But such is frequently the fate of a suggestive thinker, and particularly a dialectical thinker (Hegel himself was blessed with spiritual sons on his right and on his left). It is a measure also of the great confusion in Jewish nationalism over the precise role of religion and religious identity in the modern state of Israel. If nationalism itself is a potent brew, the addition of mystical religion may indeed prove intoxicating and even fatal.

NOTES

1. Some of the early writings of Zvi Yehudah Kook have been collected in *Le-nitivot Yisrael* (Jerusalem, 1967). For a more recent statement, see, for example, *Maariv,* 7 May 1976.

2. Biographical information on the Rav Kook is available in the *Encyclopedia Judaica,* vol. 10, cols. 1182–1187. See also I. Epstein, *Abraham Yitzhak Hocohen Kook: His Life and Times* (1951).

3. The most important expression of the "liberal" view of the Rav Kook

is in Zvi Yaron, *Mishnato shel ha-Rav Kook* (Jerusalem, 1974). Yaron, a liberal religious Zionist, sets out the major elements of the Rav Kook's thought. This essay is in large measure an argument against Yaron's interpretation of the Rav Kook and an attempt to understand how his thought could be at least as attractive to the messianic right. For a similar view of the Rav Kook as Yaron's, see J. B. Agus, *High Priest of Rebirth: The Life, Times and Thought of Abraham Isaac Kuk* (2nd ed., New York, 1972).

4. *Shdemot* 56 (Winter, 1975), pp. 142–145.

5. *Orot ha-Kodesh* (3 vols. Jerusalem, 1963–64), vol. 1, p. 145.

6. *Hazon ha-Geulah* (Jerusalem, 1941), pp. 140–1.

7. See Ber Borochov, *Nationalism and Class Struggle* (New York, 1935).

8. *Orot ha-Kodesh,* vol. 1, p. 152.

9. The metaphor appears in *Leḥishat* (1726), vol. 2. See Gershom Scholem, *The Messianic Idea in Judaism* (New York, 1971), pp. 116 and 349, n. 34.

10. *Ha-maḥshavah ha-Yisraelit* (Jerusalem, 1967) responsum from 1923.

11. *Perakim be-mishnato ha-iyunit shel ha-Rav Kook* (Jerusalem, 1965), pp. 15–16.

12. *Shevet ha-Aretz* (Jerusalem, 1965), p. 7.

13. *Ḥazon ha-Geulah,* p. 315.

14. This theme recurs frequently in the pronouncements of the leaders of Gush Emunim. See for example, the statement in Mosh Kohn, *Who's Afraid of Gush Emunim* (Jerusalem, 1975), p. 17: "I think that we have to close the options by massive settlement in the areas. When the other side sees this happening, and loses hope of our buckling under to international pressure, they'll start talking to us." Such pragmatic analyses derive from the less political notions expressed by the Rav Kook.

III

OF HUMAN LOYALTY
AND ALIENATION

ELEVEN

The Warrior God, or God, the Divine Warrior

Leonard Greenspoon

In the year 31 B.C. the land of Judea experienced a natural phenomenon with which residents of California are all too familiar—an earthquake. It was of enormous severity, "such as had not been seen before," according to the first-century Jewish historian Josephus, to whom we are indebted for this account (*Antiquities* 15.108–160).[1] Approximately 30,000 people were killed, not to mention the loss of countless head of cattle. At this very time Herod was engaged in a series of battles against Nabataean Arabs, who had temporarily gained the upper hand and then gone so far as to slay Herod's envoys sent to negotiate terms for peace.

According to a lengthy speech that Josephus constructed for Herod, used to encourage his troops prior to the next armed encounter, the Arabs interpreted the earthquake as a sign of God's disfavor, an indication that He had abandoned the Jewish forces in favor of their Arab adversaries and that He was fighting against and not along with His people. By pointing to a peculiar pattern of destruction in the recent earthquake, Herod turned the argument around and "proved" that God did indeed favor Herod's (and the Jews') cause in the soon-to-be-initiated battle: "That He [that is, God] wishes this war to be carried on and knows it to be a just one He Himself has made clear, for though thousands of persons throughout the country were killed by the earthquake, no one in the armed forces suffered any harm, and you were all unhurt. . . . Bearing in mind these things—and what is more important—that you have God as your protector at all times, go out with justice and manliness to attack" the enemy. In the combat that followed, Herod's troops were ultimately victorious.[2]

In effect, so Herod argued, the battles in which his forces were then engaged constituted a Holy War, the successful outcome of which was not to be doubted, even though the army of Judaea would have to undergo real combat and suffer real losses in order to achieve the victory of which they were assured. A phenomenon of nature, in this case an earthquake and its aftermath, provided the key for Herod's interpretation, an interpretation that the success of the Jewish forces vindicated. This was not the first time that Jews had seen God the Warrior at work through natural phenomena, nor were the Hebrews alone in associating the violence of nature with that of warfare.

This incident, raising as it does such questions as divine participation in what seems to be purely human warfare and the role of mortal soldiers in Holy War, presents clearly several of the issues with which we will deal in this paper. Since this event took place in the post-Biblical period, it also invites us to explore the ways in which Biblical concepts were carried over and further developed in communities for whom the Hebrew Bible retained a central place.

My presentation falls into two parts; my role in each is somewhat different as well. In the first part my function is similar to that of a reporter, who on occasion disseminates views of others that otherwise might go unnoticed outside of a relatively small circle of specialists. In this case, we will focus on a mythic pattern that appears to underlie the numerous references to the figure of a Divine Warrior in both Canaanite and Biblical literature, a pattern discernible also in post-Biblical writers such as Josephus. The mythic quality of this pattern should attract the active interest of those engaged in fruitful comparative studies.

In the second part of this presentation I will investigate three specific issues that arose when the concept of God as Divine Warrior, a concept we looked at in the earlier section, was applied to activities and attitudes in the sphere of human history, both Biblical and post-Biblical: (1) the difference between Holy War and other types of combat; (2) the role of human armies in Holy War; (3) the role of the "military hero" in such battles. I have already pointed out how the incident related by Josephus leads to a consideration of the first two issues. This is also true for the third of our questions, for at the end of that narrative Josephus records the following: "And so, thinking himself entitled to take great pride in his successes, Herod returned home, having acquired new prestige from this brave exploit." As we shall see, there are numerous traditions that would converge at this point in characterizing such human "pride" as unseemly at best, blasphemous at worst.

Examples in both sections will be drawn from a wide variety of texts dating from the second millenium B.C. through the third to fourth century A.D.[3]

I

Several generations of Biblical scholars, using a variety of approaches and methodologies, have succeeded in identifying the Biblical theme of God as Divine Warrior, placing this theme within the larger context of Holy Warfare, and drawing parallels between Biblical and Canaanite concepts in this regard. Harvard professor Frank Moore Cross and a number of his students, building on the work of previous and contemporary scholars, have discerned a mythic pattern that underlies both Canaanite and Biblical texts dealing with the figure of the Divine Warrior.[4] This pattern consists of two complementary themes, transmitted for the most part in vivid poetic passages from the two literatures:

Theme A: The march of the Divine Warrior to battle. 1. The divine warrior marches off to war: Driving a fiery cloud-chariot, he uses the elements of nature, such as the thunderbolt and the winds, as weapons against his enemies.

2. At his wrath, nature is in upheaval, with mountains tottering and the heavens collapsing; in effect, all nature wilts and languishes. In the foreground is the cosmogonic myth in which Chaos—represented by the deified Sea Yamm or by the flood-dragon Lothan—is defeated.

Theme B: Return of Divine Warrior to take up kingship. 1. The divine warrior, victorious over his foes, comes to his new temple on his newly won mount.

2. Nature responds to the victorious Divine Warrior. At the sound of his voice all nature awakens. As the mountains dance and the trees clap their hands, the fertility of the earth, of sea, and of womb manifests the rule of the life-sustaining Divine Warrior. (Some of the descriptions may seem a bit overblown, but are supported by the texts themselves, as I will indicate below.)

Having gone directly to a description of this pattern, I need to pull back a bit and put the entire matter in perspective. When I refer to Canaanite material, I have in mind particularly the Ugaritic texts from Ras Shamra, the decipherment of which began almost immediately after their initial discovery in the late 1920s (although it had been possible to recover the basic contours of Canaanite mythology from other sources even prior to these discoveries). In this material it is the god Baal, along with his consort Anat, who is the warrior deity par excellence. Cycles of combat against Prince Yamm and against Mot (i.e., the power of Death) can be reconstructed.

These texts take chronological priority over even the earliest Biblical material, and it is clear enough that various Biblical writers, especially in the earlier and later periods, drew from a common store of language and images, as well the property of creative Canaanite poets, to describe the God of Israel as Divine Warrior. Such use of shared motifs, epithets, and so forth supplied one of the elements within Israelite descriptions of God as Divine Warrior. To put the matter in theological terms: various writers of the Hebrew Bible sought to diffuse the supercharged language of their Canaanite neighbors through the careful appropriation of just such language in their portrayals of God. In this way, they hoped to bring into greater relief the very real differences they felt separated God from a so-called deity with whom He seemed to share a number of attributes and characteristics.

At the center of Israel's statements and beliefs concerning God as Warrior is the conviction that God does indeed reveal Himself through the processes of human history and natural phenomena visible in that history. In the context of this overarching affirmation the Hebrew writers saw God at work also when His people Israel were at war. From this point of view Israel's military history was also a recollection of one aspect of God's activity within the realm of human history, as it bears witness to numerous divine-human encounters. However, the conviction that God was fighting alongside His people, that in effect Israel's wars were God's wars, was not limited to any particular historical period or event and could be expressed as an open-ended hope for divine intervention as well as an interpretation of a contemporary or past event.

I fully agree with statements such as the following, which give appropriate emphasis to the theme of God the Warrior within the Hebrew Bible:

> The conception of God as warrior played a fundamental role in the religious and military experiences of Israel . . . it lies at the theological center. . . . The language and understanding of God as warrior dominated Israel's faith throughout its course.[5]

It has been argued that the divine name YHWH (conventionally vocalized Yahweh) initially formed part of a formula that identified the deity as "He who creates the [heavenly] armies." Unfortunately, I cannot deal here with the development of these themes within the several strata of Biblical material. Suffice it first to point to Exodus 15:3 *yhwh 'yš mlḥmh,* "The Lord is a man of war," as a succinct and unambiguous statement in this regard found in the ancient Song at the Sea, and then to turn to examples of each element from the above pattern in the Ugaritic and the Biblical material.

Canaanite (Ugaritic) passages in illustration of a mythic pattern for the Divine Warrior[6] As Baal marches off to fight Yamm his first adversary, Kothar, the divine craftsman and one of Baal's principal supporters, foresees the warrior's eventual victory:

Behold, thy enemy, O Baal,
Behold, thy enemy thou shalt smite—
Behold, thou shalt smite thy foes.

His arsenal of weapons, drawn from among natural phenomena associated with the storm, is awesome:

Seven lightning bolts he casts,
Eight magazines of thunder;
He brandishes a spear of lightning.

His voice produces earth-shattering, one might even say cosmos-shattering, results:

Baal gives forth his holy voice,
Baal repeats the utterance of his lips,
His holy voice shatters the earth.

At his roar the mountains quake,
the high places of the earth shake.

Succinctly expressed elsewhere:

Then the heavens withered and drooped
Like the loops of your garment.

As Kothar had predicted, Baal was able to overcome the untamed, chaotic force of Yamm, the Sea:

Sea fell,
His joints trembled,
Baal destroyed,
He finished off Judge River.

He sank to earth,
His frame collapsed.
Drank Sea!

Victory over death (Mot) is credited to Baal's consort Anat in the following passage:

She seized El's son Mot.
With a sword she sliced him;
With a sieve she winnowed him;
With a fire she burnt him;
With millstones she ground him.

Victory brings to Baal kingship and installation in his grand temple, which is situated on Mt. Ṣapōn:

My temple [Baal proclaims] I have built of silver.
My palace, indeed, of gold . . .

Behold, Mighty Baal lives;
Behold, the Prince, lord of earth exists.

Baal sits enthroned, his mountain like a dais,
Haddu the shepherd, like the Flood dragon,
In the midst of his mount, Divine Ṣapōn,
On the mount of his victory.

Baal's victory produces a bounteous overflow of nature's richest gifts, such that:

The heavens are raining oil,
The wadis run with mead.

Biblical passages in illustration of a mythic pattern for the Divine Warrior. We next follow this pattern through some of the Biblical material as well. Points of contact with themes and imagery also visible at Ugarit are frequent. As will be immediately noted, the various passages I juxtapose below, which are taken as particularly vivid examples of the elements of which the mythic pattern is composed, are not from one book or even from a single period. In Israel, as at Ugarit, writers selected from a variety of themes and images just those whose use and development were most meaningful in the author's particular context.[7]

A description of God as Warrior:

There is none like the god of Jeshurun,
Who rides the heavens mightily,
Who gloriously rides the clouds.
He drove out the enemy before you;
Before you he smashed the foe. (Deuteronomy 33:26f as reconstructed)

God and the natural phenomena that serve as part of the Heavenly Hosts, the army through which the Warrior wages war against his foes:

He spread apart the heavens and descended,
A storm cloud under his feet.

He rode a cherub and flew,
He soared on the wings of the wind.

He set darkness round about him,
His pavilion is the raincloud.

Cloud-banks were before him,
Before him his clouds raced by,
Hail and coals of fire.

He shot forth his arrows and scattered them,
Lightning-bolts he flashed and put them in panic. (Psalm 18 [2 Samuel 22] 10ff)

Manifestations of the wrath of God:

The god of the Glory thunders,
The voice of Yahweh is on the Waters,
Yahweh is upon the Deep Waters.

The voice of Yahweh is mighty; the voice of Yahweh is majestic.
The voice of Yahweh splinters the cedars;
Yahweh splinters the cedars of Lebanon. (Psalm 29:2ff)

The heavens roll up like a scroll,
And all their hosts languish,
As the vine leaf withers,
as the fig droops. (Isaiah 34:4)

The earth quaked and shook;
The foundations of the mountains shuddered;
They quaked when his wrath waxed hot.

Smoke rose from his nostrils,
And fire from his mouth devoured;
Coals flamed forth from him. (Psalm 18:8f)

God's victory over the chaotic forces of the Sea:

You rule enthroned on the back of Sea.
When his waves rise you calm them.

You crushed Rahab as a corpse,
With your mighty arm you despatched your enemy . . . (Psalm 89:10f)

Was it not you who smote through Rahab?
Who pierced Tannîn [the dragon]?

Was it not you who dried up Sea,
The waters of the abysmal Deep? (Isaiah 51:9f)

God's kingship and installation:

In his temple his Glory appears!
Yahweh sits enthroned on the Flooddragon;
Yahweh is enthroned, king forever. (Psalm 29:10)

You brought them, you planted them
In the mount of your heritage,
The dais of your throne
Which you made, Yahweh,
The sanctuary, Yahweh,
Which your hands created. (Exodus 15:17)

Vivid descriptions of nature's joyous reawakening at God's victory:

The desert and the steppe shall laugh,
The wilderness shall rejoice and blossom;
Like the crocus it shall burst into bloom,
And shall rejoice, yea, rejoicing and singing. . . .

Indeed waters shall break out in the desert,
And streams in the wilderness.

And glaring desert shall become a swamp,
Parched earth springs of water.

The abode of jackals shall become a pasturage.
Open land [turn into] reeds and papyrus. (Isaiah 35:1–2, 6b f)

Fall down before Yahweh who appears in holiness!

He makes Lebanon dance like a bullcalf,
Sirion like a young buffalo. . . .

The voice of Yahweh makes the deserts writhe;
Yahweh makes the Holy Desert to writhe;
Yahweh makes the hinds to writhe [that is, calve]. (Psalm 29:2, 6, 8)

The Biblical passages from which I have quoted are not for
the most part tied to any particular historical battle. As we
turn to passages where such a linkage is effected, we move into
an area where questions concerning the role of humans in warfare become relevant. Within the Hebrew Bible itself such wars
were especially to be located in the events which took place
from the Exodus, through the period of wandering in the Wilderness, until the "Conquest" of the Promised Land. These,
from the Biblical perspective, were indeed Holy Wars, in which
God as Divine Warrior fought, as did His hosts, against historical foes inimical at once to Israel and their God; in general,
God is pictured as fighting along with, not instead of, human
armies, but this is an aspect to which we must return later.

Most frequent are descriptions of God's actions on behalf of
His people at the Sea of Reeds. The following example, taken
from Exodus 15 (the Song at the Sea), serves to illustrate how
Biblical poets infused their descriptions with mythic elements
calculated to bring out those implications that, for the believer,
were inherent in the events themselves:

Your right hand, Yahweh,
Shattered the enemy . . .
At the blast of your nostrils
The waters were heaped up.

The swells mounted up as a hill;
The deeps foamed in the heart of the sea . . .
You blew with your breath,
Sea covered them . . .
You stretched out your hand,
The underworld swallowed them.

God's active use of the now-passive waters of the Sea of Reeds demonstrated that as Divine Warrior He had met and conquered the waters of Chaos, which were now reduced to the status of one among many in the divine arsenal of weapons.

In a recitation of history that made up part of a ceremony of covenant renewal described in Joshua 24, we find the following: "Then I brought you to the land of the Amorites . . . and they fought with you, and I gave them into your hand, and you took possession of their land, and I destroyed them before you . . . the men of Jericho fought against you . . . and I gave them into your hand." At Joshua 10:11 "the Lord threw down great stones from heaven" against Israel's (and His) enemies. Lastly, in a decisive battle fought under the leadership of Deborah and Barak, divine aid included the following:

From heaven fought the stars,
From their courses they fought against Sisera. (Judges 5:20).

II

Within the Hebrew Bible there is no attempt at classification of wars with respect to their degree of holiness or unholiness. However, from a close reading of the text it is apparent that not all wars fought by Israel were identical in every respect, even if we include only those which resulted in a Hebrew victory. In Deuteronomy 20, for example, a distinction is drawn according to the identity of the foe. With respect to the seven nations that occupied Canaan before its conquest, a Hebrew victory was to result in their complete destruction: "in the cities of these peoples that the Lord your God gives you for an inheritance, you shall save alive nothing that breathes, but you shall utterly destroy them . . . that they may not teach you to do according to all their abominable practices which they have done in the service of their gods, and so to sin against the Lord your God." Total destruction is also ordained against the Amalekites, a desert tribe that had been the first outside power to attack the Hebrews after their escape from Egypt (see Exodus 17): "You shall blot out the remembrance of Amalek from under heaven; you shall not forget" (Deuteronomy 25).[8]

In this regard it is instructive to recall that according to a tradition recorded in 1 Samuel 15, God's rejection of Israel's first human king Saul was linked to that monarch's sparing of an Amalekite ruler and the best of his flocks. Although Saul had his reasons, seemingly good ones at that, nothing could change the fact that he had breached the code of Holy War by substituting his own determination of what should be done for God's. We might also note that Haman, the archvillain in the book of Esther, is described as an Agagite, i.e., a descendant of King Agag, whom Saul had temporarily spared in the story just related from 1 Samuel 15.

To return to Deuteronomy 20, with respect to other nations with whom the Hebrews came into hostile contact, their spurning of Israel's overtures of peace (which could be coupled with harsh demands) would result, after their defeat, in the total destruction of adult males, but the capture and subsequent division of all else.[9] Within the literature produced and preserved by the rabbis, there is recorded considerable debate on many aspects of warfare. On the basis of their understanding of the relevant passages from Deuteronomy and elsewhere in the Hebrew Bible, certain of the rabbis devised a widely accepted distinction between obligatory wars, which adhered closely to what we have called Holy War, and option wars, which may be judged necessary in historical or even theological terms, but which nevertheless were not the results of God's express command. As we shall note in a later section, rather broad categories of exclusion were envisioned for optional wars, but for those of obligation "all go forth, even a bridegroom from his chamber and a bride from her canopy" (soṭah 44b).[10] As defined in a succinct manner by Maimonides, obligatory wars, which he termed "wars for a religious cause," included (1) the war against the seven nations; (2) that against Amalek; and (3) a war to deliver Israel from the enemy attacking it (for the last no particular Biblical passage is cited for support). Maimonides termed "optional" "a war against neighboring nations to extend the borders of Israel and to enhance his [i.e., the king's] greatness and prestige."[11]

A dispute over the classification of wars according to type did arise in connection with one category of conflict—what we would call "preventive" war: "Opinion was not divided except in the case of warring with enemies for fear that they would attack, or if they knew they were preparing to attack."[12] Rabbi Judah, who is cited by name, considered them obligatory, but the majority opinion—this is delivered anonymously in the Talmud—is that such wars are optional. By thus depriving what we call preventive, first-strike wars of the status obligatory, these Rabbinic sages, in the words of one modern commentator, "interpret 'defense' strictly, as repelling an active assault, [and] consider military action initiated by Israel to be only an Optional War."[13]

Let us return for a moment to the category of "voluntary war" and look briefly at this Talmudic statement (Soṭah 44b): "the wars waged by the House of David for territorial expansion were voluntary in the opinion of all." All voluntary/ optional wars were not condemned, but they were clearly placed in a different—and inferior—category to those of the Conquest. In this connection, we should note that within the Hebrew Bible prophetic opposition to such wars was not usually a condemnation of war per se, but rather an attack against the presumption of kings, whose efforts to obligate all to take part in combat resulted in enormous social unrest of the type that lost for the house of David control over a united people. In the earlier wars of the Conquest, such extensive internal turmoil is not recorded, and from this perspective the prophets declared that henceforth God would war not alongside His people, but against those very Hebrew leaders who sought to twist the ideology of holy warfare to their own advantage.

In the *War Scroll,* the Essene-like community at Qumran envisioned its obligatory war, of a distinctly holy nature, against the following foes: an alliance of Edom, Moab, Ammon, and Philistia, led by the Kittim of Asshur. Joined to these will be a group of "offenders against the Covenant," which effectively included all nonsectarian Jews. Other foes against whom the Sons of Light (i.e., the members of the Dead Sea community) must war are the "Kittim who dwell in Egypt" and "the kings of the north." We will look at this scroll again in the following section.[14]

I might summarize the material discussed in this section by stating that within the Hebrew Bible there are passages pointing to the recognition of various strata of war, many of which are codified in the Rabbinic material in terms of obligatory vs. optional. Actually, we should also speak of a third type of war, wherein God along with His Heavenly Hosts fought the primordial forces of Chaos. Aspects of such combat, which figured prominently in the Biblical passages cited in the first part of this paper, were in certain periods and among certain groups projected into eschatological warfare, a topic which I have been unable to treat in more than a cursory fashion within the confines of this paper.

The topics to which we now turn all relate to the following issue: the extent and nature of the participation expected of Israel in the various types of combat it did or might undergo against adversaries within the context of human history. Let us reverse the previous procedure and look first at the Rabbinic material, through which we gain some sense of the substance and character of deliberations aimed at defining the precise meaning of the various grounds for exemption offered at Deuteronomy 20: those who built a new house and did not dedicate it; those who planted a vineyard and not enjoyed its fruit; those who had betrothed a wife and not taken her—were all to go back to their houses, as were those who were "fearful and fainthearted." Each of these terms receives extensive consideration in the Talmud, but one point stands out clearly: they are understood as exemptions for voluntary/optional war only. Nevertheless, since these exemptions are defined in what I judge to be a rather broad (and also fair) manner, I think that we are dealing here with a Rabbinic reaction against the abuses referred to above with respect to wars conducted by the kings of Israel and Judah, if not also abuses from periods closer to the time of the rabbis.

Moreover, strict rules of personal hygiene, as well as ceremonial purity, were to be adhered to both in battle itself and in the war camp, for even in time of war each Israelite was told: "you shall keep yourself from every evil thing" (Deuteronomy 23). The reasons for such regulations are to be discovered in the very nature of this warfare: "the Lord your God is with you . . . the Lord your God is he that goes with you, to fight for you against your enemies, to give you the victory" (Deuteronomy 20); "Because the Lord your God walks in the midst of your camp, to save you and to give up your enemies before you, therefore your camp must be holy, that he may not see anything indecent among you, and turn away from you" (Deuteronomy 23).

Among members of the Dead Sea community, whose legal requirements for participation in warfare were quite similar to those proposed in Rabbinic literature (both took the Biblical text as their starting point), the matter of "purity" for battle was of particular significance. Their settlment at Qumran could be conceived of as an armed encampment, whose residents were purified soldiers who joined willingly with the angels in their midst to fill the battalions that obediently served under the Divine Warrior, God. The author of the *War Scroll* expressed his community's beliefs as follows: "For the Lord is holy, and the king of glory is with us—a people of saints. Mighty men and a host of angels are among those mustered with us, the mighty one of war is in our congregation, and the host of His spirits is with our steps."

Similar beliefs and regulations were also operative in the mid-second century B.C., when Judah Maccabee successfully led his forces against the attacking armies of the Seleucid king Antiochus IV, whose efforts to eradicate Judaism as a distinctive religion had received the enthusiastic support of many Jews themselves. Among our most valuable witnesses to this period are 1 and 2 Maccabees, which generally attribute the victories of their favorite Maccabean leaders to strict adherence to the canons of Holy War and trust in God as Divine Warrior. These documents also contain graphic portrayals of the martial activities of the Heavenly Hosts, such as that found in 2 Maccabees 5: "there appeared golden-clad horsemen charging through the air, in companies fully armed with lances and drawn swords."

As we have seen, Jewish communities did not determine standards of eligibility for military service in a context isolated from their understanding of the nature of both God and human society. Such a determination was, however, but preliminary to decisions, which again needed to be integrated into larger belief systems, concerning what exactly these human soldiers were supposed to do. In general, they were to fight, armed both with weapons and with the knowledge that God is on their side. As I pointed out earlier, God fights alongside, not instead of, humans. However, it was not always deemed appropriate for Israel to send all of its soldiers to battle enemy forces; further, on occasion God was not simply the decisive factor in victory, as we might expect, but the only factor. These and related questions point to the fact that the issue of human participation in warfare was a complex one, some of the subtleties of which we explore at this point.

Gideon, one of the most famous of the Biblical judges, amassed a great army to do combat against the Midianites, but God instructed him to thin out the ranks considerably, reasoning as follows: "The people with you are too many for me to give the Midianites into their hand, lest Israel vaunt themselves against me, saying, 'My own hand has delivered me' " (Judges 7). In 1 Maccabees 3 Judah is reported to have encouraged his outnumbered forces by stating: "It is easy for many to be hemmed in by few, for in the sight of Heaven there is no difference between saving by many or by few. It is not on the size of the army that victory in battle depends, but strength comes from Heaven." And yet, it does seem that as a rule the Israelite armies with whom God allied Himself were outnumbered, so as to lessen the possibility that humans might praise their own strength, instead of the Divine Warrior who allotted such strength to them, for Israelite armies were to "trust in the Almighty God, who is able with a single nod to strike down those who are coming against us and even the whole world" (2 Maccabees 8).

It was then generally necessary for humans armies to fight against overwhelming odds, in order fully to appreciate the enormity of the gift bestowed upon them. In this way they were also led to recognize the source of their strength. The divine nature of this source is generally made known in the accounts preserved for us by the fact that the decisive and determinative event in battle is frequently described in terms of what we might loosely call a "miraculous" divine intervention (which was frequently, but not always, associated with a natural phenomenon). Thus the forces at Qumran were to conduct a six-year campaign against their chief enemies, culminating in a series of seven lots of alternating victory and defeat on the last day (all of which is described in great detail). However, the seventh and decisive lot, which resulted in the annihilation of the enemy, was fought by God alone: the human troops awake to find that the multitude of the enemy were "all slain, for they have fallen there by the sword-of-God." This narrative is reminiscent of the Biblical account of the disaster that befell Sennacherib's troops as they laid siege to Jerusalem in the eighth century: "The angel of the Lord went forth, and slew 185,000 in the camp of the Assyrians; and when men arose early in the morning, behold, these were all dead bodies" (2 Kings 19).

From these and numerous other accounts (the fall of Jericho, for example), it is clear that although God could be effective without any human aid, an act of faith to God by means of human participation was generally requisite. And yet, not always—a subtheme can be constructed from passages such as

Exodus 14:14. Although we are told that at the time of the Exodus "the people of Israel went up out of the land of Egypt equipped for battle" (Exodus 13), Moses gave the following order: "The Lord will fight for you, and you have only to be still" (14:14). Thus it was that at the Sea of Reeds, clearly a crucial event in the history of the formation of Israel, the assembled humans were told not to fight, to leave it all to God.

I do not believe that in this respect at least actions (or inactions) at the Sea were meant to be paradigmatic.[15] To this degree, Josephus put things in what we might call their usual perspective by speaking of the exiting Hebrews as "unarmed folk" (*Antiquities* 2). It was not in accordance with the general scheme of things that a group of armed forces would simply do nothing when confronted by an enemy. Josephus then quotes a tradition to the effect that these Hebrews were first armed only after they had passed through the Sea of Reeds, when the weapons of the drowned Egyptians floated to their camp, thanks to "the providence of God."

However, we ought not to obscure in this way the point of the remark attributed to Moses; namely, that on some occasions, though certainly not most of those recorded, trust in God the Divine Warrior must be shown through abstention from active participation. No one ever attempted to formulate hard and fast rules in this regard, but it is noteworthy that Josephus portrays himself as having made use of such a tradition in a speech he delivered to the citizens of Jerusalem prior to its final capture by the Romans, in which he urged them to surrender at once (*War* 5). Selectively choosing examples that would prove his point, Josephus in effect overstated the case by declaring that "there is no instance of our forefathers having triumphed by arms or failed of success without them when they committed their cause to God: if they sat still they conquered as it pleased their Judge, if they fought they were invariably defeated" and "thus invariably have arms been refused to our nation, and warfare has been the sure signal for defeat." It will not do simply to "disapprove" Josephus through the citation of numerous counterexamples, when the people did take up arms to wage a successful campaign alongside God the Warrior, for what Josephus declared has the ring of theological truth: the people's faith in God, the Divine Warrior, must not at every occasion take the form of armed combat. As at the Sea of Reeds, there are times when the justice of their cause is manifest through activities of God alone. It is indeed a delicate balance—the question of the nature of human participation—but the presumption of humans and their attempts to manipulate God must most decidedly be guarded against.

Such issues are taken up again when we narrow the focus on the single individual who is usually in the position of leadership over a human army; he may be called a judge, general, king, warrior-hero, or what have you. Here there is little room for ambiguity: in a wide variety of Biblical and post-Biblical traditions there is accord on the point that God is *the* warrior, with no room for the elevation of any human to a role comparable to His. There were indeed opportunities for individual acts of considerable heroism, but even the most impressive series of such actions was not parlayed into the construction of a "military hero" of the epic proportions seen in other cultures. This downplaying, though not ignoring, of the human hero is a feature I would like to trace, if only briefly.

Within the Hebrew Bible almost every military leader about whom we are given any extensive information comes off as a flawed individual, whose flaws often rose to the surface in the context of warfare itself—this was true of Gideon, Jephthah, and Samson, from the period of the judges. David's downfall (2 Samuel 11 ff) came about through his breach of Holy War regulations (among other things), no matter that some later traditions tried to explain this away. Even good king Josiah met his death in battle (2 Kings 23), which may be accounted for theologically by suggesting that he overstepped the boundaries of divinely prescribed warfare.

"Excessive" preoccupation with the exploits of any one individual is also countered through the numerous statements, some of which we have looked at, to the effect that it is God alone to whom all praise for victory is due. Thus when the spotlight shone especially brightly on David at the occasion of his single combat against Goliath, the Hebrew Bible records his saying such things as, "The Lord who delivered me from the paw of the lion and from the paw of the bear, will deliver me from the hand of this Philistine," and "You come to me with a sword and with a spear and with a javelin; but I come to you in the name of the Lord of hosts, the God of the armies of Israel, whom you have defied" (1 Samuel 17).

David is a special case, to the extent that if any figure were going to achieve "heroic" stature, it would be he. Actually, much of the speculation, if not adulation, that might have been lavished on David in this regard was transferred to a figure who is in many respects his alter ego; namely, the Annointed One (Messiah), son of David. With respect to David himself, we find in certain Rabbinic traditions a remarkable transformation, with the result that this individual, most of whose life was occupied with fighting, became a grand figure of peace—this on the basis of his refusal to slay his pursuer Saul when the latter stopped "to relieve himself" in a cave (related in 1 Samuel 24; see also 1 Samuel 26).[16] It is likewise significant that when Rabbinic discussants sought to illustrate the verse "for the Lord your God is He that goes with you" (from Deuteronomy 20), they selected, not by chance I would suggest, two examples from the exploits of David. Thus David was to be portrayed either in terms that downplay his military activities or that emphasize the role of God in his victories.

Phineas, the grandson of Aaron, is reported to have slain an Israelite male and a Midianite woman, who were engaged in sexual intercourse (Numbers 25). Later he led an army "to execute the Lord's vengeance on Midian" (Numbers 31). The Rabbis were able to make much of the fact, recorded in the Biblical text, that with this very Phineas God made a "covenant of peace." Thus Phineas as a "man of peace" appears in a wide variety of Rabbinic sources.

With somewhat similar concerns in mind, Philo, a prolific first-century Jewish writer who lived in Alexandria, dealt with Moses' role in the initial defeat of the Amalekites and Abraham's role in the defeat of four kings (related in Genesis 14) in such a way that even what he would term a "literal" reading of such stories does not result in overglorification of these two immensely important humans. I should also add that while for Philo almost every virtue or vice is represented through the actions of one or another Biblical character, none is called forth as a prominent exemplar of ανδρεια (that is, the virtue of a warrior).

After all, within the statement "The Lord is a man of war" from Exodus 15, there is also its opposite: no one else is. This "polemical" element was clearly recognized in *Shirta,* which is a Midrashic or interpretive text on Exodus 15, representing the work of Palestinian-Jewish teachers of the first two centuries A.D. Through a series of comparisons it is clearly demonstrated that no human soldier could possibly measure up to God the Warrior: "Sometimes in a country there is a warrior fully armed, but he has no strength, no courage, no strategy, no war experience. But is is not so with Him Who Spake and the World Came to Be. On the contrary, He has strength and courage and strategy and war experience. . . ." and so it goes: every type of human warrior is found wanting in some area; God lacks nothing. It also follows that none of those who are called divine can be compared to Him or can do what He does.[17]

Let us close with a look at some examples of the fate held to be in store for human soldiers whom pride or forgetfulness impelled to strive with God for a title which cannot be shared, "man of war." Judah Goldin, from whose edition of the *Shirta* I quoted just above, has constructed a marvelously improbable theory that Exodus 15, the Song at the Sea, was composed by members of a priestly family expelled by Solomon, composed as an attack on both the pretensions of that monarch and the massive introduction under him of foreign, especially Egyptian, influence. While this attack would not have been levelled with matters of military leadership in mind, Goldin's hypothesis does serve to remind us that Israelite and Judaean kings alike were condemned when they sought to add an aura of "holiness" to conflicts that were—from the point of view of the condemners—nothing more than the result of the king's substitution of his own military leadership for that which was God's alone.

In his 1526 treatise, "Whether Soldiers, Too, Can Be Saved," Martin Luther pointed to an example of such pride in the ranks led by the Maccabees.[18] Luther, who praises David much as Rabbinic interpreters did for not laying violent hands on Saul, later speaks of God's punishment against those "who delight in war" (a phrase from Psalm 68). One of his examples is of "Joseph and Azariah [who] wanted to fight to gain honor for themselves." As recorded in 1 Macabees 5, these commanders, upon hearing of the successes of Judah and his brothers, said: "Let us also make a name for ourselves; let us go and make war on the Gentiles around us." The defeat inflicted upon those who followed Joseph and Azariah, especially when contrasted with the remarkable victories of the Maccabees in this period, was interpreted as a negative judgment on all such forays initiated for the purpose of personal glorification.

We have already viewed Herod as an example in the post-Biblical period. Our final illustration is drawn from the time of the last major armed resistance offered by Jews in antiquity, their last attempt for almost 1800 years to gain control through warfare over their national homeland. I refer to the revolt led by Bar-Kokhba between 132–135.[19] The leader of this revolt, who was actually named Shimeon bar Kosiba, was viewed as a Messianic figure by many, including Rabbi Akiba, who exclaimed: "This is the king Messiah!" Akiba's statement, we are told, was the result of Bar-Kokhba's military prowess.

The lofty expectations for this individual attributed to Akiba were, however, inconsistent with the boastful battle cry that Bar-Kokhba and his soldiers are recorded to have uttered: "O God, neither help us nor discourage us!" And, the Midrash on Lamentations continues, in this manner was Bar-Kokhba wont to interpret the passage in Psalm 60, "[Has not Thou, O God, cast us off?] And go not forth, O God, with our hosts," which in its Biblical context means something quite different from its use by Bar-Kokhba. The same story is told of two soldiers in

Bar-Kokhba's army, who decided to take Hadrian's crown and set it on their own heads. When a well-wisher said, "May the Creator be your help against them," they retorted as had their commander: "Let Him neither help us nor discourage us!" In these cases, as in every case where human presumption leads individuals or whole armies to think that victory can be achieved apart from God, defeat, inglorious if not instantaneous, was considered the appropriate end.

In the text above I have dealt with certain aspects of the figure of God as Warrior and with the ways in which Jewish perceptions of God's role in this regard played a part in shaping attitudes toward war and human participation therein. I have attempted to cover the themes of religion, myth, and nationalistic politics in the context of Israel's history through the second century. In this endeavor I have limited my efforts to the exegetical task of understanding various texts in themselves. Left largely undone is the hermeneutical work of explaining what all of this means for the modern interpreter and the people of our culture, insofar as this latter task intends to suggest how we should apply insights gained to contemporary problems. Nevertheless, as long as nations continue to beat plowshares into swords and pruning hooks into spears—and not the opposite—observations from any period of history on war and warfare will continue to have an unfortunate relevance for all of humanity.

NOTES

I want to thank the National Endowment for the Humanities, whose sponsorship of a year-long seminar on Religious Studies made it possible for me to be at Santa Barbara and thus participate in the colloquium whose papers are gathered in this volume.

In revising my paper for publication, I benefited greatly from the many perceptive comments made by colleagues in the Department of History and Religion at Clemson University, to whom I presented my work as part of the Department's Seminar.

1. Throughout this paper quotations from the work of Josephus are taken from the Loeb Classical Library translation.

2. Ancient historians such as Josephus frequently fleshed out their narra-

tives with speeches and dialogues, ranging in length from a few to several thousand words. Although this material is presented as direct discourse, it is understood that most of these "quotations" are free, but not necessarily inappropriate creations on the part of the historian or the tradition upon which he was dependent. This was not an effort to deceive the reader, ancient or modern; rather, by this means the historian sought to enliven his account and to make points that either the figure being "quoted" might actually have made or that the author felt appropriate within the context of the historical framework he was in the process of constructing.

In the case of this particular speech of Herod's, we have no way of knowing the degree to which Josephus's account reflects the *ipsissima verba* of the Jewish king. Nor is that important for our purposes. We are concerned here with the use, either by Herod or by Josephus, of traditional material dealing with God's role in Israel's wars. As such, this is a relevant example. The same holds true for direct discourse found in the Hebrew Bible, post-Biblical material such as 1 and 2 Maccabees, and Rabbinic literature.

All of these works, Josephus included, are biased, and these biases are bound to obscure, though not usually obliterate, the historical realities that their authors describe and evaluate. Again, it is not important for our purposes whether such-and-such a battle took place exactly as it is recounted in one or another source. We are much more interested, in narratives as well as in speeches, in the use, reuse, and even perversion of traditional themes and motifs in the texts with which we are dealing.

To return again to the particular account found in Josephus, we have no reason to doubt that battles did take place between Herod's troops and the Nabataeans, in which the Jewish forces eventually scored a decisive victory. With respect to the earthquake itself, we have several other witnesses, literary and archaeological, to the occurrence of this quake in either 31 or 30 B.C.

3. Recently the historian Salo W. Baron called attention to the fact that "despite the great importance, even urgency, of understanding the varying attitudes to war, those of the Jewish people, in both theory and practice, have never been satisfactorily examined. There is no significant literature on the basic Jewish ideology as it was formulated over the ages by the Bible and Talmud, by medieval rabbis and modern thinkers, as well as by the actual historical experience of Jewish participation in wars, both passively and actively." Baron's comments appear in the Introduction to *Violence and Defense in the Jewish Experience* (Philadelphia: The Jewish Publication Society of America, 1977), edited by Baron and George S. Wise, which contains papers prepared for a seminar on violence and defense in Jewish history and contemporary life, held at Tel Aviv University, August 18–September 4, 1974. A number of issues, including many related to war, are covered in this volume, which surveys the "Jewish Experience" from Biblical times through the contemporary period. Baron also calls for further "serious investigations of Jewish attitudes toward war."

A very informative, succinct account of attitudes toward "war and peace" in a wide variety of religious traditions, including Judaism, is found in John Ferguson, *War and Peace in the World's Religions* (London: Sheldon Press, 1977).

4. See expecially Frank Moore Cross, *Canaanite Myth and Hebrew Epic: Essays in the History of the Religion of Israel* (Cambridge: Harvard University Press, 1973). For material relevant to the present discussion, see especially chapters 5–7. Hereafter, this volume is abbreviated *CMHE.*

5. This evaluation is quoted from Patrick D. Miller, Jr., *The Divine Warrior in Early Israel,* Harvard Semitic Monographs 5 (Cambridge: Harvard University Press, 1973).

6. Translations of Ugaritic texts are those of Cross, *cmhe.* I have taken the liberty of altering his renderings of certain proper names, in order to present such names in their more familiar, if less correct, form. Thus Ba'l (Ugaritic: Ba'lu) in Cross's translation becomes Baal, and so forth.

7. Biblical material in this section (through the second passage from Exodus 15) is given in the form reconstructed by Cross, *CMHE,* who attempts to recover the original text underlying the later traditions through which this poetry was transmitted to us. It is instructive to compare these reconstructions with a standard translation such as that found in the Revised Standard Version (RSV), which but rarely departs from the Received/Masoretic Text.

8. Deuteronomy 13 similarly commands the complete destruction of any Hebrew city that turns from the worship of God to idolatry: "You shall surely put the inhabitants of that city to the sword, destroying it utterly, all who are in it and its cattle, with the edge of the sword. You shall gather all its spoil . . . and burn the city and all its spoil with fire, as a whole burnt offering to the Lord your God."

9. Traditional Jewish commentaries extend the obligation to offer terms of peace to conflicts against Canaanite cities and the Amalekites as well.

10. Soṭah is a tractate in the Babylonian Talmud. Although this tractate is concerned for the most part with the process by which a woman accused of infidelity establishes her innocence (see Numbers 5 in the Hebrew Bible), there is also contained therein a fairly lengthy section (42a–44b) on war and related matters. The translations of Talmudic material that appear in this paper are from the edition prepared by the Soncino Press in London.

11. Maimonides, *Mishneh Torah* 14 ("The Book of Judges"), Treatise 5 ("Kings and Wars"), chapter 5 (see further all of chapters 5–8). An annotated English translation of this work forms part of the Yale Judaica Series.

12. This quotation, from the thirteenth-century French Talmudist Menahem Meiri, is found in Maurice Lamm, "Red or Dead?" *Tradition* 4 (1962), p. 185.

13. Lamm, p. 186. Is it possible to designate the struggle against Hitler, the Soviet Union, or any other enemy as a war against Amalek? According to Lamm, p. 188, "halakhically, no such substition can be made. 'Amalek' is

the name of a specific nation. . . . Maimonides seems to accept a much broader definition of the term. This, however, does not appear to be the consensus of Halakhic opinion."

14. For a thorough and authoritative treatment of this document, see Yigael Yadin, *The Scroll of the War of the Sons of Light against the Sons of Darkness* (Oxford: Oxford University Press, 1962). His interpretations of the *War Scroll* have been followed throughout this paper.

15. On this point cf. Millard C. Lind, "Paradigm of Holy War in the Old Testament," *Biblical Research* 16 (1971), pp. 16–31.

16. On this understanding of David and certain other Biblical figures, see Reuven Kimmelman, "Non-Violence in the Talmud," *Judaism* 17 (1968), pp. 316–334.

17. The above translation and interpretation of *Shirta* are derived from Judah Goldin, *The Song at the Sea (being a Commentary on a Commentary in Two Parts)* (New Haven: Yale University Press, 1971).

The sources I have cited thus far in this section, while by far the best known, are not the only ones. When we turn to the relatively obscure second-century B.C. Jewish writer Artapanus, whose work is available only in fragments preserved by later writers, we do note greater emphasis on the military exploits of Moses. For example, to him is credited the invention of Egyptian weaponry and the leadership role in a long and successful military campaign against the Ethiopians (for the latter, see also the account in Josephus, *Antiquities* 2.238 ff). The increased prominence given to Moses's marital accomplishments is undoubtedly related to the increased participation by Jewish soldiers in the wars of the period contemporary with Artapanus himself.

However, weaponry is but one aspect of Egyptian culture and society that owes its foundation to Abraham, Jacob, Joseph, or Moses, according to Artapanus's account. These four leaders are pictured as benefactors of mankind, endowing not only the Egyptians, but through them the Greek world and beyond, with all useful knowledge of both terrestrial and celestial matters. Within this context Moses can indeed be viewed as a greater military figure than he is portrayed in the Hebrew Bible, but certainly not as a "military hero" threatening to rival God the Warrior in power or scope.

Hecataeus of Abdera, a Greek writer of the late fourth century B.C. whose work has also been preserved only in fragments, likewise gave high praise to Jewish beliefs and organization in his generally sympathetic account. In this larger context, he spoke of Moses' attention to warfare and the military training of youth. It is possible that Hecataeus, in fashioning these descriptions, had in mind a comparison between Jews and Spartans of the sort that gained currency among certain groups of the Jewish population at a somewhat later period.

For summaries of recent scholarship on Artapanus and Hecataeus, see the relevant articles in the *Encyclopaedia Judaica*. For a fuller discussion of the issues raised in this footnote I recommend the following work: Martin Hengel, *Judaism and Hellenism* (tr. John Bowden; 2 vols.; Philadelphia: Fortress Press, 1974).

18. Martin Luther, "Whether Soldiers, Too, Can Be Saved, 1526" (tr. Charles M. Jacobs; revised Robert C. Schultz) in *Luther's Works* 46, The Christian in Society III (Philadelphia: Fortress Press, 1967), pp. 89–137.

19. For a fascinating account of that historical period and of the archaeological excavations which have served to illuminate it, see Yigael Yadin, *Bar-Kokhba: The Rediscovery of the Legendary Hero of the Second Jewish Revolt against Rome* (New York: Random House, 1971). In an appendix Yadin brings together the major ancient sources, both Jewish and non-Jewish, that refer to Bar-Kokhba and the revolt. Some of the Rabbinic material appears below.

TWELVE

From Hero to Anti-Hero: The Transformation of the Warrior in Modern America*

Edward Tabor Linenthal

Robert Jay Lifton, a Yale psycho-historian who has worked with Vietnam veterans, reports that he was in Times Square on V-E day and also after the peace accords were signed "ending" major American involvement in Vietnam. He contrasts the mass joy of the one day with the desolation of the other. There were a few Vietnam vets in Times Square as our participation in the war came to a manner of closure, and one black vet exclaimed (ostensibly about Nixon), "You can tell that bastard the war isn't over yet!"[1] Six years later we may wonder if in some ways the war is still not over, and what kind of changes the trauma of the war has brought about.

I suggest that one change which appears to have taken place is a shift in perception of the nature of war and of the symbol of the warrior in America. American wars have often been symbolized as the crucial events of our history, giving birth to new worlds, worlds shaped by the martial actions of the war-

*Reprinted by permission from *Soundings-An Interdisciplinary Journal,* vol. LXIII, no. 1 (Spring 1980).

rior, especially the shedding of the blood of the enemy, or the sacrifice of one's own blood in battle. Through literature, film, stories passed on by generations of veterans, from a thousand nooks and crannies of our national memory, the mythology of American warfare has shaped our perceptions of the nature of war and the warrior in America. I would contend that the symbols that sustained us and shaped our image of war for so long failed to capture the reality of our involvement in Vietnam, and that the failure of martial imagery was largely responsible for our difficulty in depicting or "imagining" the war with any success. In this war traditional martial imagery was turned upside down. The image of the war as righteous and full of potential for a new world, and the image of the classic American warrior righteously and honorably fighting in a sacred cause, a cause which has seen the noble sacrifice of Americans in many generations, did not fit the reality of the war.

There had been other unpopular wars in American history. Samuel Eliot Morison suggests that the War of 1812 was popular when it was over, and tremendously unpopular when it was fought. The Mexican War and the war against the guerrillas in the Philippines during the Spanish-American war are other examples of wars in which the morality of American involvement has been questioned, with a zeal that equals that of the protests of the 1960s. Yet there are differences. "Victory" often swept the important moral questions aside; it reinforced those who proclaimed that these wars were part of a providential design, a notion which fit comfortably into American mythology. These wars also produced their share of heroes: Andrew Jackson, Zachary Taylor, Winfield Scott, Teddy Roosevelt, and George Dewey. None of the wars forced a general and wide-spread reworking of American martial imagery, or threatened the basic assumptions of the uniqueness and righteousness of the American fighting men.[2]

Though warriors appear as models of heroic action in many cultures, both archaic and modern, they have their own life in America. American warriors were unspoiled by the professional nature of European warriors. The "new warriors" were driven by God-given virtues, and became fighting men in an instant. The embattled farmers of Lexington and Concord were the embodiment of the citizen-soldier, characterized by Daniel Chester French's statue of a new warrior with one hand on the plow, the other grasping his flintlock.

Through the Revolutionary War one might see the hand of Providence which had guided the colonists through many crises. God's New Israel was fighting a "war of the Lord," and the burden of liberation and salvation fell on the warrior. The cause demanded sacrifice, and the warrior's death was made meaningful by the life his sacrifice gave to the cause. On April 17, 1776, Rev. Jonas Clarke said, "They bleed, they die, not in their cause only; but in the cause of this whole people—in the cause of God, their country and posterity."[3]

The poets, ministers, and artists of the Revolutionary period set a pattern for understanding and visualizing American war experience and the American warrior. Heroic models and perceptions were established in the American mind. As the Minuteman became a model for future American warriors, the Revolution became a model for the perceived course of American wars. The model of the Minuteman and the power of the formative martial events of the Revolution are adaptable to any war in our history. The model of the Revolution in the imaginations of soldiers in the Civil War linked them in the struggle to preserve what had been won in the Revolution, or to fight once again for liberty against oppression.

It became apparent during the Civil War that a nation born of strife would have to be purified before the millennium would be at hand. The warrior was once again the actor responsible for making history; his blood sacrifice would be the cleansing agent in this war of purification. In 1866, John Davidson spoke to the Legislature of New Jersey and said, "The flag of our nation flaps its pure folds . . . not torn and tattered by war, but purified by the death of our heroes and cleansed in their blood."[4] The Civil War allowed America to begin again, ransomed and redeemed. Echoing a popular mood, Elbridge J.

Cutler declared in his Phi Beta Kappa address at Harvard in 1861:

Then a red flash, like lightning, across the darkness broke, And, with a voice that shook the land, the Guns of Sumter spoke: Wake, sons of heroes, wake! The age of heroes dawns again, Truth takes in hand her ancient sword and calls her loyal men, Lo, brightly o'er the breaking day, shines freedom's holy star! Peace cannot cure the sickly time—All hail the healer, war![5]

Celebrated in battle art, historical novels, biographies, dime novels, poems, movies, etc., the Civil War truly was, as Robert Penn Warren suggests, our Homeric period, a time of heroic action, when battle was decisive and dramatic, and soldiers on both sides were perceived as models of American courage.

Worthy martial action did not cease with the conclusion of the Civil War. World War I, the "war to end war," was for many a rebirth of our heroic age, and images of past wars were points of orientation. Americans arriving in France were cast by writers as heirs of the Revolution. The famous comment attributed to General Pershing, "Lafayette, we are here," implied the completion of the circle of civilization and celebrated the triumphant return of the powerful soldiers of God's army to a still corrupt and war-torn Europe. Once again the nation was perceived as reborn through battle sacrifice. *The Chicago Evening Post* noted in July, 1917, that freedom was brought with blood and "preserved and widened through the fires of war—you cannot keep it if you will not fight for it."[6]

The image of World War I as a holy war is familiar, and it is commonly believed that we entered World War II with our eyes open, with no romantic illusions. Yet President Roosevelt noted in his war speech on December 9, 1941, that ours was a total war of ultimate good against immediate evil. As the narrator of a radio play declared, "No compromise with Satan is possible. . . . Strong in the strength of the Lord, we who fight in the people's cause will not stop until that cause is won!"[7] For many, martial action clarified the meaning and mission of

America, and the struggle once again depended on the warrior for the preservation of the transcendent principles that were imperiled. On D-Day evening, President Roosevelt offered a prayer on the combined radio networks, a prayer for the soldiers who set upon a "struggle to preserve our Republic, our religion, and our civilization, and to set free a suffering humanity."[8] Warriors, as saviors and liberators, were the agents of rebirth.

As classic American warriors, the G.I.s were twentieth-century Minutemen, citizen-soldiers reluctantly marching off to battle. The beloved correspondent, Ernie Pyle, wrote:

They weren't warriors. They were American boys who by chance of fate had wound up with guns in their hands, sneaking up a death-laden street in a strange and shattered city. . . . And even though they weren't warriors born to the kill, they won their battles. That's the point.[9]

Once again, these warriors were called upon to make the final and regenerative sacrifice for the nation. Just as the Last Stands of the Alamo and the Little Big Horn provided heroic and sacrificial models for previous generations, Bataan and Corregidor and Wake Island provided epic moral victories in this new Great Crusade. Countless heroic battles revealed the redemptive blood sacrifices made by American warriors. Robert Sherrod, walking the beaches on Tarawa, knew that the dead marines had given their lives so that others could land. "They also gave their lives for one hundred and thirty million other Americans who realize it, I fear, only dimly."[10] The blood of these warriors would bring about a new world. General Douglas MacArthur spoke during the ceremonies concluding the hostilities in September 1945, "It is my earnest hope and indeed the hope of all mankind that from this solemn occasion a better world shall emerge out of the blood and carnage."[11]

A new world would indeed emerge out of the carnage, and adherence to traditional martial images became difficult. Of course, the tension between conflicting images had existed for some time. As the nature of warfare changed, it became more difficult for traditional images to make sense of the complexities of modern warfare. The gradual emergence of total war made personal notions of sacrifice, heroism, and salvation difficult to portray.

The warrior had traditionally been a figure of singular creative power, often a symbol of a culture's highest ideals. By entering combat, a warrior was undergoing the well-known trial of heroes, and whether he died a glorious sacrificial death or killed in order to preserve, he was a purposeful figure. The acts of the warrior were assertive acts, acts which in America's sacred causes were acts not only of national but cosmic import. Warfare was perceived as a personal event, a warrior engaged in personal struggle with the enemy. The culminating image of glorious war in America might well have been Pickett's Charge, for all the elements were there. Two armies faced each other across a clearly recognizable battlefield. The aesthetic power of the assembled armies was noted by several participants. The armies fought hand to hand at the Bloody Angle, at the "High-Water Mark" of the Confederacy, a time when the fate of the nation was perceived as hanging in the balance. Clearly, this battle signified the creation of a new world, a world brought into being by the actions of the warrior. Yet, troubling ruminations about the nature of heroism and sacrifice began during the Civil War, often characterized as a transitional war, a war in which glorious images of war existed in tension with the development of weapons of mass destruction.

Mass firepower and the war of attrition in the trench fighting of 1864–65 forced sketch artists and photographers to change their concepts of warfare and the power of the heroic warrior. The views of mass death gave rise to questions regarding the meaning of sacrifice. Walt Whitman could write of the death of a soldier, but couldn't give form to the idea of war as a "slaughterhouse." Traditional notions of heroism also changed as weapons killed impersonally, from long distance. Images of mass death brought images of mass heroism. The soldier was now seen as stoically doing his duty, "his job," an expression which would gain currency during each of the world wars.

Traditional images were also tested in both world wars. The

devastation of the Western front made images of heroic sacrifice absurd, as Hemingway, Dos Passos, Trumbo, and others pointed out. While some writers used traditional images, others characterized the battlefield with words like decay, stench, putrefaction. Stanley Cooperman notes that "in place of heroes there were faceless masses of men butchering each other with little or none of the personal tests celebrated in epics."[12] Images of war as an event lacking in creative power continued into World War II. Sgt. Mack Morriss wrote of combat in the Huertgen forest, "behind them they left their dead, and the forest will stink with deadness long after the last body is removed."[13] Portrayals of battles and battlefields often resembled descriptions of World War I locations rather than the fertile fields of Gettysburg. Far from being perceived as heroic, the warrior was often seen as a victim, reduced in stature by the advent of mechanical warfare.

With the dropping of the atomic bomb, traditional martial imagery lost the last of the evocative power it had previously possessed. The difficulty of shaping A-bomb experience into usable categories is illustrated by the literature about it. The terror of the atomic apocalypse forced even science fiction literature to transfer utopias to worlds far away. Tales of future war were now transferred to other galaxies, for contemplation of future war on this planet was incomprehensible. I. F. Clarke noted that the imagination could do nothing except to describe the end of civilization. Confrontation between warriors was reduced to non-apocalyptic proportions. Attention was now turned to professional warriors who would tuilize their expertise in "limiting" warfare; thus, the demise of the warrior as heroic and regenerative figure, for no sacrifice or act of bravery could be a creative or salvific act. Soldiers in literature often turned to their own preservation as ultimate meaning. Hans Morgenthau echoes the logic of *Catch-22* and other war novels of the absurd when he states, "To defend freedom and civilization is absurd when to defend them amounts to destroying them."[14] The warrior of modern America had been stripped of his regenerative and protective power, and no longer seemed the central actor in the drama of war, but existed (almost in refuge) in various strands of popular memory.

The various events, lessons and experiences of the forties and fifties contributed to the world-view of the "Best and the Brightest," a world-view dependent on faulty models. It is within the context of these post-war models that the ritual and rhythm of American war would be destroyed and the warrior would take on shapes never before associated with the classic American warrior.

The initial impact of the Vietnam war was not evident. There was no Pearl Harbor, no major aggression against recognizable places, no armies rushing across borders. There was no psychic or symbolic jump from peace to war. Senator J. William Fullbright confessed during the Vietnam hearings that he could find no adequate models to help define our entrance into the war. The rhythm of American wars did not fit either the manner of entry or combat itself. For some soldiers, at least those who have written about their Vietnam experience, the classic script to be played out didn't work. Lifton writes that the purposes put forth for involvement

. . . are directly contradicted by the overwhelming evidence a GI encounters that *he* is the outside invader, that the government he has come to defend is justly hated by the people he has come to help, and that he, the American helper is hated . . . most of all.[15]

Michael Herr reports in *Dispatches* that growing up with war movies made the war in Vietnam at first seem *like* a war movie. "It was the same familiar violence, only moved over to another medium."[16] Novels of the war show warriors consciously trying to model themselves after popular conceptions of American warriors, even the film versions, such as John Wayne. However, fighting an enemy who did not fit any traditional image of what enemies should look like did not *feel* like the image of war Americans envisioned while growing up. Yet, in the early years especially, attempts were made to portray the soldiers as classic American warriors. Some soldiers, however, bitterly rejected any attempt at this classic formulation.

The war not only failed to produce heroic warriors, it produced new situations which prohibited many from viewing sacrifice as redemptive or regenerative. That the "body count," the statistical count of "enemy" corpses, was indicative of the success of the American mission was acknowledged by General Maxwell Taylor's comment, "We are looking for these people and destroying them at the greatest rate that has ever taken place in the history of the struggle."[17] In previous wars both soldiers and the public had viewed the killing of the enemy as regenerative, necessary for the survival and rebirth of the nation. The ritual of combat killing, even the mass casualties of bombing in World War II, were part of the symbolic process of war. In Vietnam, the popular phrase, "If it's dead, it's VC," reveals the degeneration of ritual combat killing to the illusory quantitative principle of death. One does not recognize the enemy and then kill him in combat, but first kills him and then proclaims him the enemy. Adolf Jensen explains the change, applicable to the American situation in Vietnam as well as in archaic societies.

If killing is a sacred act which involves rewards, its root meaning will be corrupted by the primitive (though human) deduction that the more killed the more benefits are engendered.[18]

Vietnam produced warriors concerned and disillusioned about their mission. It produced war narratives that reflect the clash between a memory of classic American warrior models and the reality of a war which frustrated all attempts made to symbolize it in traditional patterns. Indeed, Vietnam gave birth to a situation in which a new image of the American warrior appeared to public view for the first time: My Lai. Lt. Calley and the event of My Lai are more than a person and an event, but a symbolic experience which reveals much about the limits of the American imagination. The American warrior could now be visualized as an anti-hero, a murderer. Calley had fierce support among Americans. After he was found guilty, over one hundred thousand telegrams and letters were sent to President Nixon, reportedly ten to one in favor of Calley. In a pro-Calley rally in the Columbus, Georgia Memorial Stadium, Rev. Michael Lord said, "There was a crucifixion 2,000 years ago of a man named Jesus Christ. I don't think we need another crucifixion of a man named Rusty Calley."[19] Perhaps the most interesting response to the My Lai massacre and Calley's conviction was the popular record, "The Battle Hymn of Lt. Calley." Recorded by Tracy Nelson, it sold over two million copies. To the tune of America's most sacred martial music, "The Battle Hymn of the Republic," the song portrays the tragic fall of an American warrior-hero who has lived up to the creed of the Minutemen and has fallen victim to the betrayal of his misguided or treacherous countrymen. Calley was a symbol for all persuasions: a tragic hero, a scapegoat, a product of this unique war, a murderer. Despite the uproar over this event, the status of My Lai and Calley are not fixed in our memory. This event attacked the essence of American martial virtue and the image of the American warrior, for moral status as well as physical prowess has always been a part of the make-up of the American warrior. They have been imagined as righteous warriors, fierce in battle, yet devoid of the barbaric martial fervor of other peoples. My Lai, however, presented an image alien to our mythology, an atrocity of our own making. While certainly not the first massacre or shameful event in our martial history, it could no longer be ignored or supported by other elements of providential destiny. We possessed no categories of interpretation to make sense of it. The editors of *Newsweek* stated it plaintively:

Mindful of the comforting image of Americans at war—the friendly GI handing out candy bars to ragged victims even while mopping up an enemy-held town—the massacre . . . seems to escape comprehension.[20]

The shocking pictures of the massacre show in *Life*'s December 5, 1969 issue did not help Americans comprehend the meaning of the event. Letters to *Life* revealed that people often objected to the pictures of the event rather than to the event itself. Some saw the reports as another plot to weaken our fighting morale. Most simply couldn't accept it. An Ohio mother said, "I can't believe that a massacre was committed by our boys. It's contrary to everything I've ever believed about America." Others responded, "I can't believe our boys' hearts are that rotten."

Portrayals of the warrior were ambivalent. Tracy Kidder wrote, "Vietnam veterans have been . . . 'tarred with the brush of My Lai.' "[21] In drama, soldiers were presented as murderers or victims. Movies told of veterans bringing the war home, and portrayed the danger to society of the Vietnam vets. Traditional symbolism took refuge largely in one popular medium: country and western music. Pro-Vietnam songs were well represented in *Billboard*'s country hit list. Just as the protest music of Dylan, Baez, Country Joe, and others provided many with powerful images of peace and common public goals, country music defended our participation in the war, and praised our soldiers as heroic but tragically abandoned figures.

There were many attempts to make the war real. One of the most astonishing magazine pieces to come out of the war was the article in *Life* showing pictures of one week's dead in Vietnam. Seeking to make the war more visible the editors commented:

More than we must know how many, we must know *who*. The faces of one week's dead, unknown but to family and friends, are suddenly recognized by all in this gallery of young American faces.[22]

The popular arts made efforts to bring the war home effectively. Guerrilla theatre groups consciously adapted strategy from guerrilla warfare, striking at unsuspecting "targets" in supermarket parking lots, outside of churches, etc.

As various modes of perception were used in the struggles to give form to the Vietnam experience, images of the warrior could be removed from the battlefield, already possible to some extent in Vietnam, and to a greater extent in the future with the development of drone aircraft, killer satellites equipped with a laser ray, and the expansion of biocybernetics. This kind of ahuman technological war not only blurs the distinction between warrior and technician and makes warfare a hidden experience (which Orwell predicted in *1984*); it further blurs the difference between war and peace. The nature of warlike existence is described by Brigadier General Robert L. Scott Jr., a World War II ace and author of *God Is My Co-pilot.* "World War III started before World War II ended. We've been in it for a quarter of a century and seem to know less about it now than when we began."[23] Joseph Heller, Kurt Vonnegut, and Norman Mailer all view war as a by-product of technological society, and in Thomas Pynchon's *Gravity's Rainbow,* war is the ultimate purpose of society. The ultimate end of automated warfare appears to be the process of changing the battlefield from "wholly other" to all-encompassing reality. The technician rules in both worlds, the warrior is not to be seen. *Both he and the symbolic universe in which to look for him have vanished.*

There is another response, though this response remains a hope, a hope that the warrior will reshape his sense of mission and regenerative power. Lifton suggests that a new kind of warrior emerged from the Vietnam experience: the anti-war warrior. His mission was to reveal the meaninglessness of the war. Though the Vietnam Veterans Against the War (VVAW) were only about fifteen thousand strong out of over two million vets, they spoke with the authoritative voice of those who had made the traditional heroic journey into combat. They, unlike protesters on the campuses, knew of the mysteries about which they spoke. Their confessional, their revisioning of the mission of the warrior, was unwanted and ungratefully heard. They were seen as betraying the nation. "Our confessions of war guilt were a blasphemy to the other America, a trampling on myths of innocence and moral perfection deep-seated in the American psyche."[24] It is too soon to tell if one of these images will gain symbolic power in America and provide referents for future images of the warrior, or if in some way, traditional perceptions will live on. It remains to be seen if the shadowy figure of the Minuteman at Concord Bridge, Hawthorne's "Gray Champion," still lurks behind the figure of the modern American warrior. It seems hard to imagine. The difficulty of depicting modern warfare presents severe problems for classic perceptions of the warrior. Yet symbols live, even in degraded form, and the nostalgia for classic images of war and the warrior are strong in the American mind. Perhaps much of the key to perceptions of the warrior of the future rests on how our involvement in Vietnam is structured in American memory.

Vietnam was America's longest war, our fourth most costly in numbers dead, and third in numbers wounded. As our entrance into war was less than dramatic, our exit was less than climactic. The war appeared to have three endings: Kissinger's "Peace is at Hand" in November 1972, the Paris Peace Accords of 1973, and the final spring collapse of South Vietnam in 1975. The final years were accompanied by a series of "happy endings." The return of the POWs in February 1973, the arrival of the Vietnamese orphans in spring 1975, and the rescue of the *Mayaguez* in June 1975. That this war will be remembered is clear; *how* it will be remembered is less clear.

As we sort out the various subjects that the war opened for inspection, we will begin to understand the imprint of the war upon the American psyche. Even as that process continues, there seem to be several ways we may choose to remember the war. President Nixon wanted the war ended in a way that "Americans can look back upon not ashamed, not frustrated, not angry, but with a pride that in spite of our difficulties we have been totally unselfish."[25] Unselfishness has not come to be used a great deal in evaluating the effects of the war, but shame, frustration and anger are common components in memories of Vietnam. In the response of the VVAW, for example, we see an attempt not to wash away the feelings of guilt, or shame, but to move into the holocaust and find regenerative value in the act of confession and new identity. Similarly, Norman Cousins argues for a full-scale examination of the war, believing "the nation can survive anything except ignored and unredeemed tragedy."[26] Some simply want to forget. *Time* stated in 1975:

America did not enlist in this war for life. There cannot be an infinite cycle of protests, recriminations, and guilt. The U.S. has paid for Vietnam—many times over. A phase of American history has finished. It is time to begin anew.[27]

Presumably, America had "paid for" Vietnam by the death of its soldiers. Their sacrifice did not contribute to the rebirth of Vietnam or America, *but atoned for the guilt of America.* Thus, our agony has cleansed us of responsibility, and we may "begin anew," we are reborn. It is not a jubilant statement. It is a curious rebirth, more like a patching of the wounded than the celebration of newness.

We must turn to memory and imagination as a corrective, for a phase of American history is *not* finished. The frantic urge to forget Vietnam, to believe we have paid for it or to brush it off by suggesting all lessons have been learned is to allow the experience to seep back into our lives in powerful and subtle ways. For example, Pauline Kael writes about the Vietnamization of the American film:

The Vietnam War has barely been mentioned on the screen, but you could feel it in *Bonnie and Clyde,* and *Bullit,* and *Joe,* in *Easy Rider* and *Midnight Cowboy,* and *The Last Picture Show,* in *They Shoot Horses, Don't They?* and *The Candidate,* and *Carnal Knowledge,* and *The French Connection* and *The Godfather.* It was in good movies and bad, flops and hits—in the convictionless atmosphere, the absence of shared values, the brutalities taken for granted, the glorification of loser-heroes. It was in the harshness of the attitudes, the abrasiveness that made you wince—until, after years of it, maybe you stopped wincing. It had become normal.[28]

More recently, the war has become a "hot item." *The Deer Hunter, Coming Home,* and *Apocalypse Now* all deal with various aspects of the American experience in the war. C. D. B. Bryan's *Friendly Fire* finally found its way onto television, and was a ratings success. No doubt more movies, books, and plays will be forthcoming. It is largely in this way that our mythic image of Vietnam will be constructed. Yet even amidst some of these powerful attempts to portray the war, disturbing elements appear in our selective memory. For some, a "Vietnam Chic" has developed, a peculiar fascination with the war, a fascination that views participation in the war as an "in" experience. Vietnam Chic will do little to help develop symbols capable of absorbing and using the Vietnam experience as a tragic, yet important, part of our personal and social history. Fascination with our war experience should be directed toward resolution, not nostalgia. Our memories must absorb shattering as well as triumphant experience. That it do so in this instance is crucial, for as James Reston wrote, "Something has happened to American life—something not yet understood or agreed upon, something that is different, important, and probably enduring."[29]

Vietnam has symbolized many degenerations in American life, and among them is the degeneration of martial symbolism and ritual. From structured rites of war we have seen the loss of distinction between war and peace. From a warrior who kills to promote life and often sacrifices himself we see in recollection of Vietnam images of murder and absurd sacrifice. From war as an experience of national rebirth we experience war as a national tragedy, one that must be purged from our memory. We have yet to see how images of war and the warrior will live in post-Vietnam America, and whether we can somehow let the thrill and storybook excitement of Concord Bridge, Gettysburg, the Little Big Horn, D-Day, and Iwo Jima live in our memories without governing our perceptions of modern warfare. We must not forget the symbolic power that war and the warrior have exerted in our memories, but we must now locate regenerative and sacrificial functions elsewhere than on the battlefield, for the warrior rules there no longer. He performs no heroic acts to be mythologized, as our struggle to depict a war without structure involving warriors who were not heroes illustrates.

NOTES

1. Robert Jay Lifton, "The Postwar War," *Journal of Social Issues* 31 (1975), p. 183.

2. For further reference to these wars see Samuel Eliot Morison, Frederick Merk, and Frank Friedel, *Dissent in Three American Wars* (Cambridge: Harvard University Press, 1970).

3. Jonas Clarke, "The Fate of Blood-Thirsty Oppressors, and God's tender care of his distressed People," A Sermon preached at Lexington, 19 April 1776, *Early American Imprints* 14679, p. 28.

4. John Davidson, *Oration delivered before the Legislature of New Jersey*

upon "Our Sleeping Heroes," 22 February 1866 (Trenton, New Jersey: Printed at the *State Gazette Office,* 1866), p. 26.

5. Quoted in Elbridge Streeter Brooks, *The Story of the American Soldier in War and Peace* (Boston: D. Lothrop Company, 1889), p. 239.

6. Quoted in *Current Opinion* 63 (July 1917), p. 6.

7. William A. Bacher, ed., *The Treasury Star Parade: 27 Radio Plays,* with an introduction by Henry Morgenthau, Jr. (New York: Farrar and Rinehart, 1942), p. 379.

8. Edmund M. Kirby and Jack W. Harris, *Star-Spangled Radio,* with a foreword by David Sarnoff (Chicago: Ziff-Davis Publishing Company, 1948), p. 183.

9. Ernie Pyle, *Brave Men* (New York: Henry Holt and Company, 1943), p. 275.

10. Robert Sherrod, *Tarawa: The Story of A Battle* (New York: Duell, Sloan and Pearce, 1944), p. 113.

11. Columbia Broadcasting System, *From Pearl Harbor into Tokyo: the Story as told by war correspondents on the Air* (New York: Columbia Broadcasting System, 1945), p. 296.

12. Stanley Cooperman, *World War I and the American Novel* (Baltimore: The Johns Hopkins Press, 1967), p. 8.

13. Debs Myers, Jonathan Kilbourn and Richard Harrity, eds., *Yank— The GI Story of the War* (New York: Duell, Sloan and Pearce, 1947), p. 163.

14. Hans J. Morgenthau, "Death in the Nuclear Age," in Nathan A. Scott, Jr., ed., *The Modern Vision of Death* (Richmond: John Knox Press, 1967), p. 77.

15. Robert Jay Lifton, *Home From the War: Vietnam Veterans—Neither Victims or Executioners* (New York: Simon and Schuster, 1973), p. 40.

16. Michael Herr, *Dispatches* (New York: Alfred A. Knopf, 1977), p. 209.

17. *The Vietnam Hearings,* with an introduction by J. William Fulbright (New York: Random House, 1966), p. 192.

18. Adolf E. Jensen, *Myth and Cult Among Primitive Peoples* (Chicago: University of Chicago Press, 1963), p. 170.

19. Wayne Greenhaw, *The Making of A Hero: The Story of Lieut. William Calley Jr.* (Louisville, Kentucky: Touchstone Publishing Company, 1971), p. 191.

20. *Newsweek* (December 15, 1969), p. 35.

21. Tracy Kidder, "Soldiers of Misfortune," *Atlantic* (March 1978), p. 43.

22. "Vietnam: One Week's Dead: May 23–June 3, 1969: A Record and A Tribute," *Life* (June 27, 1969), p. 20.

23. W. W. Wood, "The Betrayed: our men in uniform want to win in Vietnam," *American Opinion* 12 (January 1969), p. 7.

24. Francis du Plessix Gray, "Slum Landlords in Eden," *Saturday Review of the Society* (December 1972), p. 73.

25. Albert Kahn, *The Unholy Hymnal* (New York: Simon and Schuster, 1971), p. 93.

26. Norman Cousins, "A Message From Indochina," *Saturday Review* (March 18, 1978), p. 4.

27. "How Should Americans Feel?" *Time* (April 14, 1975), p. 27.

28. Peter Stromberg, "A Long War's Writing: American Novels about the Fighting in Vietnam While Americans Fought" (Ph.D dissertation, Cornell University, 1974), p. 13.

29. Quoted in William Manchester, *The Glory And The Dream* (Toronto: Bantam Books, 1975), p. 1296.

THIRTEEN

The Myth of
Our Materialism

Kees W. Bolle

I would like to ask the question of how materialistic we really are. I do not mean: how much do we like *things;* nor do I mean: how materialistic are we in comparison to each other, or who is most materialistic among us. I would like to ask to what extent our "materialism" is actually related to the empirical, material world, or in what ways it may function as a mythical affair. In other words, I want to investigate the *myth* of our materialism functioning in and behind all we say and do.

Some of us, who grew up in the countryside, remember from the "good old days" how villages in close proximity could mistrust each other, call each other names, and find sundry nasty ways to express their antagonism toward one another. It was not a matter of individuals, but of entire communities set against each other, in spite of ongoing relationships, commercial, cultural, and social—and even through marriages. Those of us who have always lived in big cities, and have heard about gang wars only from newspapers and movies, may think of such antagonisms as survivals of a dim and primitive past, extant only in remote places. But it is a sobering thought that globally all of us are still involved in such suspiciousnesses and name-calling, without apologies and without regrets.

We in the West, in all our collectivity, are called "materialistic" by well-meaning, educated Hindus and Buddhists. The designation is so commonly applied and we are so used to it that we have to make a special effort to realize that in its blunt, indiscriminate use it is exactly like the qualification "lazy" applied by Westerners to all Indians, or like the term "savage" used until very recently by learned men to refer to all peoples who had no share in the large historical and religious traditions of the world. That we are so often called materialistic may serve as a special stimulus for thought on our materialism. Obviously, the designation is not merely a geographic reference to the industrialized areas of Europe and America.

The collective nature of the materialism we are dimly aware of, and the collective sense with which "outsiders" assign the label to us, indeed exclude all consideration of greater or lesser degrees of individual materialistic adherency. Our problem is deeper and more encompassing than that of psychological makeup and comparisons. Indeed, the problem is fundamental. Our materialism is something that affects and even determines all of us, our thoughts and our emotions. It is as if we had *inherited* a manner of thinking and feeling. In fact, we have.

What is our materialism, fundamentally? A number of thinkers, who have contributed to our positive and eager grasp on the material world around us, could be examined. One name stands out: Karl Marx. Marx is not merely the patriarch of the Soviet Union and a number of "peoples' republics," but also a major exponent of Western thought. Sizing up Marx's materialism means understanding more of ourselves.

Let us recall some of the striking features of Marx's thought. In the first place, Marx's thought is not mere thought about the world as it exists. He quite consciously presents his ideas as means to change the world. Hence, the relation to matter is not mere theory, but involvement. Secondly, and immediately related to the passionate involvement in the material world, is

Marx's certainty that the world will be truly *transformed*. This is Marx's expectation of the classless society. That society will take us literally beyond the societies all of us exist in now, which are characterized by opposition and conflict between those who have and those who have not (or who have a great deal less). The dialectic of history will lead to the great revolution with scientific inevitability. It is the proletarians, those who do not own the means of production, who will bring about the revolution and usher in the new, classless age.

We should not be glib in pointing out the religious structure of Marxism. This is not to deny that religious features exist. Several scholars have described them to us,[1] or at least indicated Marxism's semblance to religion.[2] Most concisely, Eliade summed up the similarities in barely a page. The "proletariat" have exactly the role of the "elect" or "anointed" in other myths. The proletariat are the Just who will play the crucial redemptive role in bringing about the new world. Marx's classless society is a precise equivalent of the Golden Age, which in many traditions lies at the beginning and the end of history. The messianic form Marx gave to this mythology derives from Jewish and Christian ideology.[3]

The absolute goal of history in Marx's theories resembles the hope Jews and Christians had nurtured for many hundreds of years, which flared up from time to time in passionate millenarian movements. There is the burning conviction—is it not a faith?—that Good will be completely victorious over Evil.

I do not want to detract from religious interpretations of Marx and Marxism, but I feel that something more must be added to make them convincing. Pointing out Marx's Jewish parentage, the obvious religious features of his work, his eschatological ideas and so on, will never suffice in a discussion with a Marxist, or, for that matter, with any intellectual historian. One might as well make a list of equally obvious religious features in Sartre's existentialism, or in the cult of baseball or the Indianapolis 500, or in Republican and Democratic conventions. Surely, those features are there, even some very crucial ones. But what difference does it all make?

The intriguing thing about Marx as a protagonist of our type of materialism is that he was so obviously wrong and yet gained an enormous following. To explain the vast influence of that form of materialism that is inseparable from Marx's name we need an altogether different frame of understanding than that which his critics have provided.

The truly religious, mythological impetus of Marxism begins to show itself when we realize how invulnerable it has been to learned, scientific, specialized criticism. Some devastating critiques have been launched against Marx's work. Max Weber, one of the pioneers of modern sociology, criticized Marx principally because social phenomena, to be explained, need more than a straightforward, uncompromisingly materialistic method. Furthermore, it is unscientific to foretell the future or to claim to be able to do so.[4] In Weber's wake, the sociologist of religion, Joachim Wach, has pointed out that religious facts are among the determinants of a society and these cannot often be understood merely as byproducts of an economic process.[5] The vast majority of philosophers have not even deigned to look at Marxism as a system worthy of a critique. Marxism, presented as an all-encompassing system, was too puerile, too inconsistent, too dependent on illusory assumptions. Benedetto Croce did take the trouble to mount an attack, demonstrating the inadequacy of Marxism's narrow basis: not merely matter, but *economic* matter—a conspicuously inadequate foundation for explaining all of human history.[6]

The most devastating rebuttal of Marx that I know came from an economic perspective. It was made in James Burnham's *The Managerial Revolution*[7] and destroyed the cornerstone of which Marx was so sure. Burnham demonstrated that Marx's economic predictions had been thwarted by history itself. The development of the stockmarket had refuted Marx's certainty that the world's capital would be piled up in the hands of fewer and fewer people. The opposite had happened. On top of that, actual power was no longer identical with the largest share, but with the voice of the managers of any large business concern. And finally—the deathblow, equally unpopular among

Marxists and anti-Marxists—the actual development in the communist world and the capitalist world had turned out to be the same. What one calls "managers" the other calls "commissars," but they function alike. Contrary to official "ideology," the two systems are not diametrically opposed at all.

And here, I believe, we may begin to glimpse the myth of materialism. Only rarely has it been stated that Marxism and capitalism are made of the same stuff. Only occasionally has a poet or a solitary original student of society and human values clearly addressed himself to this theme.[8] I am convinced it is a theme that will ring truer and truer in our time. The myth of materialism is pervasive, in the manner in which only a myth can be pervasive. It absolutely ignores the walls people build around their political camps.

Having noted the solid critical arguments against Marxism, we may now observe some of the truly religious, mythological features of this materialism. As in the case of all great mythologies, we note two revealing facts. First, we find a number of poets who expressed the myth in unmistakable and often splendid forms. Second, we find that the myth reverberates surprisingly well in the most divergent circumstances and diverse cultures.

POETRY

There is a bit of poetry in Marx's mature writings, in spite of his economic determinism. Everyone has heard of his reference to religion as an *opium*. He made that reference by the end of 1843 in his *Introduction to the Critique of Hegel's Philosophy of Law*. But how many people have actually read it in its context and reflected on it? "Religion is the sigh of the oppressed creature, the heart of a heartless world, the soul of a soulless environment. It is the opium of the people." Religion, the opium of the people. Let it be noted that this is what Marx said. It is not the statement often quoted—Lenin's emendation: "opium for the people!"[9] Marx did not describe religion as some sort of deceit coolly foisted upon man. On the contrary, Marx exclaims that religion is the only means of expression open to man in the miserable circumstances in which he finds himself; the only manner in which he may exist. This vision of Marx has proved to be much more seminal than the nitty-gritty of his economic theories. Since religion is man's principal expression, it is also the principal documentation we have in history. Primarily for this reason, and not simply because he retained some of the theological excrescences of his student years or was conditioned by external Jewish or Christian influences, Marx refers to religious facts throughout his writings.

It is also in this context that we should understand Marx's description of Christianity as the *fitting* religion for a commodity-producing existence: capitalism. Marx does not mock or scorn religion. Not only is religion in general the stuff without which no development of history is ever documented, but it has its specific forms to provide specific consolations under specific pressures and miseries.

Marx's view of religion is interwoven with his science of history, and the famous statement about opium presents it not without poetry. This view is completed in the imagery of the purpose of the dialectic of history. When the purpose of the dialectic is achieved, everything will change. Not only will society be classless, because the class struggle will have reached its conclusion, but that new society will know no religion. It will no longer need to console itself.

It should be obvious that this grand vision is far more than the leftover of a Jewish or Christian upbringing. The classless society of the eschatological imagery is part and parcel of Marx's (supposedly) scientific system of history. History will reach its end.

It is exceedingly important to see that these ideas are not external to Marxism and not merely there because Marx was a Westerner. All this may be the case, and any historian of ideas may emphasize it. However, the religious importance of Marx cannot be fathomed in this way. This symbolism of the final stage of history goes beyond any progression which might be expected in the history of ideas.

It is striking that the importance Marx attributed to religion and the importance of religionlessness-in-the-end escaped most of the best-known orthodox Marxists. Among them are Bebel and Liebknecht in Germany.[10] Marx's compassion, his insight into the necessity of consolation, is missing in them. Unlike Marx, they like to mock and deride. But while the great political leaders among the Marxists turned out to have inherited little of Marx's vision, the Marxist inspiration of ever-new forms among poets is truly remarkable. The vision of the future holds them spellbound, time and again anticipating prophetically the goal of history Marx heralded.

We owe some of the most splendid "Marxist" poetry to Herman Gorter (1864–1927), a Dutch poet who was also a politician. In two of his poems he envisioned a man and a woman as they would be in the world to come. It is Marx's vision of the goal of history, but anticipated vividly, transformed from a theory into a live presence.

Out of a new world a woman dressed
in a dignified and elegant garment steps forth.
She is serene like no one else ever.
Her eye is radiant like the day.

She has not a single ornament
of timidity, not a single illusion.
She is pure like glass,
as if she was born just like that.

She holds her arms at a pure angle,
her shawl falls in the fairest rays,
and the clearest light of her throat, her mouth,
plays around her wholesome, perfect face.
. . . .
Out of a new world a man dressed
in a tight cloak steps forth.
He has a brilliance never seen before,
a head radiant like the day.

He has not a single ornament
of servility, not a single illusion.
He is pure the way a man
grown up naked can possibly be.

His arm clenches in a pure fist.
His leg moves in a pure footstep.
A strong and pure passion encircles
his proud and chaste face.[11]

Marx's great appeal is immediately related to the fervor of his expectation. Fervent, prophetic, yet theoretical, it is in poets like Gorter that the appeal created a new code that was most effective in addressing large gatherings. A remarkable feature of the new man and woman is that they bear no mark of servility or of timidity. Much less poetically, but most characteristically, Marx himself is on record as sharing that abhorrence of servility. In Marx's old age, one of his daughters asked him to fill out a questionnaire in which it was asked: "Which vice do you detest most?" Marx wrote down: *servility*.[12] Marxism inspired Gorter and many others to great articulateness in depicting freedom. Ultimately, man will be, and even now he must be seen as free from submission, cringing, self-contempt. This freedom from all such vices, from timidity, servility, and from illusions—this freedom obviously depicts the final time without religion. It may be useful to remember that here we can see another aspect of *our* materialism in the non-Marxist West. It is a cliché among ourselves to speak of the "dignity of man" as something to which we are entitled. But how do we *know* that economic means and changes create such dignity? We have no evidence of any scientific sort. All we have (regardless of our precise political sympathies) is a certainty of the type expressed by Gorter.

It is not as if Gorter and other poets simply echoed Marx. The inspiration Marx exerted had unexpected consequences in their writings.

The greatest prophetic poet at the gate of the twentieth century is the Frenchman Charles Péguy (1873–1914). Patriot, feeling himself part of the real country tradition of France, its peasants and conscientious workmen, increasingly a conscious Catholic, he was also set in motion by the then-young proletarian movement. He was killed in the Battle of the Marne, in the first year of World War I. In his all too brief life, he wrote two long poems about his heroine, Saint Joan of Arc. The first Joan he envisaged was his "socialist" Joan. Here Joan was the great revolutionary, impelled by mankind's suffering, to transform the world. His second Joan has come to realize that the suffering of the world is more complex and more profound. Suffering does not cease when hunger is stilled. It continues mysteriously, if not satanically, when all material needs are taken care of.

Péguy was passionately involved in the controversies surrounding Dreyfus, the Jewish officer falsely accused of treason and justified only after a long process that left the entire country in moral shambles. In one of his essays Péguy sang the praises of Bernard-Lazare, the journalist who had first brought the outrage of Dreyfus's unjust condemnation to the attention of the French. Bernard-Lazare died at the age of forty, ignored and in poverty.

Were people such as Péguy socialists? Yes, but the Marxian economic base becomes less and less conspicuous. It is instead a materialism of which only the thorough spiritual concern, the compassion, stand out. What we have (at the same because and in spite of Marx) is a most uneconomic concreteness of vision of details that cannot be caught in a formula. Péguy ends his glorification of Bernard-Lazare with this meditation: "I feel no need of unifying the world. The more I see of the world, the more I discover that free men and free events are varied." [13]

Péguy was a friend of Jaurès, the famous socialist leader, yet came close to despising him after Jaurès turned into a mere politician. Péguy wrote an essay on Jaurès and ended with a reflection on the inadequacy of political organization: "When I was small I believed that groups worked. Today we know that groups do not work. They create agitation." [14]

I am not quoting a man who is merely disappointed, but a man who has learned the wisdom of a vision-of-the-end-and-purpose-of-all-suffering, visible to us now in all its concrete reality only in scattered rays. This, we hear from Péguy, is precisely what history as we are experiencing it is all about.

Reviewing the Dreyfus case, Péguy can say things that do justice to the precise historical details, as in Bernard-Lazare's in-
volvment, while at the same time illumining the meaning of
history.

The disregard of Israel for prophets, and despite this the guidance of Israel
by the prophets: this is the whole history of Israel.

The disregard of sinners for saints and despite this the salvation of sinners
by saints, this is the whole of Christian history. [15]

In all of the history of Marxism, its politicians and popular
leaders, the economics of Marx has received rather little attention. As an educator, Rosa Luxemburg (1870–1919) was among
the few who occupied themselves with the economic theory of
Marx. [16] We are fully informed of the lives and works of the
great men and women in the Marxist tradition. Most of them
wrote autobiographies. It is striking that the details of the basic
materialistic assumptions occupied so little of their attention.
Péguy's acid portrayal of Jaurès' change into a mere politician
could well serve as a close-up of other great socialist leaders.
The great and leading ideas with which they stirred the masses
are those of education, hope, the new world, freedom. The
poetic contribution to Marxism is precisely the creation of a
language that seemed to make the details of the foundation
certain without the politicians' ever having to spell them out.

Not only historians of religions and mythologists, or critical
minds like James Burnham, but also general political and cultural historians are gradually waking up to the fact that Marxism is not a phenomenon that can be understood in isolation.
A critical study today cannot view Marx anymore as an exception, but must see him as one facet of a much broader movement, in which we find culturally the romantics, politically the
nationalists, imperialists and colonists, and, last but not least,
religiously the organizers of missionary institutions. [17] They are
all carried by the mighty stream of evolutionism, the undying
dream of a world moving constantly upward in its course, and
finding its fulfilment in the West. In all these ideas the importance of matter was beyond doubt. Did not the industrial de-

velopment indicate that importance? Did not the course of history, entrusting the destiny of the world to the hands of the colonial powers, prove the point? This comprehensive view of nineteenth-century history gives a new understanding of our common inheritance: the myth of materialism. But there is more to speak of than the poetic forms given to the myth by Marxist poets, and we must go beyond even the widest context of a western history of ideas.

THE MYTH OF MATERIALISM WORLDWIDE

The overwhelming importance of matter, of material conditions, of the production of goods, has impelled unforeseen forces all over the earth. Ever since the nineteenth-century colonialist expansion and missionary efforts began, the material possessions of a growing industrial society impressed the entire world. Although we take all sorts of commodities for granted, we may still be able to imagine what a priceless possession a pocket-knife could be even a few generations ago, for a Tom Sawyer of Huckleberry Finn. How much more impressive was a camping knife of Birmingham steel for an Australian aborigine, whom this object suddenly lifted out of the Stone Age.

Before we think too much on this marvellous progress of our world and thereby feed on our own myth in its most naive form, it is necessary to call to mind something less self-congratulatory. The most felicitous utterings of poets should not cause us to forget the singularly greedy nature of materialism. In Marxism the basic axiom remains: matter determines the quality of human life.

We have seen that this axiom received scant attention among Marxists. In fact, the dogma had so many adherents in diverse circles, not only among Marxists, that little need was felt for elaboration. Even if the commitment to materialism was expressed not at all, or not in such a blunt way, it functioned across the board; of course among industrialists and businessmen, but also among government officials in the colonies and among missionaries. The most striking characteristic of a living myth is that it functions even when it is not talked about. It literally goes without saying. The myth of materialism in the nineteenth century was almost unchallenged. (Its most severe and eloquent critic, Sören Kierkegaard, remained virtually unknown.)

At the present time we speak of the "Third World," meaning those regions in which the material, industrialized progress of Europe and North America has not taken place. It is an ugly, superstitious term, as it suggests that one part of the world can be adequately described by saying that it belongs neither to the Warsaw Pact nor to the NATO alliance; it fits neither in the "free" nor the Communist world, and that makes it "third."[18] This ugly concept is rooted in the earlier superstition that the largest part of the planet was meant to be governed, cared for, and led to salvation by the nations and missionary societies of the West.

When we search for a structure in the myths of materialism, I believe we must revise completely our customary mythological divisions of the world. In the entire world of the nineteenth and twentieth centuries, a certain uniformity becomes visible in regions that in historical, cultural, and economic matters have nothing in common. Certainly, I am aware that the picture I want to draw would have offended Karl Marx as much as Adam Smith, or Hegel, or E. B. Tylor, or Darwin, or Rudyard Kipling. I want to suggest that some of the most "primitive" myths born in the acculturation of Melanesian, Papua, North and South American, Siberian, and other tribes are made of the very stuff of which *our* materialism consists.

It is generally recognized that contacts between the well-equipped Western tradesman, soldier, or missionary and the "primitives" triggered novel expectations among the latter. The cargo cults have received a good deal of scholarly attention, and their general features are well-known.[19] The term "cargo cult" itself is one of the most descriptive terms modern social studies have invented. In some parts of the Southern Pacific world, American bases were established during World War II. The riches of industrial society overwhelmed the native populations. A series of crises broke out after the war had ended and the troops, their airplanes, their equipment, their cigarettes, and their canned foods left. Would they return? New ideologies were born, anticipating a return of the ancestors, a renewal of the world, an end of toil.

The dramatic cargo cults are not different in structure from numerous movements that have occurred in other industrially and economically undeveloped parts of the world. In all cases, we find movements on the fringes of or touched by the material wealth of the rich nations. In all cases, the transformation of the traditional myths centers in the expectation of a perfect future.

Naturally, scholarship of a more or less Marxist persuasion became fascinated with the subject. It is an obvious case, after all, of the opposition of "haves" and "have-nots." Moreover, these millenarian cults clinch the case for religion as an ideology meant to make life bearable.[20] It does seem inconsistent, however, not to turn this same fascination towards Marxism itself. The most cursory glance can detect a resemblance between Marxism and cargo cults. A perfect future lies in store for the "have-nots," once they have assimilated the possessions and power of the "haves." In a wider, historical perspective, all classical details of millenarianism are found in the cargo cults as well as in Marxism. Moreover, the two share features that have been added to the old pattern in recent times.

What is so generally and vaguely referred to as "our" materialism has a certain structure that is most articulately expressed in Marxism and sundry millennial movements born in the period of high capitalism and colonialism. What are the features typifying this peculiar conglomeration?

The first feature, already touched on, is that they are what they are because they are triggered by Christianity. I do not think that we should give too much weight to the biblical ideas of the coming kingdom of God, and certainly not in such a manner as to suggest that Karl Marx and various cargo cult leaders had borrowed the idea for concealed purposes of their own. No one has tried to pull the wool over anyone else's eyes.

What happened instead is that people on the fringes of Christianity picked up precisely those notions of expectation and hope that had lost their vitality for the Christians with whom they came in contact. In the (external) mission fields, it is even possible to say that there was a hypocrisy among missionaries that did not escape the natives.[21] The hope they spoke of did not seem to function in their lives. The expectation of the new world did not make any difference to their acts. But what seemed a mere dead weight of formulas became revitalized in millenarian myths and cults. So it did in Marx and Marxism.

The second peculiar feature of "our" materialism is that its interest in material goods is relatively new. To be sure, we know of the promise of a land of milk and honey, and we know of fairy tale motifs concerning fried pigeons flying into one's mouth, and the like—but those are imageries of a paradisal nostalgia as universal as the symbolism of north, south, east, and west, or of sun and moon, or male and female. Christianity itself was born as a millenarian movement, but we must wait for the nineteenth century to find an eschatology in which the expectation of commodities for everyone has the major part. This makes Marxism not so much an offshoot of Christianity, as many have argued, but a mythology with reverberations and parallels over the entire planet, expressed in a variety of materialistically oriented millenarian movements. The ancient millenarianism of Jesus Christ—who, after all, did say that we would always have the poor among us—is not too conspicuously continued in these nineteenth-and twentieth-century messianisms. The reason the churches failed in understanding the meaning of hope is ultimately a theological subject, which does not occupy us here. What is relevant is that time and again Marxists have expressed wonderment or outrage that Christians did not embrace Marxism. Would it not have made the Christian faith real and perfect? So it seemed even to Rosa Luxemburg.[22]

Thirdly, there is a conspicuous feature to our materialism that everyone can observe: syncretism (or, more generally, acculturation processes). Syncretism, the molding together of elements that are heterogeneous, sometimes even opposed to each other, into one religious system, characterizes Marxism as well as other recent millennial movements and does so in all details in which it characterizes the other eschatological materialisms around the globe. The word acculturation is not out of place in a description of Marxism. After all, Marx, in calling for action, did not merely analyze history in terms of a class struggle, but brought about the class struggle with the means of production as its stake. Inevitably, this was not a mere affair of economic confrontation, but a broader, forced and forceful give and take of cultural features at large. Marx himself could hardly have foreseen the plans and achievements of groups with such battlecries as "equal opportunity," or the institution of consumer advocates, or labels proclaiming the approval of *Good Housekeeping*. The desire for and availability of industrial products, the desire for powers and functions, and for individual rights to choose—these were themselves new visions for the proletarian class. People came to assign themselves to classes in terms of Marx's new code. The key word remains *material*, but the process of change is an acculturation, i.e. an acceptance of another group's culture in a situation of conflict or stress.

The word syncretism is quite accurate in the case of Marx. A crucial term used by Marx is "alienation." It fills the need to describe every economically and socially caused emptiness and misery in which man is doomed to turn to religion for consolation. The word has its origin in Jewish and Christian theological discussions. Men are alienated from God, fallen from grace.[23] It is the most concrete, realistic description the scientific Marx can find to indicate the condition of a man who is not yet enlightened and who turns to religion.

The peculiar mishmash of a scientific, or, more accurately, positivistic jargon, with notions of a clear religious, transcendental type, are properly called syncretistic. The cardinal syncretistic example of the classless society, the very goal of history, has already occupied us. It is the crown of transcendental concepts, existing in a system that prides itself in its this-worldliness.

Syncretism is a persistent feature of "primitive" millennial movements in the nineteenth and twentieth centuries. In most cases, the expected return of the dead represents a rejuvenation of traditional myth. The preoccupation with material goods, and in several cases the expectation of the renewal of the world itself, is a new addition, filtered in from Christianity. More precisely, as in the case of Marxism, it is the addition that in a new manner triggered a whole new movement.

CONCLUSION

We chose Marxism as an example of our common myth of materialism. It is useful to remember that we could as well have used any theory of classical high capitalism. The conclusions would remain basically the same.

The first is that logically, the assumption that the quality of human life is completely determined by material conditions is as absurd now as when the first theory of materialism was designed. Yet as a functioning, living myth, materialism is not affected by this (or any other) logical or empirical objection. The certainty that the myth must be so is religiously held beyond doubt. That, I believe, is the nucleus of our materialism.

The open confession of materialism may be principally a Marxist contribution, but the myth projecting the definite future material change of the world occupies a wide territory. Not only has it played its part in missionary enterprises and thereby contributed to millennial movements in Brazil, parts of Africa, Melanesia, and so on, but these movements themselves, no matter in what particular conditions they arose, must be seen in the same future-oriented materialistic context.

It is important to realize that we must not continue the customary endeavors to "explain" Marx as a late exponent of biblical eschatology. We cannot do that to Marx or Marxism any more than we can do it to the sort of materialism that may not happen to be Marxist but is our own. If we persisted in this mistake, we should have to offer the same supposed explanation of other nineteenth-century movements that are equally future-oriented: nationalism, colonialism, imperialism.

A concluding note must be added. It is a sure sign that a myth is beginning to lose some of its self-evidence when we can begin to discuss it intellectually. We actually begin to see somewhat the contours of our myth of materialism. However, let us not be hasty and begin to dream of the demise of our myth.

It is frightening to realize that all spiritual criticism launched by Kierkegaard against anything resembling a myth of materialism fell on deaf ears. What of Kierkegaard's meditation that all that really matters is growing in poverty and weakness? If Marx could have listened to that, it obviously would have had no meaning for him whatsoever. Is the present age so different?

Who could actually come out today with anything resembling a spiritual critique? Marx may be proven wrong in all respects, yet the myth of materialism of which he was a major exponent is very much alive. Not too long ago, when the Pope hinted at the blessings of poverty to a Mexican audience made up of good Christians and many priests, he was booed. He would be booed anywhere in our world today.

The myth of materialism may begin to open here and there to little doubts or small attacks, but the myth is alive and flourishing. It is ours. Should not poverty be removed first of all? Doesn't all the rest take care of itself?

NOTES

1. See, for instance, R.C. Zaehner, "A New Buddha and a New Tao," in R.C. Zaehner, ed., *The Concise Encyclopaedia of Living Faiths* (London: Hutchinson, 1959); Ninian Smart, *The Religious Experience of Mankind* (New York: Scribner, 1969), p. 37.

2. Joachim Wach, *The Comparative Study of Religions* (New York: Columbia University Press, 1958), p. 37.

3. Mircea Eliade, *Myths, Dreams and Mysteries* (New York: Harper, 1967), pp. 25–26.

4. See W.G. Runciman's introduction to *Weber, Selections in Translation*, transl. by Eric Matthews (Cambridge, Cambridge University Press, 1978), p. 4.

5. Joachim Wach, *Sociology of Religion* (London: Kegan Paul, 1947), pp. 12, 54.

6. Benedetto Croce, "Christianity for Our Time: An Argument Against Historical Materialism," in Charles G. Abbot, *The Drift of Civilization* (New York: Simon and Schuster, 1929), p. 61.

7. James Burnham, *The Managerial Revolution: What is Happening in the World* (New York: The John Day Company, 1941).

8. I am thinking of Charles Péguy and of E. Rosenstock Huessy in particular.

9. Owen Chadwick, *The Secularization of the European Mind in the Nineteenth Century* (Cambridge: Cambridge University Press, 1975), p. 49.

10. See especially August Bebel, *Aus meinem Leben,* two volumes (Stuttgart: Dietz, 1910, 1911).

11. Herman Gorter, *Verzen* (Amsterdam: Versluys, 1903) afd. iv.

12. Chadwick, p. 58.

13. Translation by Julian Green in *Charles Péguy, Men and Saints* (London: Kegan Paul, 1947), p. 133. Text in "Casse-cou," *Cahiers de la Quinzaine* II, 7 (1901).

14. Translation by Julian Green, *Men and Saints,* p. 159. Text in "Personnalités," *Cahiers de la Quinzaine* III, 12 (1902).

15. Translation by Julian Green, *Men and Saints,* p. 141. Complete text in "Notre jeunesse," *Cahiers de la Quinzaine* XI, 12 (1910). Reprinted in Bibliotheque de la Pleiade, Péguy, *Oeuvres en prose 1910–1914,* p. 553.

16. See Rosa Luxemburg, *The Accumulation of Capital,* translated by Agnes Schwarzschild, introduction by Joan Robinson (New York: Monthly Review Press, 1968). First German publication 1913.

17. See Karl Hammer, *Weltmission und Kolonialismus: Sendungsideen des 19. Jahrhunderts im Konflikt* (München: Kösel-Verlag,1978).

18. See the critique of this tripartitioning of the world by Paul Mus, "Situation du Tiers Monde" (first published in 1960) in Paul Mus, *L'angle de l'Asie* (Paris: Hermann, 1977), pp. 83–97.

19. See Sylvia Thrupp, ed., *Millennial Dreams in Action, Essays in Comparative Study* (The Hague: Mouton, 1962).

20. Vittorio Lanternari, *The Religions of the Oppressed: A Study of Modern Messianic Cults,* translated by Lisa Sergio (New York: Knopf, 1963).

21. Mircea Eliade, "Cargo-Cults and Cosmic Regeneration," in Thrupp, p. 143.

22. Rosa Luxemburg, "Socialism and the Churches," in Mary-Alice Waters, ed., *Rosa Luxemburg Speaks* (New York: Pathfinder Press, 1970), pp. 131–153.

23. Chadwick, p. 63.

Conclusion

Ninian Smart

We have in this collection explored some of the theoretical and historical relations between modern nationalism and religion. It may be useful to point forward to some further lines of enquiry.

It is worth noting that the fruits of an interplay between the study of religions and the discipline of political science themselves show that at certain points the distinction between the fields is problematic. The distinction between politics and religion (and there is of course some validity in it) may itself be made too sharp in our culture for ideological reasons. This is where Kees Bolle's concluding essay has an important message. If there is an area of enquiry that may be called "worldview analysis," covering both traditional religions and secular worldviews, some old questions take on a new look. For instance, the Moral Majority is seen as syncretistic, bonding elements of Protestant Christianity and American patriotism and civil religion. The division between Church and State becomes the division between worldview-imposing organizations and the State (thus if secularism in one sense of the term means such separation, the Soviet Union is not secularist). Further, the rubric of worldview analysis would not build in any particular preformed slants on religion, which sometimes skew analysis.

Thus, because in the West, and most clearly in the United States, the distinction between Church and State has become well-developed, it is easy to slip into the thought that religion is what concerns the individual in his own pursuit of integrity and happiness while politics essentially covers the public domain. But this "privatization" of the concept of religion ignores some vitally important facts.

First, and notably, it neglects the way in which other cultures do not thus privatize religion—Islam is the most conspicuous example. Thus the modern Western model just does not apply in many areas. Second, and perhaps more importantly from the point of view of the way we ought to reflect in the future about these matters, it neglects the way in which the privatization of religion itself may reflect a wider worldview, or *Weltanschauung*. The notion that faith speaks to the individual in a context of pluralism and choice itself is a notion in a total worldview that finds a place for religion as one possible element in a more comprehensive social cosmology. Thus we should not artificially separate religion from the theory of toleration and choice that surrounds it in such societies. For instance, there is a conflict between the claims of Christianity and Islam over the divinity of Christ and many other matters, but in the contemporary world the conflict more deeply is between differing theories of society, as between Islamic conservatism and the typical Western treatment of religion.

This is a conflict between Islam as traditionally interpreted and Christianity as now (in some societies) expressed. But of course the very tension between existential meaning and the need to modernize, and to adapt to change, itself produces new intermediate syntheses. Thus an important area for reflection about future trends in living worldviews is that which concerns the power of "modernist" religion, in its various forms: liberal Christianity (and its variant "liberation theology" as expressed in Catholic social action in Latin America); modernist Islam, whether of the more Westernized form as in Nasser's Egypt or its more conservative variety, as with Bani-Sadr; neo-Buddhism in Japan; independent Christianity in Africa, etc.

Methodologically, the history of religions and more widely religious studies may have some insights to offer political science. If I here dwell on these rather than the trade that might occur in the opposite direction, it is partly because the study of religion in its modern form has not yet entered sufficiently into the thinking of the social sciences (mainly because it is too easily identified with the older style of theological tradition).

Thus first—as this collection partially indicates—there is much investment in the modern study of religion in the phenomenological approach, i.e. the attempt to delineate the world from the standpoint of the agent or believer. This leads to a way of trying not merely to analyze the structure of the belief system but also to bring out its impact, in feeling and symbolism. This exercise is not peculiar to the study of religion, but for various reasons it is now strongly emphasized as an ingredient in the task of delineating the various religious traditions. It is clear that this involves a self-awareness too, for one has to know something of the peculiarity of our own cultural and conceptual apparatus in order to see that our categories will not apply directly to another worldview. We need to examine ourselves clearly in order to understand others. Thus the comparative method is built in to the phenomenological approach. I have argued here for the rejection of any sharp distinction between religious and secular worldviews, and that the rejection itself rids us of an inappropriate model drawn from the content of a particular phase of Western culture as a universal distinction. It is an example of "bracketing out" our own cultural assumptions.

Second, partly because the study of religion, by ridding itself of certain earlier encumbrances drawn from Christian theology, also has a strong drive towards description (albeit description which brings out the feel and impact of a set of ideas and practices), questions are raised about the theory in the social sciences. Thus it seems inappropriate to bring theory-laden expressions too early into the descriptive exercise. This allows us to treat of (say) the Marxist theory of international relations as more on a par with the Christian theological interpretation of history than with a phenomenological delineation of religious history. I have partly explored these issues in regard to projection theories in the social sciences (which in describing phenomena in a certain way already build, one might even say project, the theory into that which it is due to explain) in *The Science of Religion and the Sociology of Knowledge* (Princeton: Princeton University Press, 1973).

Third, the study of religion is much concerned with the analysis and explication of symbols. There is fruitful territory to be explored in regard to the religious or quasi-religious symbolism of secular movements (e.g., Nazism). The theory of rites of passage is relevant to the analysis of the psychic logic of the revolution: destroying the old society and transubstantiating it into the new. Thus I would look forward to a meeting of the disciplines in the joint analysis of traditional and secular symbolic motifs.

Fourth, the study of religion, and of new religious movements in particular (a fruitful and flourishing area), makes much use, whether explicitly or implicitly, of the category of syncretism. The interaction between religious cultures has some interesting effects, and many new growths are the consequence of such interaction. Here one harks back to Hegel's dialectic as being an early way of trying to present such interactions. There is a need to look upon political forms in a similar way. Thus it is possible to speak of syncretism not just between religions but between worldviews, and this may be a syncretism of the traditional and transcendental on the one hand and of the secular and "this-worldly" on the other. Consider, for instance, the blend between neo-Hinduism and important elements in Western political ideology, which has produced the present Indian outlook. A fruitful question is concerned with the degree to which deep cultural attitudes conduce to certain types of ideology. For instance, Hindu traditional pluralism contributes to a sense of democratic pluralism in modern India.

There are other themes that need further exploration. Thus we may ask what place religions and ideologies may play in multi-ethnic societies. At its broadest the multi-ethnic society corresponds to an empire. The Soviet Union and Ethiopia are instances of empires that in their post-revolutionary phase would not recognize the title (and indeed they repudiate some of the prestensions of the imperial past). Yet the logic of the multi-ethnic situation persists, only now an older, overtly religious ideology that could bind at least some of the peoples together (Orthodoxy or Coptic Christianity) has given place to Marxism as a new legitimation for the State.

Smaller ethnic groups across the globe have also been host to a large number of new religious movements, stimulated by the impact of the West on traditional society. Very often they take the form of independent churches (independent, that is, of Christian mainstream denominations and of missionary control). They are one symptom of the need to strike a bargain between the modernizing forces of the West and traditional identity. There is here a fruitful area of enquiry into the relationship of the new movements in the processes of nation-building in the typical multi-ethnic society of Africa (but we may cite other countries of the same sort such as Papua New Guinea).

We may also note that modern communications have tended to reinforce the transnational character of traditional religion. This sometimes gives them a special political leverage. The visit of the Pope to Argentina and Great Britain in 1982 brought to a greater level of consciousness the paradox of members of the same faith fighting one another. The ecumenical movement in Christianity has been an element in creating a new transnational peace movement in America, Europe, and elsewhere. It is obvious that Islam's sense of identity has been reinforced by modern methods of realizing the pilgrimage, while the transnational character of Judaism has been an obvious ongoing pressure on United States foreign policies. The time may thus be ripe for a general study of transnational entities, whether churches, or loose religious confederations, or multinational corporations with their own ideological outlook.

But in the end, so much of our discussions in this volume have concerned the nature of, and varieties of, nationalism.

The use of symbolic analysis in this area is a useful reminder to us of the powerful nonrational forces that shape our identities. It might be useful to adapt the language of Paul Tillich, who defined religion as ultimate concern, and think of what constitutes for a given population the institution of ultimate concern. For some it is the family, but for so many citizens of today's world it is the nation. It is the nation that in gathering taxes and marshalling armies demands deep sacrifices of its sons and daughters. But what lies beyond the nation-state? Maybe one of the world's major problems is that it is less easy to create symbolic resonances in the wider units. We do not think of ourselves very deeply as citizens of the world, and lesser coalitions ("the free world," "Europe," and so on) have rather feeble purchase on the imagination of their members. It seems that it is chiefly the transnational religions that may have the symbolic resources to strengthen bonds beyond national boundaries.

But though religions may be transnational they may also acquire, in a global perspective, sectarian characteristics. Thus Shi'a Islam, even though it has become the established religion of Iran, and is reaching out towards similar objectives in Iraq and elsewhere, is sectarian in the sense that it wishes to maintain a relatively isolated and pure existence within the frame of the global economy and politics. So a further question that needs exploring is how far religions, even if in theory universal, can have a globally universal influence. We seem here to be moving towards a loose kind of religious federalism in which the religions establish themselves in various regions and cultures of the world and tacitly allow others to coexist, at least elsewhere. However, there are elements in conservative Islam and Marxism that show a less federalist face, while the steady systematization of the world's economic processes and modes of communication faces all the worldviews with new challenges of adaptation to this new situation.

The lessons the political scientist may learn from the historian of religion and the worldview analyst can be reciprocated. The academic division between the two disciplines here is reinforced by the tendency (natural enough) for students of religion to "spiritualize" religions. Often the concentration is upon the experiences that are central to the formation of the great faiths— experiences of conversion, the numinous, enlightenment, and so on; or it is upon the hidden meanings of myth; or upon doctrines that try to delineate the transcendent and its relations to events in this world. Too little is religion seen in its political dimension. Thus the process of Christianization of northern Europe is imperfectly understood unless it is clear why rulers found the new faith a useful ideology for shaping political power, and often Buddhist origins are seen independently of the socio-political changes occurring in the Gangetic region (a point about which we are reminded by the recent writings of Trevor Ling). It would be healthy both in historical and contemporary contexts if there were a more politically realistic approach to the meaning of religion.

But the heart of this book is about nationalism. Since it happens that national sovereignty is one of the major factors in present global and regional instability it is hoped that this volume will suggest new ways to understand some of the features of it, and so indirectly help toward a more settled and serene world.

Index